Border Watch

Anthropology, Culture and Society

Series Editors:
Professor Vered Amit, Concordia University
and
Dr Jon P. Mitchell, University of Sussex

Recent titles:

money
norms + values +
expectations

– constellation of social
relationships

BEHAVIOUR complexity of interactions +
negotiations BETWEEN +
AMONG GROUPS

BORDER WATCH

Cultures of Immigration, Detention and Control

slippages in norms
and behaviour

Socially constructed

Alexandra Hall

why and how?
Intro – complexity
interactions
in IRC

3 themes,
aspects,
relationships

context
of

structural
realities

rules structure of
rules

– resistance +
moralities

– morality
– power
→ sense of self
– ethnicity / race / gender
– bodywatching
– ideology

. freedom?
– citizenship
   ("the other")
– monitor, levels of
– knowledge and
   / power
fear of the
unknown
– discipline
– making idea of
   border more
   abstract / porous

PlutoPress
www.plutobooks.com

who is
Hull, what is
her context?

First published 2012 by Pluto Press
345 Archway Road, London N6 5AA

www.plutobooks.com

Distributed in the United States of America exclusively by
Palgrave Macmillan, a division of St. Martin's Press LLC,
175 Fifth Avenue, New York, NY 10010

British Library Cataloguing in Publication Data
A catalogue record for this book is available from the British Library

ISBN	978 0 7453 2724 2	Hardback
ISBN	978 0 7453 2723 5	Paperback
ISBN	978 1 8496 4716 8	PDF eBook
ISBN	978 1 8496 4718 2	Kindle eBook
ISBN	978 1 8496 4717 5	EPUB eBook

Library of Congress Cataloging in Publication Data applied for

This book is printed on paper suitable for recycling and made from fully managed
and sustained forest sources. Logging, pulping and manufacturing processes are
expected to conform to the environmental standards of the country of origin.

10   9   8   7   6   5   4   3   2   1

Designed and produced for Pluto Press by Chase Publishing Services Ltd
Typeset from disk by Stanford DTP Services, Northampton, England
Simultaneously printed digitally by CPI Antony Rowe, Chippenham, UK and
Edwards Bros in the United States of America

Contents

Series Preface

Anthropology is a discipline based upon in-depth ethnographic works that deal with wider theoretical issues in the context of particular, local conditions – to paraphrase an important volume from the series: *large issues* explored in *small places*. This series has a particular mission: to publish work that moves away from an old-style descriptive ethnography that is strongly area-studies oriented, and offer genuine theoretical arguments that are of interest to a much wider readership, but which are nevertheless located and grounded in solid ethnographic research. If anthropology is to argue itself a place in the contemporary intellectual world, then it must surely be through such research.

We start from the question: 'What can this ethnographic material tell us about the bigger theoretical issues that concern the social sciences?' rather than 'What can these theoretical ideas tell us about the ethnographic context?' Put this way round, such work becomes *about* large issues, *set in* a (relatively) small place, rather than detailed description of a small place for its own sake. As Clifford Geertz once said, 'Anthropologists don't study villages; they study *in* villages.'

By place, we mean not only geographical locale, but also other types of 'place' – within political, economic, religious or other social systems. We therefore publish work based on ethnography within political and religious movements, occupational or class groups, among youth, development agencies, and nationalist movements; but also work that is more thematically based – on kinship, landscape, the state, violence, corruption, the self. The series publishes four kinds of volume: ethnographic monographs; comparative texts; edited collections; and shorter, polemical essays.

We publish work from all traditions of anthropology, and all parts of the world, which combines theoretical debate with empirical evidence to demonstrate anthropology's unique position in contemporary scholarship and the contemporary world.

Professor Vered Amit
Dr Jon P. Mitchell

Acknowledgements

First of all, my sincere thanks go to all the officers, staff and management at 'Locksdon' immigration removal centre.

The fieldwork and writing of this book were aided by the encouragement and support of many people along the way. I am extremely grateful to Lisette Josephides at Queen's University Belfast for years of guidance, help and friendship. I would also like to thank Louise Amoore at Durham University, who has been a real inspiration and support. At Queen's, thanks go to Paloma Gay y Blasco for her help during fieldwork, and Hastings Donnan. Thanks also to Thomas Hylland Eriksen and to Kay Milton. At Sheffield Sociology I would like to thank Jenny Hockey and Victoria Robinson. At Durham Geography particular thanks go to (past and present) members of Room 414. Thanks also to Marieke de Goede and Mara Wesseling at the University of Amsterdam. I am extremely grateful to Anne Beech and Will Viney at Pluto Press for their endless patience and support.

An extra special big thanks to Divya Tolia Kelly.

I would also like to thank my family: my father and stepmother for help during fieldwork and my mother for all her early encouragement.

Most of all, I would like to thank Mark Powell for his friendship, for his constant love and support, and for our life together. This book is dedicated to him, and to our daughter, Connie.

Would you buy a flower that looks like this?

1
Introduction: Going Inside

Locksdon immigration removal centre accommodates men who have been detained under UK immigration law. The centre is a cluster of buildings set behind an imposing perimeter wall topped with razor wire. For Locksdon officers, staff and visitors, entry to the establishment is through a small door in the wall that leads into the gate area. For people who find themselves detained at Locksdon, entry is in the back of an escort contractor's van, often at the end of a long and exhausting journey. Inside the centre walls, detainees getting out of the escort van, like staff coming through the gate to start their shift, find themselves in an open quadrangle, with an administration building to the left and the main centre straight ahead. Detainees will spend only a few moments in the fresh air, stretching their arms and legs, before being taken by the private security contractors into the reception area, where they will undergo a series of checks before being admitted to the establishment. Locksdon officers and staff, on the other hand, will use keys attached to a key pouch to pass through a series of time delay gates and doors to gain access to the main centre.

Once inside the centre, new detainees and staff members alike confront a long corridor with doors leading off to various offices and departments – the visits centre, the multifaith centre, dormitories, gymnasium, dining hall and kitchen, education department, health department and offices used by immigration officers. Depending on the time of day, the main corridor is either silent and deserted, or busy with detainees moving and talking in groups and staff bustling in and out of offices. The smell is always the same – disinfectant, bleach, institution. As an officer walks towards the centre office to discover his or her detail for the shift, he or she might encounter a new detainee carrying his 'in possession' belongings in a large box and being led to a dormitory which will be his 'home' for the following days, weeks or months.

What kind of place is a detention centre for those who live and work there? What kind of life is led behind the walls? What strategies of control and government are at play in detention? And what forms of contestation and resistance?

This book is concerned with these questions through an examination of the daily life and everyday practices of immigration detention, focusing on the immigration removal centre that I have called Locksdon.[1] My starting point is that the practice of detaining asylum seekers, undocumented migrants and 'illegal' immigrants in the West is shaped by, and makes explicit, a series of boundaries between insider/outsider, citizen/other, secure/dangerous, deserving and undeserving. This book is concerned with the lived meaning, expression, contestation and reproduction of these boundaries and hierarchies in the everyday routines at Locksdon. This book does not address itself directly to the experiences of those detained.[2] Rather it places centrally those people charged with the enactment of practices of detention: Locksdon's officers. This book will show how the officers' experience of their work, their understandings of detention populations, their interactions with one another and with detainees, and their discretionary judgements produce and reproduce the secure detention regime, with ramifications for those who find themselves detained. This book's premise is that understanding the act of detention and its political effects on individual lives requires knowledge of the ways in which the secure regime is produced within daily, even banal, social practices and interactions.

Immigration detention only periodically comes to public attention in the UK, usually through media reports of crises within the detention estate: the 2002 fire at Yarl's Wood, for example; riots and disturbances at Harmondsworth in 2004 and 2006; hunger strikes and protests by detainees, and the death of a man being forcibly deported in October 2010. These reports briefly reveal a hidden world of 'cultures of control', indeterminate lengths of detention, dawn immigration raids and forced removals. News about crises in the detention estate is frequently accompanied by statements from state authorities which justify detention as a crucial and necessary part of a robust border. Just as frequently, non-governmental organisations (NGOs) and advocacy groups condemn detention (especially in the case of asylum seekers, or children and families) as an excessive, punitive and brutal method of dealing with vulnerable and traumatised populations (see, for instance, Burnett et al. 2010; London Detainee Support Group 2009, 2010). Despite these criticisms, detention capacity has been enlarged in the UK over the last decade, with two new immigration removal centres (Brook House and HMP Morton Hall) being added to the estate since 2009. At the end of March 2002, as fieldwork for this book began, there were 1370 people subject to immigration law being held in secure establishments in Britain. The numbers fluctuate, but on 1 December 2011 there were 2419 people held in immigration detention (Home Office 2002a, 2011).

Under UK immigration law (the 1971 Immigration Act) a person can be detained pending a deportation order and removal. According to guidelines, the act of detaining someone under UK immigration law is considered an 'appropriate' measure to: effect removal; establish a person's identity or basis of claim; or where there is a perceived likelihood of a failure to comply with the conditions of temporary admission or release. In the case of asylum seekers, people may be detained to enable a 'rapid decision' to be taken on an asylum/human rights claim. Detention is viewed as vital for 'effective' state immigration control, but guidelines for frontline staff nonetheless state there should be a presumption 'in favour of temporary admission or release' (UKBA 2012: 55.20 and chapter 57). In practice, the decision to detain is taken at a port of entry, or after an initial encounter with an immigration officer, for a variety of discretionary reasons (Weber and Gelsthorpe 2000). Far from being a 'last resort', people may find themselves detained at any stage of an asylum claim or appeal, or petition to remain. The guidelines stipulating 'presumption in favour of release' and detention for the 'shortest possible time' (UKBA 2012) are in tension with frontline border officers' duty to protect the 'public from harm' in the case of those people subject to immigration law who have been convicted of criminal offences, for example.[3]

The men held at Locksdon may be appealing against negative immigration or asylum decisions, finding themselves detained for months or even years during this process. They may have exhausted the appeals process and be facing imminent removal. People in the detention estate may have an asylum case which has been considered 'unfounded' or liable to be 'fast-tracked'. People may also enter the detention estate from prison after having served a criminal sentence or after being issued with a deportation notice. Some people in detention have been picked up by the authorities (often for a petty misdemeanour) after overstaying a visa, or after working or living without official immigration status in Britain (sometimes for many months or years, or even decades). People are moved around the detention estate for various logistical or administrative reasons. Some detainees will be granted bail, or will gain leave to remain and even eventual citizenship. While all detainees held in detention can apply for bail to the Asylum and Immigration Tribunal, in practice many men, women and children face indefinite and unchallengeable detention periods. The men held at Locksdon are part of a growing detainee population in Europe and the West, held in various accommodation and induction units, secure detention facilities or holding centres.[4]

Detention has become increasingly controversial over the last two decades, as the power to detain non-nationals under national immigration law, but also in the name of counter-terror, has been steadily entrenched across western states.[5] Detention has become an important entry point for debate about the contemporary international political terrain shaped by the 'war on terror'. Detention brings to mind high-profile cases like Guantánamo Bay, the secretive practices of extraordinary rendition and the pre-charge detention of people suspected of terrorist involvement who could not be convicted under normal juridical procedures. In the UK, for instance, the Home Secretary has the power to detain people suspected of being 'a terrorist' under the Terrorism Act 2000, when doing so is 'conducive to the public good' and for reasons of national security. The 'evidence' for detention is frequently provided by security agencies and police in secret or closed hearings, and is based on material that could not be used to secure conviction in a regular court of law (see Amnesty International 2011; Carlile 2009). The detention of people deemed a security risk 'outside' legal norms across the West raises crucial questions about how sovereign power operates across multiple domains of contemporary life (Diken and Laustsen 2005; Gregory 2006; Guild 2003; Minca 2005; Salter 2008; Tyler 2006).

Detention has therefore come to epitomise the exceptional measures that are unleashed in the name of protecting national security, and for managing populations of out-of-place, potentially risky immigrants, asylum seekers and refugees. Yet despite increased concern with the topic, relatively little has been written about the detailed operation of detention, or about the individuals who make detention work at the grassroots (though see Gill 2009; Makaremi 2008; Pratt 2001, 2005). In part this is due to the occlusion and securitisation of administrative immigration detention facilities in the international context, which has made their functions notoriously difficult to examine empirically. This book, then, contributes to the interdisciplinary literature on detention by examining individuals in social, cultural and political context as a means of understanding the 'micro-physics' of power (Foucault 1977: 26) at work in contemporary detention.

BORDER SECURITY

Locksdon immigration removal centre (hereafter IRC) is operated by Her Majesty's Prison Service under contract to the UK immigration authorities. Four of the UK's thirteen IRCs are run by the Prison Service, while the rest are managed by private security contractors for profit (see Bacon 2005).[6] Locksdon is operated under the *Detention Centre Rules* (2001) and, unlike some IRCs, holds only male detainees. The centre is staffed by approximately forty-five prison officers and ten operational support grade (OSG) staff.[7] Both wear prison uniform. There are also administrative and training workers, estates staff, four nurses, on-site immigration officers, a chaplain and education staff from a nearby Adult Education College,[8] as well as two Prison Officer physical exercise instructors (PEIs).

Officers at Locksdon frequently argued that the detainees being moved around the detention estate were unknown: 'we don't know who they are, what they've done' and 'it's better to be too secure than not secure enough'. The problem of the unknown, unidentified detainee at Locksdon is a prominent one. It draws forth a secure, surveillant regime that seeks to control men's movements and interactions around the centre. One of the central themes of this book is the way in which security and mobility are related in Locksdon, and how security becomes embodied and achieved through officers' decisions and actions. My starting point is that the control and organisation of people's movement across UK borders is intertwined with the production and protection of security, which I see to be a shifting and contested concept. Detention crystallises the problematic relationship between certain kinds of movement and projects of security. I am concerned with security as a social and cultural category, expressed and experienced within daily life in the IRC.

It is not new to suggest that migration has become 'securitised' in the West (see, for instance, Huysmans 2006; Squire 2009). In the European context, the acceleration and diversification of migration into and within member states over the last two decades, coupled with the dissolving of internal borders, has produced a paradoxical relationship between liberalisation of the markets, liberty of movement and the security of citizens. Immigration and asylum have become ever more prominent in national domestic politics since the end of the Cold War, frequently conjoined with concerns about employment and welfare, and with an increasingly 'schizophrenic' and suspicious stance taken towards asylum seekers and 'economic migrants' (Gibney 2001; 2004; Schuster 2003a, 2003b). The 'war on terror' and fear of the Islamic fundamentalist has exacerbated this suspicion and the politicisation and securitisation of migration. Europe has seen a steady rise in exclusionary nationalist politics – what Derrida (2001: 53) calls 'purifying reactions' – as well as a gradual conjoining of immigration and terrorist threats with border security initiatives. The current security climate, argues Bigo (2001, 2008) is characterised by interpenetration of 'internal' and 'external' security, producing an indistinct, contingent border like a Möbius strip, where the battles against crime, immigration and terrorism become blurred within a context of 'unease'.

In 2002, the year fieldwork for this book began, Locksdon was feeling the effects of a tumultuous period in the UK immigration and asylum system. The terrorist attacks in New York and Washington had kickstarted the 'war on terror' and a series of 'shake-ups' of the UK's border. There had also been a series of recent asylum controversies: the Sangatte crisis of 2001–2 (where asylum seekers repeatedly tried to use the Channel Tunnel to enter Britain from the camp near the French tunnel terminal) had sparked a diplomatic furore between Britain and France. The 'bogus asylum seeker' featured prominently in media reports about an immigration system deemed 'out of control'. In the British detention estate, the 2002 Nationality, Immigration and Asylum Act was swinging into force and Locksdon was negotiating the full transition from prison to IRC. New Labour's immigration reforms had, since 1997, aimed to facilitate 'beneficial' economic migration within a modernised immigration system, while stepping up the exclusion of 'undeserving' asylum seekers and threatening mobile people (see Bloch and Schuster 2005; Flynn 2005; Sales 2005; Walters 2004). This vision of an orchestrated and 'tightly managed' system described in the White Paper, *Secure Borders, Safe Haven* (Home Office 2002a) placed detention (alongside dispersal and deportation) as a crucial pillar of the 'robust but fair' border. So, while detention had been an aspect of UK border governance regimes throughout the twentieth century, through the 1990s and 2000s, it emerged as a 'normalised' technique of control (Bloch and Schuster 2005).[9]

If internal and external security become intertwined in techniques to target the immigrant/terrorist, as Bigo (2001, 2008) argues, then interdisciplinary interest has increasingly moved away from the idea of a state-centric view of security towards a more nuanced account of the practices enacted in the name of security (see, for instance, Buzan and Wæver 1997). The issue here is not how a situation of security is attained in the international and national context via military or police action, but how certain domains of life and populations become understood and governed as security problems. In relation to contemporary security-migration complexes, as Guild (2009: 3) puts it, the crucial question is how an individual becomes placed within 'a set of state structural frameworks' and 'categorised as a threat to security and to state control of migration'. Or, as Bigo has it 'Who is doing an (in)securitisation move, under what conditions, towards whom, and with what consequences?' (2008: 5). These questions, applied to the context of detention, move attention away from detention as a *response* to 'illegality' or 'threat' among groups of mobile people (asylum seeker, refugee, economic migrant). Rather, the question becomes how detention creates, targets and produces populations of insecurity, undesirability and illegality. That is, detention is a technique of government through which individuals and mobile populations become managed as illegal, undesirable or threatening.

Foucault's notion of governmentality perfectly captures the productive relationships of power through which subjects and social groups become constituted via political interventions which appear to be reactions to self-evident political or social phenomena. Foucault contrasted governmentality with sovereignty, understood as a direct form of power associated with force, law and violence applied to juridical sovereign subjects. He was concerned to uncover the multiple and indefinite networks of power deeply rooted in the social nexus that create the possibilities for certain kinds of identities to emerge (Foucault 2000 120–3). Governmentality is a dispersed operation of power that works through multiple institutions, organisations, individuals and relationships. It is the modulation and shaping of people's conduct through the diffuse orchestration of relations between people and things for certain ends, by 'having a hold on things that seem far removed from the population, but which, through calculation, analysis, and reflection, one knows can have an effect on it' (Foucault 2007: 72). Government is:

> The ensemble formed by institutions, procedures, analyses and reflections, calculations, and tactics that allow the exercise of this very specific, albeit very complex, power that has the population as its target, political economy as its major form of knowledge, and apparatuses of security as its essential technical instrument. (Foucault 2007: 108)

These 'apparatuses of security' were, for Foucault, associated with the emergence of liberalism as a particular orientation to social, economic and political contingency in the West. Security, specifically, is not concerned with prohibiting things from happening, but with governing by 'letting things happen' so that the consequences and effects of different outcomes might be played off against one another (Foucault 2007: 45, 47). As Giorgio Agamben summarises:

> Whereas disciplinary power isolates and closes off territories, measures of security lead to an opening and to globalisation; whereas the law wants to prevent and prescribe, security wants to intervene in ongoing processes to direct them. In short, discipline wants to produce order, security wants to govern disorder. (2002: 2)

Governmentality, then, is a problematising form of power: it does not intervene upon social, political or economic problems already constituted, but brings these problems into being through targeted action meant to intervene upon them (Dean 1999; Miller and Rose 2008; Rose 1999). Knowledge, expertise and representation are central to the way in which 'problematic' or 'threatening' people are governed across fields of social, political, economic and moral life – how they become intelligible, 'rendered thinkable, calculable, and manageable' (Inda 2006: 5, 7) and so amenable to intervention.

What is important here for a consideration of Locksdon and detention is, first, the 'intimate link between knowing and doing, thinking and acting, representing and intervening' at work in efforts to govern mobile people (Inda 2006: 23; see also Inda 2005). The detention of 'illegal' or 'risky' mobile people (the failed asylum seeker, the economic migrant, the possible terrorist) is the application of political, legal and moral categorisations produced within shifting knowledge regimes, legal developments and interventions across time and space. The status of being 'detainable' in any western state is created by law's tactical productivity as it is strategically implemented to differentiate between mobilities and subjects within historically constituted contexts (De Genova 2002, 2004, 2007). Far from being a rationalised system of legal categories, norms and procedures, the legal system that governs mobility in any context resembles 'an experimental machine' (Douzinas 2007: 123): it constantly changes, is inconsistent and contradictory, and is frequently reactive rather than proactive. This means that categories such as 'the refugee' are constructed 'in practice'

(Harvey 2000: 137–49) through the pragmatic interpretation of officials, whose decision-making is shaped by prevailing social, economic, political and institutional contexts. So, the framing of 'problematic' mobile populations tends to oppose them to categories of citizenship, creating a series of binary distinctions: between responsible citizenship and irresponsible 'others'; between civility and incivility; between genuine and bogus; between legality and illegality; between deserving and undeserving (see Coutin 2007, 2010, 2011; Heyman and Smart 1999; Inda 2006). At Locksdon, legalistic immigration categories ('asylum seeker', 'refugee') collapse into meaningful working categories. At Locksdon, the people awaiting immigration decisions or deportation on immigration or security grounds are known as 'detainees'. I am concerned in this book with 'detainability' as it is articulated and understood within the specific context of Locksdon: as a socio-political condition it is produced, embodied and resisted by detainees, and draws forth a response from officers that is bound up with security and their own sense of identity as citizens, officers and persons.

Second, the concept of governmentality disrupts notions of 'the state' as a coherent and reified actor. The modern state, claimed Foucault, does not have the 'unity' usually attributed to it. It is more usefully seen as a 'mythicised abstraction' and 'composite reality': a crystallisation of power relationships into which people become integrated in objectifying ways (2000: 220–1, 332–4), and an 'exercise in legitimation, in moral regulation' (Abrams 1988: 771). On one hand, the rise of international and supranational alliances, and webs of regional and global governance (in Europe, for instance) make 'the state' less able to singularly define its domestic affairs and defend the security of its territorial border. New international authorities, private authorities and novel, reinvigorated sovereignties are emerging that appear to herald the disintegration of state power (Cowen and Gilbert 2007; Edkins et al., 2004; Gregory and Pred 2007). On the other hand, defending territorial borders and protecting the nation are one of the ways through which the security states 'writes itself' (Campbell 1998). 'New' terrorist threats have been associated with the bolstering of state militarism and force within public spaces and the border (Andreas and Biersteker 2003; Andreas and Snyder 2000; Newman 2001). The ability of the state to align nation, territory and citizenship is, on the one hand, challenged by the 'disruptions, transgressions and dislocations' of mobile people: their movements and their rights-claims (Squire 2009: 5). Yet it is through what De Genova

(2002: 437) calls the 'spectacle' of enforcement at the border (like detention) that 'the state' is brought into being, materialised in the effects it has on individual lives. This is despite the dispersal of state effects within fields of governmentality, and despite global migration being managed by international coalitions of public and private authorities, humanitarian organisations and inter- and intra-state alliances (Lui 2004; Nyers 2006; Walters 2002).

My concern in this book is to de-unify the state in Foucault's terms by focusing on the practices of actors embodying 'its' power at capillary points (Foucault 1977). Government, here, is not 'self-enacting or all-encompassing' (Heyman 2004: 494); as Herzfeld (1992: 156) argues, there is no autonomous state 'except in the hands of those who create and execute its ostensibly self-supporting teleology'. Prison officers at Locksdon are designated state agents, 'proxy sovereigns' able to wield authority and physical force over detainees in the name of preventing injury or a disturbance, and my interest is in how this authority is understood, experienced, applied and expressed. A consideration of Locksdon staff, then, exceeds what Heyman (2004: 491) calls 'broad-brush' analyses of power and bureaucracy, one which places centrally 'the way bureaucrats go about their work, especially in the zone between official policy and unofficial routine and discretion' (2004: 491). At stake in this zone is the prosaic operation of power in context, and, as I shall argue, the possibility of ethical encounter in the divided routines of the secure detention establishment. This book is very much concerned with the experiential, embodied practices of detention, and with subjectivities – 'complex structures of thought, feeling and reflection' (Ortner 2006: 115). Foucault reminds us that there is no necessary coherence or clear directionality to power relations and effects. It becomes vital to grasp how people act upon others, what desires they have, how persons are objectified and how rationalities become implemented in relationships, criss-crossing, annulling and reinforcing one another (Foucault 2000: 345). Also, I would add, it is vital to tease apart social and cultural meanings within relationships of power and control. In this way, the everyday life of detention and a consideration of individuals in their social context is not separable from some more important or profound realm of 'the political'. Rather, an examination of 'the everyday' is to take seriously the way in which governmental control is produced through the actions of people in context, and how these actions affect individuals' lived experience.

The detention centre epitomises what Foucault (1977, 2007) referred to as biopolitical and disciplinary power. In the detention centre, detainees' bodies, health and physical state become thoroughly invested by politics – the responsibility of the institution and the site for multiple battles for control. The detainees, and staff, become subject to a disciplinary regime that aims to fix, arrange and train individuals in time and space to achieve an ordered, secure establishment. Discipline in Foucault's sense is an objectifying form of power that takes the human body as its prime focus, seeking normalisation through knowledge, perfection through scrutiny and economy through training (Foucault 2000: 339). Yet if the everyday life of detention is where power and control penetrates individual bodies and the textures of social life, it is also where power *and resistance* play out agonistically. Foucault's insight was that power is always accompanied by (in fact cannot exist without) resistance. Locating these points of resistance can shed light on the way in which power relations operate (Abu-Lughod 1990; Foucault 1977). Everyday life in Locksdon, then, is not simply an arena of control and domination, but, as I shall show, also a lively place of diversion, resistance, 'clandestine forms' and 'play' (Certeau 1984: xiv–xv, 25). The detention centre regime as an apparatus of control is constantly being undone and contested by staff and detainees alike.

BORDER DECISIONS

Locksdon officers often compared life at Locksdon to life in a 'real nick': working with immigration detainees was like 'babysitting' in comparison to working with convicted criminals in a prison. Despite the key differences between prison and immigration detention that will emerge through the book, there were many overlaps and similarities in the daily work. Officers would frequently describe the difficulty of negotiating what one officer described as 'wiggly lines' – the exercise of discretion in highly visible contexts. Indeed, one of the concerns of this book is to demonstrate how detention and criminality are related within a distinct dynamic of control within Locksdon: the use of Prison Service establishments for the accommodation of people detained under immigration law continually blurs the line between penalty and administrative detention.

On the one hand, officers have no real authority over crucial border decisions – about which detainees are granted leave to remain, for instance, or which are released from detention, or expelled from Britain. On the other hand, Locksdon officers must make swift decisions about the men in their control all the time: about when to use force, for instance, or when to monitor a man as a suicide risk, or when to separate him from the regime for his, and others', 'protection'. These decisions, as I will argue, are *sovereign* decisions that produce an ambiguous political space and political vulnerability among detainees. The philosopher Giorgio Agamben places 'the decision' centrally in his delineation of sovereign power. After Schmitt, he sees sovereign power to be located within the decision on 'the exception' and its production of a vulnerable and powerless condition, a condition he calls 'bare life'. Bare life is a biopolitical state where a person is stripped of political status and becomes abject: unworthy, excludable, undesirable. Bare life is held in an ambiguous relationship between inclusion and exclusion in the political order, which Agamben calls a zone of indistinction. So, while the creation of political order appears to recognise people via political status (citizens as bearers of rights), natural life is never wholly excluded but rather held in an 'inclusive exclusion (an exceptio)' (1998: 7). Agamben explains the exception through a discussion of the figure of *homo sacer* from archaic Roman law. *Homo sacer* was a subject who had committed an infraction and who had been banished from the political community, a person excluded from the law and who could not be sacrificed, but who could be killed with impunity and who could not claim rights and protections. Agamben draws on Carl Schmitt to relate the sovereign ban and the banned life of *homo sacer* to declarations of emergency and the identification of the figure of the enemy: 'sovereign is he who decides on the state of exception' (1998: 11). This decision to declare an exception is a decision to 'suspend the validity of the law' (1998: 15) in an extraordinary situation. In this way, the creation of the rule of law hinges on a power of decision that is itself outside or above the law. Sovereign power, after Agamben, is an ordering (of space, relations, politics, law) that does not simply demarcate a juridical and territorial order, but also governs by 'taking outside' – excluding people yet retaining a hold upon them, and maintaining certain subjects in a banned relationship. In being able to decide on the exception (when the normal law is suspended, when a political emergency requires 'special measures') sovereign power is both inside and outside law. As Humphrey (2004) argues, the menace of sovereign power rests on its capacity to snuff out bare life without regard to its sacral quality.

For Agamben, it is the camp (he used the wartime Nazi camp as his example) that forms the material manifestation of the indistinct zone of biopolitics and the exception. The camp is the place where people are 'taken outside' yet governed more tightly, where sovereign power intervenes directly on bodies and individual lives which do not have the normal protection of law, and where people become reduced to 'bare life'. Importantly, for Agamben, the camp is not 'an anomaly belonging to the past ... but the hidden matrix and nomos of the political space in which we are still living' (1998: 166). The concentration camps, Agamben argued, were originally created through the temporary suspension of the law in order to preserve the law in a declared state of emergency, but they went on to become a 'permanent spatial arrangement' where the rule of law and exception blurred and everything became possible (1998: 169–70). Camp inhabitants became pure bare life, *homines sacri*, subject to the full force of sovereign power over their very lives, but unprotected by it.

Agamben's delineation of the camp, the exception and sovereign power have been widely engaged to illuminate the dynamics of contemporary camps – terrorist detention centres, refugee camps, holding centres and removal centres – but also the more generalised working of sovereign political power in contemporary times (Diken 2004; Diken and Laustsen 2005; Gregory 2006; Johns 2005; Minca 2005). For Judith Butler, notably, detention (she uses Guantánamo Bay as her example) is where the resurgence of contemporary sovereign power is most visible. Foucault (2007) did not see governmentality as *replacing* sovereignty, but rather maintained that these distinct forms of power intertwine in their effects and operation. For Butler, sovereign power is increasingly dislocated from the core agencies of the state and juridical authorities, and is found in the suspension of law and the exercise of prerogative power in the name of security and emergency by what she calls 'petty sovereigns' – executive administrators and managerial officials, whose discretionary power is heightened yet unmoored from systems of legitimacy and accountability (2004: 54–5). We have seen a revitalisation of sovereign power within the war on terror, she argues, not only in the sense described above – as traditional state agencies' capacities are bolstered and entrenched in the name of security – but also novel and 'rogue' forms of sovereign power which, for Butler (2004: 54), are resurging 'with the vengeance of an anachronism that refuses to die'. Crucially, the possibilities that pertain to declarations of security and emergency usher in exceptional powers of exclusion, seep into everyday contexts and become normalised.

Moreover, the camp betrays the way in which sovereign power is deeply entangled with the politics of the nation: the camp becomes the 'logical consequence and an almost necessary correlate of a world fully divided into territorial, nation-states' (Walters 2002: 285), a 'lasting crisis' in the relationship between territory, state and nation (Agamben 2006: 113–14). Ordering political life according to sovereign territorial nation-states, and basing 'universal' political inclusion on belonging ordered by birth, requires zones where those who do not belong on these terms may be relegated. That is, sovereign power can only 'produce a homogenous and pure "people" by the exclusion of all that do not count as people in its terms' (Edkins 2007: 78). The refugee, particularly, emerges as a 'political excess' and 'limit concept' (Nyers 2006: xiii–xv) against which modern accounts of 'the political' (community, citizenship, rights) draw their sense, and yet are simultaneously made precarious. The refugee, by 'breaking up the identity between man and citizen, between nativity and nationality … throws into crisis the original fiction of sovereignty' (Agamben 2006: 5), becomes both the 'constitutive outside of sovereignty and the element that threatens its disruption from within' (Edkins 2007: 86). Without the protection of a state, without membership of a national community, the refugee exposes the limits of 'universal' citizen rights and protections, revealing them to be unevenly applied and based on exclusions. As a category of protection, then, being a refugee is consistently framed as a temporary condition, 'solved' by either repatriation or naturalisation. Detention is a crucial part of the (forcible) reallocation and organisation of bodies within this 'national order', what Walters (2002) calls a 'technology of citizenship' (see also De Genova and Peutz 2010). In the UK, detention is officially linked to removal and the failure or end of an immigration case claim, and the official renaming of detention centres as 'removal centres' in 2002 reflects this. In sum, the possibility of political life – of inclusion, of law, and of rights and protections for some within this political order – operates only through making 'exceptions' of those who do not count and do not belong. Sovereign power, argue Edkins and Pin-Fat (2004) 'draws lines' between lives: between politically recognisable lives and excludable 'bare' lives.

For my purposes, I see the decision to 'take outside' (with all of the consequences that entails) to be a central 'problematic' of life inside Locksdon. First, in the sense of being a problem of discretion and judgement for officers, on which the security of the establishment and people's very lives depend, and, second, in the sense of diagnosing how sovereign power is devolved, embodied and unleashed in social life. As Humphrey (2004) argues, Agamben's philosophical approach is general and prescriptive, but anthropology takes a less abstract and programmatic tack, exploring the social characteristics and actualities of relations under sovereignty. This book is concerned with officers' decisions and the 'drawing of lines', and how everyday decisions emerge from physical sensations of risk and emotional states of anger, from disorientation and frustration related to a desire to punish, from normative pressures and obligations to colleagues. This book, then, looks at the way the banal decisions of detention frequently suspend the 'normal regime' in favour of punitive and retaliatory action. These decisions are taken within discretionary judgements by officers. Discretion, as Pratt and Sossin (2009: 306) argue, is 'ultimately a political issue, not simply a legal one'; it is as much to do with cultural norms, working protocols and social experience as it is about rule-based legalistic categories. As Heyman (2009: 367) puts it, discretion 'is not a formless domain of uncontrolled action, but ... an analysable domain of patterned actions that significantly affect law and administration'; these actions may 'draw on existing lines of social inequality and constitute and reinforce them' (2009: 367, 388). At Locksdon, as I shall show, the power to use force is lawfully conferred on officers in order to prevent a detained person from injuring himself or others, damaging property or creating a disturbance, but in its moment of application becomes embodied as physical force and experienced as a castigatory measure to retain control over detainees.

I see the detention centre as a border zone. First, in the sense that Agamben describes – a place that is at once inside and outside, where distinctive forms of power shape life. Makaremi (2010: 9) argues that, faced with new forms of mobility and the interpenetration of domestic and international security, states increasingly 'thicken' the border 'into spaces where people live, are confined, selected, displaced' (see also Squire 2011). The detention centre is, literally, the national border 'stretched' and displaced away from the territorial edge, inhabited by people whose identity and status are in question and around whom multiple bordering procedures flourish. At border areas, people experience 'state' and 'nation' in tangible ways, through the physical intrusions of technologies and the overt classification of people according to politico-legal complexes

(Donnan and Wilson 1998: 1–10, 16, 1999). The detention centre is a border zone, second, in its spatialised isolating practices which aim to create distance from 'others' who threaten the desired social order (Bauman 1993: 162, 237). Detention actively inscribes differences, distance and otherness. The relegation of anomalous people (and those charged with their care) to certain places and enclosures, with associated barriers, prohibitions and constraints, is a ubiquitous feature of modern social life (Sibley 1995: ix). These practices become even more accentuated in the management of national 'outsiders', where the security of the majority appears to justify the confinement of the few (Bashford and Strange 2003: 4). Isin and Rygiel (2007) argue that contemporary holding zones, frontiers, refugee camps and camp-like spaces do not aim to eliminate people reduced to bare life and stripped of political status, as in Agamben's camp, but to interrupt, curtail or disrupt the possibility of being a political being – of acting politically and of claiming rights of citizenship – by rendering people inaudible and invisible through spatial exclusion, for example, or measures preventing people from reaching sovereign territories to claim rights, or literal confinement. These spaces are abject: 'spaces of inexistence' where people are 'condemned to inexistent states of transient permanence in which they are made inaudible and invisible' (2007: 198). Isin and Rygiel call for attention to be paid to the precise processes enacted in various camp-like places, and for knowledge of the efforts and practices through which a politically abject state – cast out, unworthy, lowly, unwanted, excluded – is inscribed and resisted. In the detention centre, the national boundary between inclusion and exclusion, security and insecurity is worked through in banal encounters between officers and detainees, and is intertwined with other boundaries. The detention centre as border zone is the place where the relationship between inside and outside is constantly in question and becomes intensified, where moralised discourses about exclusion and 'deservingness' permeate physical space and social relations, and where ideas about threat, security and order become physically experienced and expressed.

BORDER ETHICS

The 2001 *Detention Centre Rules* (para. 1, 2) state that:

> The purpose of detention centres shall be to provide for the secure but humane accommodation of detained persons in a relaxed

regime with as much freedom of movement and association as possible, consistent with maintaining a safe and secure environment, and to encourage and assist detained persons to make the most productive use of their time, while respecting in particular their dignity and the right to individual expression.

Due recognition will be given at detention centres to the need for awareness of the particular anxieties to which detained persons may be subject and the sensitivity that this will require, especially when handling issues of cultural diversity

In practice, and as this book will argue, the production of a 'secure but humane' regime is fraught with difficulties. If the nature of barriers and their policing suggests much about expert imaginaries of confined populations (Bashford and Strange 2003: 8), then the use of removal centres as tools of control frames detention populations as security threats, system abusers, absconders and criminals. HM Inspectorate of Prisons' immigration removal centre inspections reports regularly criticise detention centre facilities for failing to deal sensitively with the 'particular anxieties' of detainees.[10] If suspicion and security are key elements in the governance of immigration and asylum, then they coalesce most acutely in detention, and in the practices at Locksdon.

Officers and staff at removal centres like Locksdon find themselves dealing with constantly shifting populations of men with disparate backgrounds, experiences and histories. As I will show, Locksdon was a divided social context, with boundaries between officer and detainee, officer and manager, inside and outside constantly at issue in daily life. These boundaries were related to the production of security within the regime. The structure of the secure regime at Locksdon utilised various technologies of surveillance and control (CCTV cameras, visual vigilance, bureaucratic procedures) that objectified detainees as abstracted 'bodies' to be organised in time and space. One of the effects of Locksdon's regime, I will argue, despite its obsessive attention to detail, was the production of inattention and indifference, where individuals were not recognised as persons. Detainees became interchangeable, part of a mass of men to be managed and 'processed'. During my fieldwork, for instance, officers were criticised by management for using the term 'fed' to refer to detainees' mealtimes (as in, 'Well, I suppose we'd better get them fed'). For the officers, such language reflected their work as they saw and experienced it: the correct and efficient fulfilment of a variety of procedures pertaining to the detainees. The regime at Locksdon –

concerned as it is with security – frequently obliterated the possibility of recognising detainees' personal, individual circumstances, to which officers remained largely indifferent. The specific problems, needs and histories of those who might find themselves at Locksdon – depression, trauma, experience of persecution – were, despite well-meaning staff, not easily accommodated within the everyday life of detention. Yet, despite the fractured and indifferent context, as I will argue, officers also embodied responsibility and accountability in relation to the men in their control, a responsibility and accountability that was ethical in character.

On one hand, then, the immigration and asylum system of which Locksdon can be seen as a part is a classic bureaucratic assemblage. As Herzfeld (1992) has argued, the ritualistic, formalistic nature of national state bureaucratic action tends to produce a transcendent aura of finality and certainty that hides the arbitrariness of the boundaries it seeks to uphold. As Herzfeld argues, national bureaucracy fosters solidarity among fellow nationals at the same time as it produces a 'logical' indifference to outsiders: laws and procedures that appear benign, universal and egalitarian hold the seeds of hierarchy, indifference and exclusion. We see this clearly in the bureaucratic administration of the rule of law, for instance, where abstract, rational, universal principles become in their enactment indifferent to the plight of the individual, frequently unable to address the unique singularity of a person's life and experience, providing an excuse for inaction rather than the justice to which they aspire (Bauman 1993; Douzinas 2002: 13; Herzfeld 1992).

In the case of immigration rules and procedures, the 'moral cosmology of belonging' of the national order is made explicit (Malkki 1995a, 1995b; Nyers 2006), a cosmology which creates an overarching geo-political framework and 'moral cartography' which produces in turn 'radical circumspection of the kinds of persons and groups recognised as worthy subjects of moral solicitude' (Shapiro 1999: 61). Put simply, the British asylum and immigration system relegates people outside the sphere of moral concern in the name of 'self-evident' national borders, bureaucratic efficiency and the rational administration of legal rights. Here we might turn to Bauman's discussion (after Levinas) of how organisational cultures and bureaucratic regimes keep moral responsibility 'afloat' by rendering individuals 'speechless in the face of assigned tasks and procedural rules' (1993: 125–6). The disassembly of people into traits or parts that can be acted upon, processed and administered 'effaces the face' of the moral person and makes possible immoral acts (Bauman, 1993: 127). I am concerned in this book with the way in which detention utilises technologies of control to divide and disassemble detainees, reducing them to a series of biological processes or transforming them into objects to be processed, and how this produces the conditions for them to be placed beyond moral solicitude.

On the other hand, the discretionary power that officers held – about designating a threat to security, about the use of force, about protecting the regime – always contained the potential for a response to the detainee that recognises him as more than 'detainee'. Social life at the centre was characterised by antagonism and tensions between detainees and officers, but could also produce encounters of respect, generosity or solicitude. The emergence of encounters like these in the inhospitable conditions of the detention centre have much to tell us about what Kristeva (1991: 96) has called 'the confrontation between political reason and moral reason'. The politicised categories and abstractions through which we become intelligible to bureaucratic technologies are exceeded by the approach of the other, in Levinas's term. This approach might provoke indifference, apathy or practices to 'place [the other] under my categories and use him for my purposes' (Wild 1979: 13). It might, alternatively, provoke 'a real response, a responsible answer' that seeks to 'share his world [the world of the other] by speaking to him' (Wild 1979: 14). I am concerned in this book with the way in which the everyday life of detention throws up moral situations where officers cannot help but be responsible for 'the other' and cannot help but recognise the arbitrariness of the lines dividing them from the detainees.

Anthropology has tended to approach the study of ethical systems in terms of moralities. The discipline has emphasised the multiplicity, inclusiveness and plurality of moral discourse and practice. It has also focused on the differential values that are associated with different persons within communities (for example men and women) as well as the 'conflicts of premises and values that may emerge at the meeting of different moral orders' (Howell 1997: 4–11; see also Caplan 2003: 4; Heyman 2000). Many anthropological studies have approached morality 'from an angle', through considerations of social norms, social control, religion, pollution, honour and shame and conceptualisations of evil (Caplan 2003: 3; and see Parkin 1985). Anthropologists have generally aimed to discern the link between values which are derived from a larger metaphysical whole and actual behaviour and practice, and the dynamic relationship

between moral ideals and practice. Specific cultural predisposi-
tions and perceptions of personhood, agency and sociality inform
moral relations between groups and persons: ethnographic detail
can reveal the plurality, contestation and negotiation within moral
action by considering moral agents in concrete social situations
(Howell 1997: 14).

Given traditional anthropological concerns with context and
relativism, anthropologists have appeared reticent in defining what
could be meant by morality 'cross-culturally', beyond that it is 'a
form of socially sanctioned behaviour' (Parkin 1985: 5). Morality
has been conceptualised as an 'evaluation of conduct in relation
to esteemed or despised human qualities' (Humphrey 1997: 25)
and 'a form of embodied knowledge' enabling action in the social
world (Howell 1997: 11). It has also been described as linked to
'the happiness or misery of those involved', where well-being and
happiness are culturally produced and defined (Parkin 1985: 6).
These definitions seek to reflect morality as not only supporting
and perpetuating social structure (as Durkheim argued), but as a
complex of cultural assumptions about personhood; what counts
as appropriate behaviour by and towards someone under different
conditions and how this informs the creation of selfhood and social
relationships (Parkin 1985: 4, 6). Other scholars have sought to find
the basis of morality that transcends cultural and social boundaries,
and have focused on what is shared ontologically by all humans
(see Josephides 2003a, 2003b).

This book is concerned with moral norms in the centre – local
assumptions and elaborations of what it meant to 'do good' and
'be good'. I will discuss, for instance, the friendship and solidarity
that existed between officers and colleagues, and the way they
shaped moral action in everyday working life. My interest is
also in what I describe as 'ethical moments' in centre life. These
ethical encounters are in stark contrast to the antagonistic and
divisive social relations that existed between officers and detainees.
At times, the boundaries that shaped and emerged from life in
detention were dissolved and transcended by expressions of concern
and care, and by 'unmediated recognition and generous action
without calculation' (Josephides 2010: 390). I will examine these
fragile relationships as 'cosmopolitan', being grounded in shared
capacities such as empathy and embodied vulnerability. The way
that human mobility is governed relies on the apparently self-evident
distinctions between citizens and others, between legal and illegal,
distinctions which are more accurately seen as being created within

sovereign decisions. This is never more the case than in the 'zone of indistinction' of detention centres like Locksdon, where there is much at stake in policing boundaries between inclusion and exclusion. Yet it is in places like Locksdon that the coordination between physical and social/cognitive proximity is broken (Bauman 1993: 152). The detention regime is certainly objectifying, as I will demonstrate, but the everyday life of detention frequently exceeds the clear boundaries that are supposed to separate officers and detainees, citizens and others, political 'inside' and 'outside'.

ENTERING LOCKSDON

Locksdon IRC is operated by the Prison Service and has a hierarchical 'rank' structure: normal grade officers, senior officers (SOs), principal officers (POs), deputy managers and managers.[11] SOs and normal grade officers are responsible for the daily regime, while POs and governors are responsible for managerial duties. At the time of my fieldwork, officers tended to come from working-class backgrounds – few had been to college and many of the men had skilled 'manual trades' – and the majority of officers at Locksdon had served in the armed forces. A career in the Prison Service is a 'well-trodden' route for men and women leaving the forces, although Prison Service recruitment initiatives in recent years have favoured a more inclusive mix of backgrounds. Officers operated the regime on a shift basis. Only normal grade officers worked night shifts. Officers were detailed to work alternate weekends and tended to be detailed with the same people on night shifts. They had two rest days a week, not necessarily together. At the time of my fieldwork, the Locksdon regime was divided into a morning period, lunch, an afternoon period, tea, an evening period and lock-up. These periods were interspersed with roll checks, when detainees were counted and locked into their dormitories for staff breaks and overnight. During the daytime, normal grade officers could be detailed to work in one of the following areas:

- Reception, where detainees passed in and out of the establishment. This involved carrying out the various procedures accompanying the movement of detainees into and out of the establishment.
- The exercise yard, where detainees took air and exercise. This involved monitoring detainees 'associating' in a small courtyard.

- The education department. This involved pat-down searching detainees entering and leaving the education department, the library or music room.
- 'Visits', where friends, families, volunteers and lawyers could visit detainees. This work involved accompanying visitors and detainees to the Visits building, searching them and monitoring the Visits room.
- Immigration department. The immigration liaison officer (ILO) processed incoming and outgoing faxes from detainees to their solicitors and other immigration detention establishments, arranged for detainee interviews with immigration officers and coordinated detainee enquiries.
- The sports field, acting as back-up security for the PEIs who were refereeing sports matches.
- The centre office. The centre officer staffed the desk at the centre office, dealing with detainees' queries and keeping the roll board correct when detainees came and went from Locksdon.
- Audits, the task of checking that the establishment's various procedures for routine and emergency scenarios were all in place and up to date.

On night shifts staff performed regular dormitory and perimeter checks and were responsible for coordinating aid in case of an emergency. They were most likely to be present during a possible escape attempt, suicide attempt or disturbance. Apart from these duties, they were not detailed to do any special task. Staff could be called in to boost officer numbers in an emergency situation at any time.

The establishment was visited regularly by a Visiting Committee, an independent body which offered an 'outside' eye to assess the standards of care at Locksdon and to provide an ear to staff and detainees alike. There was also a volunteer group that visited and befriended detainees, and there were weekly visits made by Citizen's Advice Bureau workers, who operated a 'drop-in' clinic for detainees. Local leaders from all faiths would visit to lead acts of worship and to be available to detainees. There were regular Detainee Consultative Committee meetings, where problems with the regime could be raised and detainees could also address their problems or grievances to the manager directly, on application. Locksdon provided laundry services and a barber visited weekly.

Having secured the manager's approval for fieldwork, and having undergone a security check, it was agreed that I could spend two or three days a week at Locksdon. I was able to move unaccompanied around Locksdon to observe and talk to staff as they went about their work. Despite having secured the centre manager's permission to conduct research, obtaining the officers' consent to my long-term presence was an ongoing negotiation. In the Prison Service, observation and research are associated with audits and inspections, with connotations of judgement and examination. Officers frequently expressed frustration that they were commonly portrayed (in the media, for example) as 'brutes' or 'animals'. I later learned that I was the subject of an SIR (Security Intelligence Report) in the first few weeks of my fieldwork because officers suspected I was an undercover journalist. The IRC is a place of multiple boundaries – between staff and detainees, officers and managers, staff and outsiders. Gaining the officers' trust involved appreciating these boundaries and the way they shaped and ordered life within the centre: specifically, it involved tactically distancing myself from management and also from the detainees.

Initially, officers were 'detailed' to show me around the establishment and talk to me about things that they thought might interest a 'student': the race relations and equal opportunities work, detainee meetings, provision for worship. I soon wanted to escape this managed routine, and I told the deputy governor that I required no special 'babysitting'. The fact that I had no clear role in a place of work meant I was often watching men and women in their daily routines and this, of course, made people awkward at first. Before long, however, I had negotiated a habitual round of the establishment that involved spending time in different departments. I talked to the officers as they coped with the mundane and the fraught aspects of their work, as they laughed and argued with colleagues and detainees, and outside work as they socialised.

This book, then, takes an ethnographic approach to detention. Ethnography is what Ortner (2006: 42–3) calls 'an intellectual (and moral) positionality': it is 'a constructive and interpretive mode' and a 'bodily process in space and time' which aims to produce 'understanding through richness, texture, and detail, rather than parsimony, refinement and (in the sense used by mathematicians) elegance'. It looks at 'concrete manifestations' (Inda 2005: 11) of power – how specific inclusions and exclusions materialise in specific practices and contexts, their effects and consequences, their embedding in the dense, humdrum everyday. It aims for what Geertz classically called 'thick description' (1973: 10) that goes beyond surfaces to expose implicit meanings. As an approach to Locksdon, at issue is the way in which certain subject positions and identities – detainee, asylum seeker, citizen – are formed from the intersections of discourses and practices, but also the way in which subjects create and shape those discourses and practices in turn: there is a tension between people's practices and the contexts of culture, society and politics in which they find themselves (Aretxaga 1997: 19; Ortner 2006: 2). Subjects, as Ortner argues, occupy particular positions in the socio-political order, but also have complex subjectivities – feelings and fears, desires and affects, thoughts and perceptions – that are shaped within social and cultural formations, but shape these formations in turn.

The production of ethnographic knowledge is always situated and contextualised. I have used the past tense to describe life at Locksdon to reflect the spatio-temporal specificity of this research, though I would argue that the themes and 'problems' of detention are pervasive in detention (though this does not mean that working practices at Locksdon are not in constant development and have not changed year on year). Ethnographic knowledge, as well as being positioned in time and space, emerges from the distinct positionality of the researcher. The positioned production of knowledge within long-term fieldwork and the relationships that are forged have ethical implications. Participant observation involves the researcher becoming suspended somewhere between stranger/friend, involvement/detachment, empathetic engagement and 'objective observation' (see Crick 1992: 189–90; Powdermaker 1966: 9, 13). The 'friendships' that emerge during fieldwork are imbued with utility and what Strathern (1987) has described as the arrogance of authorship: anthropological knowledge appears to be 'extracted' from selves, relationships, work or products (Strathern 1987: 21–3), and this contrasts sharply with the ideals of friendship in the western context. There are many understandings of the term 'friend', of course: the ideals of equality and equivalence associated with western friendship frequently camouflage various kinds of vulnerability, revelation, secrecy and inequality (Pahl 2000; Paine 1999). For many men and women at Locksdon, the fluid lines between colleagues and friends, and the tightly knitted relationships at the centre, did not allow for a clear separation between being mates and being colleagues. Indeed, the everyday expression of amicability at Locksdon was part of 'being there'.

Entering the social world of Locksdon was to encounter a dense set of friendships, obligations and histories which played out across and within the working practices and protocols of centre life. My knowledge of Locksdon was 'extracted' from these social relations in which I was temporarily embroiled. At first, officers simply could not understand what I was doing at Locksdon and were asking 'Are you still here?' in the weeks leading up to my departure a year later. In time-honoured fashion, it was when I was befriended by a 'maverick gatekeeper', Drew, that my position eased. Once Drew had declared that I was 'switched on' (had common sense) and 'was a good laugh' (did not react badly to bawdy jokes), more officers were easier around me. Kauffman (1988; see also Waldram 1998) notes that observers in secure environments are often seen as intruders. The process of securing access and cooperation in a divisive prison environment involves multiple negotiations and a careful 'presentation of self' (Goffman 1969). The governor's permission to conduct research at Locksdon did not give me the officers' own permission, and gaining officers' trust involved tactically distancing myself from management and also from the detainees. Staff were more relaxed when I had demonstrated that the information I discussed with them did not get passed on to management.

More specifically, Agar (1980: 41) notes that people will always categorise or contextualise the ethnographer in a way that affects attitudes to him or her. My gender was an important structuring factor in my acceptance (and non-acceptance) at Locksdon and the relationships I made with (certain) officers. Locksdon was, and is, a predominantly male environment and most of my informants were male and aged between 35 and 55. In the research process, gender differences set up different patterns of social relations and can create differential access to domains of knowledge. Indeed, some places were rendered literally invisible and inaccessible to me: the male officers' changing rooms, some of the masculine spaces of male sociality within and outside Locksdon. Yet other insights and spaces opened up: officers would talk to me about feelings of uncertainty and fear in a way that did not come out in the boisterous 'public' face they presented at Locksdon. Locksdon was an environment where salacious gossip and illicit affairs were a regular part of life, and it was an environment where people were highly visible. Women had to tread a careful line between friendliness and impropriety. My own experiences of the difficulties this presented gave me insights into what it was like for women (and men) to work at Locksdon. Jackson (1989) argues that we use our own experience to grasp the experience of others. In the detention environment, where bodily dispositions of mistrust and vigilance permeate social life, my own experiences of vigilance offered me insights into what life was like for the officers.

* * *

The next chapter begins to describe and discuss life at Locksdon. It considers the modes of visual control that permeated life at Locksdon, and the efforts that officers undertook to achieve 'security' and an orderly, predictable detention regime. It examines looking and seeing as embodied practices which secured the detainee body in detention. Chapter 3 places the relations between officers at Locksdon at its centre, and provides an account of the IRC as a place of gender politics, friendship, familiarity and tension. Understanding what 'loyalty' and 'solidarity' meant in the context of work at Locksdon is central to understanding the way the regime worked. Chapter 4 discusses resistance, disruption and subversion within the IRC, and explores what happened when the regime was threatened by indiscipline in the form of detainees' bodily contestation or organised protest. Chapter 5 explores staff discretion and judgement in light of Agamben's account of sovereign power, particularly around the mobilisation of force. In the context of daily work, the staff at Locksdon constantly made decisions and judgements. The way in which these decisions drew the line between acceptable and unacceptable, norm and anomaly, and between norm and exception was crucial to the operation of the detention centre. Chapter 6 is concerned with the possibility of an ethical response within discretionary judgement.

2
Visual Practice and the Secure Regime

Ed Davies was a long-serving officer at Locksdon. He had joined the Prison Service after serving in the army, like many of his colleagues, and he had been content to stay as a normal grade officer rather than 'going for promotion' and 'joining management', despite his experience. Ed was popular with his colleagues but he was known to be temperamental: sometimes he was talkative and humorous, sometimes he was remote and unapproachable. There were rumours of problems at home, depression perhaps. Ed appeared to be particularly affected by the working environment at Locksdon, which he summed up as having 'everyone in your face all the time'. He would frequently withdraw from the regime – finding work to do that would take him away from the confrontations of the centre or literally hiding in a quiet office or disused room until roll check. At lunchtimes and other breaks, he would sometimes retire to his car in the car park, where passing staff members would spot him sipping tea from a flask and listening to the radio.

The conversations I had with Ed typically revolved around 'Immigration' being 'hopeless' – the authorities losing men in the detention estate, needlessly moving people between IRCs, failing to deport detainees despite them waiting months in detention. Ed, like many of his colleagues, frequently talked about feeling a loss of control over the detainees and the centre. The pressing issue confronting officers at Locksdon, Ed told me, was that the Prison Service rules were being gradually taken away from staff, not only at Locksdon, which was operating under the *Detention Centre Rules* (2001), but also more generally in prisons. For instance, the 'carrot and stick' system whereby governors (managers) could add or subtract sentence time according to prisoners' behaviour had disappeared. It used to be the case, Ed told me, that officers could open a prisoner's letters, for instance, and they would know before the prisoner did whether there was a problem at home – 'a Dear John letter, or bad news'. That way, officers could make allowances and manage difficulties as they arose:

You wouldn't have to roll about on the floor [deploy control and restraint techniques] – most problems could just be sorted out very easily with an extra phone call, a letter home. Some would say you were being soft but you were just using your head. There isn't enough of that sort of thing now.

In the context of Locksdon, Ed implied, the loss of 'the ways we have' (to control people) was particularly problematic given the uncertainty that surrounded the men in their care and control. Officers perceived the detainees passing through Locksdon to be unknown – without a verifiable identity, history or biography. In a prison, convicted inmates arrive at an establishment with a history of prior convictions, psychological reports, 'expert assessments' and sentence procedures. Detainees, in comparison, would arrive at Locksdon with little or no documentary evidence, either because it did not exist or because it had not been transferred by the immigration authorities or police, for instance. As a result, there were often large gaps in authoritative knowledge about a new detainee's history and past behaviour. As another officer explained:

These people [detainees] could be anyone. We have no idea who they are and what they are doing here. I'm not saying that some of them aren't genuine, but do we know who they are? They could be ex-soldiers. We've had a few of them. One guy was interviewed by the Special Branch and got taken away – he was wanted for some war crime in Serbia or something. These guys – they may be wanted by the local mafia, they may be on the run from somewhere. They may have killed their granny, pissed off the family, the local gangs. They may have been involved in all kinds of stuff. All they have to do is get on a plane, get rid of their passport and arrive in Britain. Once they're here they just give a name and we have no way of knowing who they are. Immigration don't know. They haven't got a clue. And they wind up in here. (Male officer)

One day Ed remarked to me, quite out of the blue, and as if by way of explanation, 'In this job, you have to be a bodywatcher. You have to notice things about people.' 'Bodywatching', I will argue in this chapter, captures the staff's daily confrontation with what will always remain unknowable about the men at detention, distilled into a set of suspicious, precautionary and vigilant dispositions. Bodywatching was the watchful and suspicious practice of observation that surreptitiously assessed detainees, colleagues and other inhabitants of the IRC, a socially and culturally saturated examination in time and space that constituted (for the officers) the frontier of the battle between security and insecurity at Locksdon. This chapter discusses bodywatching as a set of embodied visual habits, which constantly 'read' the detainee's body as a site where intent and proclivity could be discerned ahead of time, and where control could be inscribed.

I will show that, at Locksdon, the relationship between confinement and vision that Foucault (1977) placed centrally in his description of 'disciplinary power' was intertwined with specific local concerns about securing the regime. For Foucault, the prison exemplified the way in which the objectifying, disinterested gaze of the Enlightenment was bound up with the production of modern subjecthood. In his discussion of Jeremy Bentham's panopticon, Foucault argued that subjecting criminal inmates to constant, surveillant observation inculcated projects of (self-)reformation and reorganisation among them. In a broader sense, discipline takes the human body as 'an instrument or intermediary' of training the subject, placing it 'in a system of constraints and privations, obligations and prohibitions' (Foucault 1977: 11) in order to produce efficiency from inefficiency, order from disorder, and productivity from idleness. Disciplinary power simultaneously forms and regulates, invests and materialises the body and the subject. Yet despite visual practice being central to discipline, Foucault said very little about the kinds of efforts, embodied habits and technologies of the self that were required to produce the panoptic regime or sustain attentive vigilance (see Aretxaga 1997; Feldman 1991).

At Locksdon, vision was a disciplinary practice of power, control and resistance that was unevenly experienced and applied. The paradigm of the authoritative, cool and disinterested gaze associated with Foucault's panopticon dissolved in the detention regime into suspicion, anxiety and mistrust. The visual efforts of detention became a matter of training, refining and disciplining officers' visual habits as 'a layer of the body' (Crary 1994: 22). Vision, in the western epistemological tradition, has been privileged as the most prominent, credible and trustworthy of the senses (see Jay 2002; Mitchell 2005). It is through being made visible that subjects engage in projects of self-reformation in Foucault's disciplinary sense. It is also by embodying vision as the 'superior, most reliable' of the senses (Bal 2003: 13) that the individual is constituted. Yet the superiority of vision has also been undercut with a historical mistrust of the 'congenital sensory frailty' of humankind (see Stafford 1993). That is, the visual is related to the production of 'objective' and 'truthful' knowledge, but the visual is also located within shifting multisensory bodily subjectivity (Cooley 2004; Jay 1993; Mitchell 2002; 2005). As Crary argues, visual attention is thus the 'making productive' of 'faulty, unreliable ... arbitrary' vision; attention is a constellation of active visual efforts combining engagement and disengagement, concentration, and embodied dispositions (1994: 2, 21). This chapter, then, is concerned with vision at Locksdon – with the way officers looked at the detainees, the way the detainee was registered within a scopic regime, the way that the gaze shaped relationships between and among officers and detainees, and the way officers experienced the watchfulness of the establishment.

IDENTITY AND RECOGNITION

Reception

A new detainee entered Locksdon via 'reception', which designated a spatial area of the centre, and also a particular induction procedure. Reception was a series of processes that sought to make a newly arrived detainee known and visible to the establishment. A new detainee had to be *identified* to the regime before he could be admitted: he had to be registered within the establishment's records, his defining physical features had to be inscribed in documents and his character had to be noted via consideration of his demeanour. At the time of my fieldwork, the reception routine was as follows. Reception officers would check the IS91 (immigration detention order) 'against the body' by checking the detainee's names, date of birth and nationality.[1] The officers would then conduct a cursory 'rub down' body search by hand or electronic device to check for concealed weapons or contraband and they would temporarily remove all 'in possession items'. They would check a detainee's property had arrived with him and would order a meal if the man had not eaten. If several detainees arrived together, they would be placed in what the officers called 'the dirty room'. This did not mean dirty in the sense of filth (though many detainees were physically dirty after being picked up on clandestine journeys or having spent nights in police holding cells) but in Douglas's (1966) sense of being liminal, 'polluting' and ambiguous. New arrivals had yet to be checked by Locksdon officers (who did not consider the prior checks made by security escort contractors to be reliable) and were thus possibly contaminating to the orderly, secure and controlled regime inside. New arrivals could be carrying a weapon, they could be unhealthy or a risk to themselves or others.

Officers brought out the detainees one by one from the 'dirty room' to submit to the reception procedures. The detainee was strip-searched[2] behind a curtain to ensure he was not carrying a concealed weapon. The new arrival was measured, photographed and his eye colour, face shape, hair shade and distinguishing body marks (tattoos, scars and birthmarks) were logged on a personal summary sheet along with other personal identifying detail. Once he had dressed again, a man's fingerprints were digitally recorded and a series of photographs was taken for Locksdon records.[3] His possessions were searched: his money and valuables were securely deposited, his stored property was bagged and labelled and his 'in possession' items (including clothes) were logged. He was issued with a set of establishment rules in his native language, a detainee ID card, a phone card and a set of standard issue clothes and toiletries if he needed them.

Amid the rituals of reception, officers had to ask a new arrival whether he had ever attempted suicide or self-harm, and 'Do you feel like doing so now?' It was always an incongruous and grotesque moment: the detainee often did not understand the question, and the officer was forced to *mime* his meaning to secure a response from the detainee. In the concentrated rush of getting the man through the reception procedure, the question was a mirror to the impersonal process, a fleeting acknowledgement of the detainee's individual circumstances and shock at being detained. Officers admitted to me that the detainees were highly unlikely to admit suicidal feelings to them, and that they would be more likely to 'open up' to the nurses during the health check. After officers had finished the forms and documents, the detainee was placed in the 'clean room', signifying he had been initiated into the secure inner world of Locksdon. Staff had now assumed responsibility for him. There was a toilet, a TV and a phone in the clean room; the first chance a man may have had to contact friends or family. The nurse met with the detainee in private and filled in a parallel set of health documents with details of his medication and health problems, if any. He was able to access medical services in the establishment's health centre or at a hospital if necessary. Finally, the reception procedure instructed officers to 'locate the body in relevant bed space' – to lead the man carrying his possessions into the main centre and his dormitory.

Locksdon's reception mirrored a classic rite of passage (Turner 1969; van Gennep 1960). A new arrival was 'mortified' and was suspended in a position of liminal ambiguity (in the dirty room), before being plunged into a new grid of meaning where the 'total institution' assumed full responsibility for him (Goffman 1961). Reception was a puncture point through which previous associations, histories and circumstances fell away and the man was fixed with a new identity as 'detainee'. Reception procedures were exactly identical for all newcomers, and they became highly routinised and repetitive. There were a number of designated reception officers who would regularly work together, and reception became a choreographed performance or ritual, a polished set of actions. When less experienced officers had to cover reception duties, the process became markedly slower and less efficient, demonstrating the proficiency that regular reception staff acquired. The whole reception process (at best, when performed by experienced staff and when the detainee had a small amount of luggage and was cooperative) took at least twenty minutes and was identical with each man. Reception staff would often find themselves processing detainees in and out of the establishment simultaneously. When detainees left, the rituals described above were reversed: the man's possessions, clothes, valuables were returned to him and officers closed the various files associated with him.[4]

Anthropological work on religious and bureaucratic ritual (as a set of stipulated, repetitive acts) has shown it to have multiple political, symbolic and communicative registers. Ritual is concerned (among other things) with authority and authorisation, with limiting the possibility of improvisation and 'alternative utterances' (Bloch 2003: Herzfeld 1992). Ritual is performed, but it is also performative in Butler's sense, materialising the authority from which it emerges (1990, 1993). Indeed, it is through the ritualised, repetitive demands of the border – to present passports, apply for visa, submit to security checks, offer biometrics – that the security state 'writes itself' (Campbell 1998; see also Amoore and Hall 2010).

At Locksdon, similarly, the bureaucratic ritualised practices of reception made manifest the regime at Locksdon and the kinds of control it was to exert on the new arrival. Reception was intolerant of digressions and the unexpected:

> Detainees come through here [reception] and they say it's against their human rights. I say, And? In a way I agree. I wouldn't want to be cooped up in there [dirty room] for hours. But what else can

I do? People are coming and going, going and coming all the time. They can't go to pray, they can't go to the dormitories. I tell them they're not allowed, they haven't been processed. (Male officer)

More accurately, reception used digressions from a desired norm (compliant, obedient, quiet) to gain traction on detainees trying to resist its demands. The precise, repetitious nature of the procedures meant that staff's attention was immediately focused on a new detainee's reaction, identifying the man who might be 'trouble', the man whose 'attitude' was wrong, the man who needed to be 'kept an eye on', or the man who was confused and disoriented. Distressed men would be paired with detainees from their own country (if possible), or might be visited by an immigration officer to explain their situation. Aggressive men who 'kicked off' or complained were pulled instantly into focus, and their 'punishment' was the deliberately meticulous and pedantic application of the rules: as one officer put it, 'Listen, mate, I don't care, all right? Stop whining. We're just going to get on with the job here, and the longer you spend yakking, the longer it'll take us all. If you're all right with me, I'll be all right with you.' From the very start of his stay at Locksdon, the detainee was made to understand that his comfort was linked to his compliance.

Reception was also the moment when Locksdon's 'optical paradigm of power' and 'scopic regime' (Feldman 1991: 205) was revealed. Incarceration, Feldman notes, involves the 'stratification of sensory capacities and sensate subjects' whereby 'vision is denied the observed object' (1991: 205). The enforced exposure of the detainee at reception (through the strip search, through the windows of the dirty room, through the exposure of his luggage) marked his initiation into the layered visual economy of the IRC, where he would be made visible to the officers but would not be able to return the gaze. This visibility was an examination in Foucault's (1977: 185) terms: a normalising, calculative process which 'manifests the subjection of those who are perceived as objects and the objectification of those who are subjected'. Reception posited the detainee's body and behaviour centrally within a set of normative ideals, and the visual extraction of knowledge was central to the exercise of power:

The examination combines the techniques of an observing hierarchy and those of a normalising judgment. It is a normalising gaze, a surveillance that makes it possible to qualify, to classify and to punish. It establishes over individuals a visibility through which one differentiates them and judges them. That is why in all the mechanisms of discipline the examination is highly ritualised. In it are combined the ceremony of power and the form of the experiment, the deployment of force and the establishment of truth. (Foucault 1977: 184)

In exposing the detainee via searches, officers were concerned to transform physical particularities and signs into clues about a man's history and capability. Historically, the criminal 'sciences' have posited that character and proclivity were 'readable' from human anatomy (Stafford 1993: 107) – from skulls in the eighteenth-century 'science' of phrenology or face shape in the work of the physiognomists, for example. The body's measurements were once believed (if properly interpreted) to form a paradigm for predicting deviance – in the nineteenth-century criminal photographic portraiture of Francis Galton, for example (see Daston and Galison 1992: 103; Sekula 1986: 11). The body's marks and surfaces (tattoos, scars, wounds) are *still* thought to offer clues about its 'trades, occupations, calamities' (Sekula 1986: 33) in penal contexts. The visual scrutiny of Locksdon detainees at reception did not attend to the marks of persecution or violence that might accompany an asylum seeker (though these were registered by the routine health check with the on-site nurse). Rather, officers were concerned to apply their prison experience to a man's physical marks: a tattoo could signal criminal gang membership, a wound could signal a history of violent altercations, or the potential for self-harm, and a needle mark could indicate drug use.

Despite the intricate reception procedures, the efforts to identify the man in his particularity were frequently incomplete and unachievable. In many ways, it was a spectacle that simply exposed what the officers would never know about the men arriving at Locksdon. The awareness of a possible gap between stated identity and genuine identity was part of the officers' suspicion towards their charges, and one of the differences between work at Locksdon and work at a prison. In a prison, a newly convicted inmate has, in Foucault's (1977) terms, been examined by experts and classified according to a series of criminal taxonomies of deviancies, pathologies and tendencies. The prisoner is allocated to a suitable facility and a range of appropriate security procedures swing into action. An immigration detainee, in contrast, would often arrive at Locksdon with little information, if any, and what documents did arrive were often incorrect or unreliable, with confusion between different calendars and name spellings.[5] The detainees' immigration case notes did not necessarily accompany him on his initial reception – although they often arrived via the visiting immigration officers. Occasionally staff received details of a man's behaviour at other establishments (for example if he had attacked staff, or self-harmed, or whether he had spent time in a prison for a conviction). The sense of not knowing who the detainees were and what threat they posed was a concern for the officers, who felt that their personal safety and their ability to do their job was being compromised.

> [With convicted prisoners] you know what the guy's done, what he's in for, his history, everything. You can make out a sentence plan for him, you can build up relationships, you can make some progress, see him through. With these guys [detainees] you can't communicate with some of them, they may be gone in a few days, there's no history for them, it's just not the same (Male officer)

The officers' (penal) expertise filled the gaps in reliable knowledge around the detainees. Prison experience shaped the officers' performance of their job, as well as their outlook on the men in their care and on one another. The social world of a prison, as perceived by the people inside it, is a volatile and capricious place, and officers held experience-hardened views of the capabilities of desperate or frustrated people. As one officer put it, 'it can be all quiet, then suddenly there is another side, there is tension and a real atmosphere'. The threat of physical violence was a prominent factor of life in Locksdon, and officers knew that distressed men could become volatile, especially in confusing, unfamiliar surroundings. Officers developed a 'sixth sense' about impending trouble or 'toxic' troublemaker detainees. Working with people 'who could be anyone', officers developed their visual and intuitive 'bodywatching' skills wherein the detainee body became a text to be deciphered.

'Bodywatching' reduced the detainee to a 'body'. A man was literally referred to as a 'body' in procedural documentation, formal and informal instructions and conversations among staff. For example, a reception officer would ring the centre office and announce that he had 'two bodies to locate' in the dormitories or an immigration officer would ask a colleague about the possibility of checking bio-facts against 'the body'. The term 'body' designated a dual importance: the body as *object* within the IRC, to be organised, managed, tracked, surveilled and located, but also the body that might *betray itself* and provide some clues of a man's intent. It was this body that the officers were trained to observe and scrutinise.

VIGILANCE AND SECURITY

The detainee in the regime: body-objects

Once inside the establishment, the 'meticulous observation of detail' and close 'monitoring of time, space and movement' (Foucault 1977: 181–2) continued. The regime at Locksdon stipulated that the detainees (and officers) were arranged according to the time of day and the activity in which they were engaged. The regime was run to a tight timetable that rarely wavered and which structured and divided the day into blocks of activity. There was a morning roll check, when officers took over from night staff, to check all men were accounted for.[6] After breakfast, detainees vacated their dormitories while cleaning took place. In the morning period until lunch the detainees were encouraged to use the sports facilities and attend classes provided by the education department. They could also fulfil appointments at the health care centre, or with immigration officers, or attend religious services organised by the chaplain. They could buy items at the canteen shop, take air in the exercise yard (a lawn area with benches), watch TV, visit friends in other dormitories or play pool. There was another roll check at lunchtime, when detainees were locked in their dormitories for an hour while staff took lunch breaks.[7] After staff breaks, the dormitories were unlocked and detainees made their way to the canteen for lunch, watched by huddles of officers leaning against the walls and positioned at the hotplates where kitchen staff served lunch. Mealtimes were flashpoints. Detainees expressed frustration through complaints about food and there were several violent incidents in the dining hall during 2002–3 (see chapter 4). After lunch, the regime activities resumed for the afternoon – men received visits from friends and families in the visitors' centre ('Visits'), returned to classes or joined in with activities in the gym. There was another roll check in the late afternoon and the detainees were locked in their dormitories again while staff took tea breaks. Then it was dinnertime and the detainees were 'fed'. There were then several hours when the detainees were free to do what they pleased – staff would organise bingo nights, or put on a film – before final roll check and the end of the day, when detainees were confined to their dormitories until the following morning.

The notion of observation as spectatorship – especially prominent in the prison – conjures an image of a stationary, immobile and spatially fixed observer whose gaze ranges over a given area. Locksdon officers periodically occupied certain fixed vantage points around the establishment from which they observed the circulations of the establishment. The Visits officer, for example, would sit on a raised platform within the Visits hall, where he or she had full, direct sight of the large room where detainees and their visitors sat on colour coded chairs. The officer had a direct view over the hall, but also a mediated view via two cameras which could be trained and zoomed onto the room's inaccessible corners. The aim was to prevent 'contraband' or money being passed between visitors and detainees. In the exercise yard, too, an officer sat in a small hut from where he or she could see most of the courtyard and the men sitting, walking and talking. For Locksdon officers, the work of a secure environment at its most basic level meant making sure no-one escaped and everyone was accounted for at all times. As the officer watched the detainees move into, out of and around the establishment's zones, he or she had to count and log them passing in and out. If there was a suspected escape, or a sudden emergency, he or she was expected to be able to produce a 'number' for a particular zone. This work required the officers' attention to glance over the surface of individual men, reducing them to itemised 'body-objects' that could be accounted for numerically as they circulated in time and space. The accounting of 'bodies' was epitomised at the periodic roll checks, when the detainee population was tallied. Rather than watching and counting men as they moved, roll checks involved the detainees moving to their dormitories where they were head counted by officers. The numerical coding produced a transposable detainee – the detainee became interchangeable with other men, an object among other objects to be accounted for and tracked.[8]

For many practical, mundane aspects of the job, there was absolutely no interest for the officers in detainees' personal details. Individuality and uniqueness among the detainees (at worst) threatened the uniformity and predictability of the regime, or (at best) simply made the day flow more pleasantly. Individual detainees were just a few of many who passed through Locksdon. Numbers changed every day and men stayed up to a year or only a night. There was little incentive to engage with many of the detainees. One officer expressed this aspect of de-individualisation and objectification in stark terms:

I don't even think of them as human beings. That sounds bad doesn't it, but rather I don't really think of them personally in that way. I mean, I don't notice if they're good-looking or what they look like. I just wouldn't really notice that, wouldn't fancy them or anything. It doesn't even register. They're ... well, they're just detainees. (Female officer)

Many practical concerns of the officers' job, then, encouraged them to regard the detainees as abstract bodies to be monitored and controlled, bodies around whom various practices and procedures revolved. In Heyman's (1995) terms, part of the organisational 'thought-work' of Locksdon thus required officers to account for detainees as objects in time and space. The officers' use of the de-individualised term 'body' reflected this visual abstraction and objectification and their experience of their job. The routines and practices at Locksdon (provision of food, surveillance of movement, roll check) were *acted upon* these bodies-as-objects and the officers' job was the correct and efficient fulfilment of these routines. This was for the security and well-being of the detainees, the officers and everyone in the establishment. Detainees became de-individualised as bodily objects associated with an aggregate of personal characteristics that had direct relevance for the officer's job: violent, cooperative, helpful, insolent.

The detainee in the regime: deciphering the body

The visual practice that required an overview of detainee bodies-as-objects was joined with other attentive visualities. The architecture of Locksdon did not produce the hyper-transparency of Foucault's panoptic paradigm, but was understood by the officers as a series of zones (centre, gym, Visits, education) joined by corridors, gates and doors. These zones were associated with certain kinds of visibility and invisibility: officers, detainees and staff alike came to know the places to chat quietly with friends, to escape the noise of the centre. The Locksdon officer was required to be attentive and observant as he or she moved around the establishment. Indeed, the ideal attentiveness was produced via energetic, pro-active movement that probed the occluded corners of the centre. Far from being an immobile spectator or fixed observer, the officer's working routine involved formalised and informal checks and searches. During these checks, officers' eyes were trained on the hidden sites of the establishment (dormitory bedposts, detainees' possessions, detainees' cupboards and boxes, under the beds, the mattresses, the ceilings, the bars, the locks) that could hold a concealed weapon or contraband. Signs of damage, wear and tear, or intervention on locks and window bars could indicate suspicious activity (an attempt to escape or hide contraband) and were duly noted. During the night shift, again, officers were required to periodically check the perimeter fence, and monitor the dormitories of sleeping men to check for suspicious activity.

On one hand, then, bodywatching aimed to fix and order detainee bodies in the classic disciplinary sense: it sought to inculcate an orderly physical circulation around the establishment, it sought to gain a panoramic view over men's position, it sought to draw detainees towards a desired norm of compliant behaviour. Yet bodywatching also relied on circulating bodies to secure the regime, where the body of the detainee in everyday movement would betray intent, meaning and purpose. In this alternative practice of bodywatching, no observation was too small to be considered 'evidence' of possible indiscipline, violence or disorder. The static, compliant and 'disciplined' body would give nothing away: it was the moving, conversing, interacting body that Locksdon's regime acted upon, and it was through circulations and actions that the risky detainee would give himself away.

When Ed Davies told me that 'you have to notice things about people', this was what he was implying. Officers *noticed* things about people and understood what they saw within an effort to maintain security, as an ordered, predictable, safe regime. 'Bodywatching' was a culturally learned, embodied, trained disposition that reflected a suspicious and precautionary vigilance towards signs of possible indiscipline and security breaches such as infringement of the rules, escape plans or attempts, bullying, insolence or abuse. The attentive mobile officer had to spread and disperse his or her vision outwards, not just in the sense of counting bodies-as-objects, but in the sense of catching glimpses of surreptitious activity from the corner of the eye, an out-of-the-ordinary event or gathering, or bodies moving away from one another in haste, or remaining static too long, or being out of place and time. In addition, the officer would train his or her visual attentiveness to particular individuals as they moved around the establishment, following him and his activities by 'keeping an eye'. Both these modes of visual practice were bound to an awareness and expectation of other bodies in time and space that was *more* than visual and became, instead, a 'gut feeling' which registered norms and deviations in movement and behaviour, and which directed the gaze.[9] Officers would frequently describe how they 'knew' trouble was brewing, that they 'could feel it brewing' or 'bubbling under the surface'. This feeling was frequently related to the unusual or unexpected movement of detainees, of men 'running up and down corridors', of 'gathering in groups' or 'sneaking around'.

The development of attentiveness and vigilance formed a large part of the job for Locksdon officers. Their alert gaze was inculcated via official prison training mechanisms (how to search for contraband for instance), but was also inculcated via working routines, experience on the job and expectations of colleagues. At the heart of life in a secure centre like Locksdon is the notion that people may be always more than they seem. The officers held experience-hardened views of what people in general were capable of. More than just cynicism, the officers had personal experience of the dangerous capabilities of people (in life, through their experiences with violent criminals, and in detention, through their experiences with prisoners). At Locksdon, mistrust formed the habitus of officers in the sense that Bourdieu (1977: 72) described: habitus is the embodiment of regularities and tendencies and a 'socialised subjectivity' enabling agents to cope with changing situations. It is a system of durable dispositions produced within objective conditions and reproducing those conditions in turn. The officers *learned* and developed a particular kind of suspicious, observant and watchful visual practice as a 'technology of the self' (Daston and Galison 2007: 234). This watchfulness extended also to fellow staff members, who had to be scrutinised for 'inappropriate' relationships with detainees or for mistakes in the job.

At Locksdon, moreover, the constitution of 'the officer' was directly related to the embodiment of proper visual attentiveness, an attentiveness which in turn individuated staff. Foucault's notion of governmentality challenges us to understand how power relations act to 'produce and reproduce subjects, their practices and beliefs, in relation to specific policy aims' (Butler 2004: 52). One junior officer, for instance, was reprimanded by senior colleagues for doing a colleague's LBB checks (locks, bolts and bars). Being an officer at Locksdon involved taking responsibility for allocated tasks, including visual checks, which were logged in various records and could thus be traced back to individuals. Responsibility for these checks could not be transferred without authorisation. Security within the regime emerged from every officer being individually accountable for generating visual knowledge of detainees and the establishment: 'we're only as good as the knowledge we're gathering', as one officer put it, or 'What is at the centre of security? UR.' The ideal, vigilant officer missed no important detail of the detainees' or fellow officers' behaviour, exposing suspicious behaviour within the most apparently innocuous activity, and it was the ability and authority to do so that constituted him or her as officer.

The body of 'the other'

In a description of an outbreak of violence and unrest at Locksdon, one senior officer reflected to me:

> That's what it's like here. It can suddenly become very volatile. Take the Africans. I remember once when I first started, I saw a group of them coming down the corridor, shouting and waving their hands. I have to tell you I was frightened. It's in their culture to wave their arms about and be loud, but when you first see it, you don't know what to think. Usually if you can get one on their own, you can quieten them down and it's quite easy to get stuff sorted out. But at first it terrifies you. The last thing you want to do is to start shouting and screaming yourself, because it just inflames the situation.

The visual surveillance at Locksdon produced, and shaped in turn, stereotyped schema that organised knowledge about detainees according to notions of skin colour, 'race', cultural difference, national origin and gender. Officers were fond of saying 'I don't see race, I just see attitude.' The officers were aware that generalising about nationalities ('the Africans', 'the Turks', 'the Jamaicans', 'the Chinese') might be construed as prejudice and racism. They were always keen to point out to me that their opinions were based on the *evidence that presented itself*, on *what they saw*, rather than blanket prejudice based on skin colour. Nevertheless, the knowledge that officers built up around detainees at Locksdon centred on the different potentialities and capacities of different nationalities, and the different effects they had on the regime. A series of stereotypes emerged for ordering daily experience of the detainees. 'The Africans', for example, were generally 'like children' – emotional, moody, unreasonable, demanding. However, there were 'bad' Africans (Nigerians) and 'good' Africans: 'I've never come across one [Nigerian] that wasn't dodgy. But guys from Ghana – they always seem all right.' Algerian detainees were 'known' to be violent and disruptive; the Chinese 'kept themselves to themselves'; the Turks 'looked after their own'; 'Jamaicans' were 'trouble' and had 'bad attitudes'. Odd 'acceptable' individuals did nothing to dispel the stereotypes about nationalities, and were seen to be exceptions to the rule.

> [Other Jamican detainees] told me that people from Jamaica hate 'em ['dreads'] too. I'm sure there's lots of good people from Jamaica, but we sure as hell don't see any of them here. You've seen the way the system works. Some might say it's racist because there's always some Jamaican guy banged up in the Seg Unit. But you've seen, we just go on what we see, and they're always in the middle of trouble. (Male officer)

The otherness of the detainees was marked on the body via skin colour and manifested through the body and its movements, which in turn produced evidence of detainees' 'different mindset'. The 'Africans', as in the example above, were often described as having a 'different culture' that was expressed through different physicalities: chanting, or having glassy eyes, or 'going into trances' or running with a strange rhythm when distressed or angry. Even as officers rationalised that 'it was just their way of being angry' their response was frequently 'not knowing what to do to calm them down'.

The detainee body was also potentially unhealthy and possibly diseased. Many detainees come from Africa and Asia, and the nurses in the health department spoke regularly to me of their concern that detainees could unknowingly have HIV. They had all come across men who had tested positive and also men who refused to be tested and who had girlfriends or wives in the UK. At the time of the SARS outbreak in spring 2003, there was extra vigilance surrounding detainees arriving from Asia. There was also a case of TB at the centre, and all detainees were escorted to the local hospital for x-rays. Officers took seriously the threat of infection or contagion through contact with the detainees. For example, a female officer was bitten by a detainee during a C&R (control and restraint) operation. The bite drew blood and the officer had to undergo an HIV test. The detainee body, as 'other', embodied alien and 'disgusting' habits. Many officers and establishment cleaning staff complained at many detainees' habit of coughing up phlegm and spitting it on the floor, or not using perfumed deodorants and shower gels as is the western custom, and so being 'smelly'.

The 'evidence' that the officers gleaned from the detainees and their everyday behaviour was thus concerned with categorising 'the other' within discourses that tended to distance, differentiate and reduce – a generalising tendency that Said (1978) called orientalism. Anthropological accounts of the practices of orientalism in colonial and postcolonial contexts, for instance, have noted the ways in which political, economic and social boundaries become coded and expressed through 'racial' or ethnic markers of difference, in intersection with 'cultural competences, sexual proclivities, psychological dispositions, and cultivated habits' (Stoler 1996; see also Stoler 1991). For instance, the notion of imperial bourgeois civility in colonial times (understood as a matter of self-control, self-discipline and self-determination) was contrasted against subjugated, colonised 'others'. These others came to be located within what Foucault calls a 'grid of intelligibility' – a hierarchy of distinctions in perception and practice that conflated, substituted and 'collapsed the categories of racial, class and sexual others strategically and at different times' (Stoler 1996: 11).

Contemporary notions of alterity are haunted by these imperial 'grids of intelligibility', but have ostensibly moved away from 'race' and towards 'culture' as the significant basis for the organisation of difference (see Stolcke 1995). Categorising people according to collective identities (a 'different mindset', 'it's in their culture') reifies the complex processes by which individuals negotiate identification, and portrays religion and culture as unchanging and deterministic monoliths (Appiah 1994). 'Culture' is frequently essentialised and reduced to a 'package' of behaviours and customs within which people are trapped (Wikan 1999). At Locksdon, periodic crises about losing control, about security and 'toxic' mixes of different nationalities, and about particular troublemaker detainees, became expressed within constantly adjusted 'grids of intelligibility' about cultural and 'racial' difference. As I shall discuss in more detail later in the book, the 'otherness' of the detainee (unruly, emotional, undisciplined) was contrasted with the officers' own disciplined, active and rational identity (see chapters 3 and 4).

The Obs book

The awareness of bodies in time and space, and the practised 'instincts' of the experienced officer, solidified into a scopic regime that paid attention to every detail, one which took up '[t]he smallest infraction … with all the more care for it being small' (Foucault 2007: 45). Every encounter, passing glance or chance glimpse provided an opportunity to notice something *specific* about a detainee: something anomalous, suspicious or out of place. Incidents involving individual detainees were noted in a man's personal file:

'live' files for current detainees were kept in the centre office, while 'dead' files for ex-detainees were transferred to the administration building. The staff 'Obs book' (Observations book) was a written inscription of this ongoing scrutiny, where staff wrote up notes and observations about detainees and events during their shift in chronological order:

> Detainee — caught smoking in corridor. I told him to put it out. Detainee blew smoke in my face, told me I could do nothing if he wanted to smoke. Eventually went back into dorm. Detainee has bad attitude and has shown aggression towards staff. Could pose possible threat of disorder in future.
>
> Detainee — seen watching perimeter fence out of window and discussing something with Detainee — when I passed. Possible security risk.
>
> Detainee — seemed very miserable at lunchtime. Friend reported was talking of suicide and refused to eat at lunch and tea. SH2052[10] opened.

In the Obs book, the officers' attentiveness was transformed into a textual record of vigilance. Staff observations of mundane encounters, transgressions and insolence became inscribed as 'evidence' of possible security problems. This attentiveness was disciplinary and normalising in Foucault's sense, making it possible to measure and compare differences and discrepancies. An insolent or disruptive detainee would be moved away from his friends as 'punishment'; a violent man would be segregated to 'cool off'; a depressed man would be moved together with his friends, or referred to health care for special attention.

The knowledge of the Obs book was associated with other security-relevant knowledge. For instance, any observation that indicated a possible security threat (like a detainee watching the perimeter fence, or being found repeatedly in the 'wrong' dormitory, or in possession of a weapon) warranted the opening of an SIR (Security Intelligence Report). This file gave details of the detainee who had been observed, what he had been observed doing, when and with whom. The document was transferred to the Security Office where SIRs were collated and where 'profiles' were built of individuals. For example, one detainee being routinely searched on his way out of the education department, was found to have £500 sewn into his trouser waistband. He was 'given the benefit of the doubt', told he was not allowed to hold cash at Locksdon, and had the money put into his account to be spent using his canteen card. On a subsequent occasion, the same detainee was found to have another large sum secreted in his clothes and this time the matter was classified as a security risk: Where was he getting the money? Were visitors bringing it in? Was he planning to escape? Was he using the money to bribe or coerce fellow detainees? Or staff?

The detainees' suspicious behaviour, as well as any incidents and known 'accomplices' and associates (inside the establishment or outside) were written on a white board. The white board was the watchful establishment rendered visual: the links, relationships, actions and possible plans of the detainees were laid out so that patterns could be discerned across time. In the Security Office, the detainee under suspicion became abstracted and reduced to a function of his association with a number of security-relevant incidents that had come to the attention of the officers. At the time of my fieldwork, the Security Office was staffed by a fixed-post senior officer and four designated officers. The senior officer explained to me:

> We are trying to build intelligence, knowledge. We're trying to build a picture of what is happening in the establishment at any time. This means we are doing our job properly, we're one step ahead. If there haven't been any SIRs in a while, it means we're getting lazy, we're losing our grip, getting sloppy. (Male senior officer)

This officer frequently complained that staff were not as vigilant as they should be. After a bout of indiscipline, or an escape attempt, he noted, staff 'would suddenly notice things again', but security reports would soon dwindle. A lack of security reports meant either a perfectly docile detainee population, or, more likely, a staff cohort who 'were not picking up on odd behaviour'.

Keeping the initiative

The generation of security intelligence, then, the disciplinary bodywatching (which took note of events unfolding and which asserted a normalising, surveillant watchfulness), blurred into a precautionary, anticipatory and pre-emptive mode of vision, where 'seeing becomes an act of foreseeing, pre-empting or anticipating' (Amoore 2007a: 221). Visual practices within Locksdon were ultimately concerned with staying 'one step ahead'. The officers understood and experienced this forward-looking vigilance as 'keeping the initiative'. 'Keeping the initiative' was a physical sensation of proactively 'being in control': it was an ideal of a perfectly ordered establishment where staff did not 'let things slip', where the detainees were not allowed to 'get the upper hand' and where everyone was where they were supposed to be at all times, with no 'trouble' or confrontation. The loss of initiative, as I have described, was physically experienced by officers as a 'gut feeling': a sense of colleagues becoming lax or sloppy, of detainees 'pushing the rules', of things 'slipping'. Keeping the initiative was a sensation of good order and organisation, using the clues gleaned from everyday visual practices to act upon emerging moods and indiscipline before threats could come to fruition.

As a mode of action in the face of the future, pre-emption operates on uncertainty, an uncertainty that is not simply due to a lack of knowledge, but 'because the threat has not only not yet fully formed ... it has not yet even emerged' (Massumi 2007: 13). While precautionary measures (embodied in the precautionary principle) intervene on threats that are already determined (even if those threats are uncertain), seeking to halt their progression (see Anderson 2010; de Goede and Randalls 2009), pre-emption targets the *potential* for threats to emerge. The pre-emptive strike acts against a range of unspecified uncertainties and thus incites the potential future: it 'brings the future into the present' and produces a 'sovereign closure of the foregone event' (Massumi 2005: 7, 8). The 'war on terror' has been marked by the emergence of various precautionary, anticipatory and pre-emptive responses in the name of homeland security (see Amoore and de Goede, 2008a, 2008b; Aradau and van Munster 2007).

At Locksdon, the problem posed by the anomalous and potentially threatening detainee called forth a precautionary regime which worked to prevent and pre-empt 'trouble'. For Massumi (2005: 8), affect (notably fear) is central to the way that possible future threats take effect in the present, standing as a 'mechanism of linkage'. In pre-emption, an event's consequences precede it, as if it had already occurred, but without the fear that threat creates, threat would have no effect (see Anderson 2007; Massumi 2005: 8). The broad but undefined fear or anxiety that is said to characterise the securitised domains of contemporary everyday life (see Isin 2004) crystallised into an embodied, existential experience of insecurity and trepidation at Locksdon. For the officers, work in Locksdon produced a bodily proximity to a population deemed 'risky' or 'illegal' but also unknowable. Detention constitutes a disorienting, confusing and terrifying experience for those who are forcibly confined, of course; the testimonies of those who have been detained attest to this. Detention also provokes anxiety and unease among those whose are charged with the care and control of 'unknowable' detainees. It was not the case that officers at Locksdon worked in a continual state of dread and anxiety. Rather, officers were frequently given cause to reflect on the fragility of the security in the establishment, and their own vulnerability:

> One day, during a quiet moment, officers exchanged stories about infamous names they had come into contact with in their work in prisons. The conversation turned to an incident involving a female officer at a certain prison who had been taken hostage and repeatedly raped by an armed prisoner. Other officers, fearful for her life, had been forced to stand by during the attacks, negotiating with the prisoner. A new female officer at Locksdon appeared shocked by the stories. One of the officers took the opportunity to put her straight: 'It could happen here, you know. Don't be fooled by them. Some of these guys in here are capable of that, and worse. We have no idea what they've done. My advice to you? Watch your back.' He told her that on that very morning, a handmade weapon had been found in a detainee's possession: a wire coat hanger embedded in a piece of wood. The woman looked shocked. 'You wouldn't believe it, would you? I mean, I was having a chat with him the other day, we'd begun to form a relationship,' she said. Later that day, several officers made comments to me about this particular female officer. One told me, 'What crap is she on about? Relationship? You must be having a laugh. She hasn't got a clue. She needs to get a grip. There's no bloody point trying to be their friend.'

In the face of this existential danger, officers engaged in precautionary measures to avoid the realisation of certain 'knowable' threats: detailed searches for contraband and dangerous items; logging of personal belongings to remove the possibility of bullying; night-time perimeter searches to hunt out possible hidden weapons thrown over the fence; regular head counts; body searches on the way into and out of Visits or education to close down the potential for smuggling. Pre-emption, on the other hand, worked through a more nebulous and subjective mode. It acted on future uncertainty itself – through 'feelings' about certain mixes of character, or a laxness in the regime, or a period of suspicious 'quiet' that came before an outbreak of unrest. In their desire to 'keep the initiative', the officers acted on what would always remain unknown about the detainees and the future. Every encounter was executed with one eye on possible future consequences, to 'stop something before it happens'. Pre-emption could involve a careful and kindly word with a new arrival 'to make sure he doesn't end up putting his fist through a wall, or someone else'. It could also involve making sure detainees 'know who's in charge here' by stringently enforcing rules to quash insubordination or, more spectacularly, the swift removal of a 'troublemaker' detainee who had come to the attention of the officers. I will return to these themes throughout the book.

CONCLUSION

This chapter has argued that the 'unknown detainee' was understood as a problem of security at Locksdon. The detainee was frequently unidentified, or unidentifiable, with no accompanying history or official documentation. The unknown detainee at Locksdon drew forth a secure regime which sought to annul his threat. I have examined the ways in which officers' habits of watching detainees filled the 'unknown' gaps in knowledge around detainees. These visual techniques aimed at knowing or uncovering proclivity, tendency and potential by tracking and deciphering the body. The body in detention was understood as duplicitous (people could always be more than they seem) but also became a location of certainty (the body would give itself away if watched carefully enough). The particular mode of attending to the body of the detainee at Locksdon was 'bodywatching' – a suspicious, mistrustful and cautious gaze. The dispassionate, authoritative gaze associated with incarceration was revealed, contra Foucault, to be an embodied, uncertain and burdensome set of visual habits. This active, mobile and searching gaze was one which bore the residue of experience with convicted criminals, and often applied the same suspicious, punitive logic to detainee populations.

Bodywatching was objectifying and de-individualising. It was an abstracting visual apprehension, one which organised, and was shaped by, a desire to know the detainee not as a person and individuals, but as objects to secure. In his introduction to Levinas's *Totality and Infinity*, Wild (1979) discusses vision as a means of knowing the other in social life. Vision, he argues, is related to an egocentric, systemising and totalising way of relating to people, objects and the world, one which aims for 'an all-inclusive, panoramic view of all things, including the other in a neutral, impersonal light' (Wild 1979: 16). Vision as a mode of encountering the other tends towards categorisation, subordination, even manipulation, and its 'neutrality' and 'objectivity' hides its ambivalent power. As a technology of control within detention, as the case of Locksdon demonstrates, bodywatching arranges unequal relationships between detainees and officers. Edkins (2011), in her discussion of the camps and trauma, describes a politics that 'misses the person': this is a politics that treats the person as object, functionally as a 'what' rather than a 'who'. Isin and Rygiel (2007: 184) similarly describe the detention centre as an 'abject space', a site where people are treated 'neither as subjects (of discipline) nor objects (of elimination) but as those without presence, without existence, as inexistent'. Bodywatching, despite the close attention it paid to detainees, missed the person in Edkins' terms, and was productive instead of inattention and indifference.

Locksdon officers often talked to me about 'not being able to do their job properly'. In a prison, officers act as personal officers for a number of prisoners, organising sentence plans and carrying out periodic reviews of a prisoner's progress, arranging training, therapy, education and so on according to the penal administration's aims of rehabilitation (see Garland 1990, 2001). In a prison, 'dynamic security' is maintained via careful negotiation of these relationships with inmates, which create unspoken webs of obligation and reciprocity that can be brought to bear in volatile situations. In a prison environment, the de-individualising effects of the structured institutional environment are tempered in part by these relationships. This aspect of life in total institutions is not developed by Foucault in his account of 'austere' institutions. Locksdon officers described life in a prison as hectic and volatile, but full of laughter, 'wind-ups, set-ups and send-ups'. Work in a prison is satisfying in terms of this personal interaction and rapport. There was a mere shadow of this boisterous prison banter at Locksdon. Language barriers meant that humour could not be shared in the same way. What remained was a sharp differentiation between 'them' and 'us', with little sense of shared sociality or commonality with the detainees. This resulted in boredom and apathy among staff, with repercussions for detainees, who were rendered ever more 'other'. Interaction was reduced to the administration of the regime.

As the sovereign and 'noblest sense' (Fabian 1983: 106), the visual holds a unique place in the sovereign work at the border, in the production of certain kinds of authoritative border knowledge about 'illegality', 'deservingness', 'risk' and 'threat'. For instance, decisions about immigration status and the conferral of asylum protection frequently pivot on claimants' credibility, in the frequent absence of verifiable knowledge (see Good 2004a, 2004b, 2007; Kelly 2009; Thomas 2006, 2008). The conferral of immigration 'status' is related (at least in part) to the perception by officials of 'correct' (that is, socially, culturally and gender-appropriate) behaviour on the part of applicants (see Crawley 1999; Indra 1999; Spijkerboer 2000; Weber and Gelsthorpe 2000). Visual appraisal colonises the gaps between authoritative identification and verifiable facts. The trained, expert and alert human eye is considered more crucial than ever for securing public spaces and everyday frontiers of the 'war on terror'. It is citizen-subjects' 'vigilant visuality' that marks the thresholds of normal and risky in daily life (see Amoore 2007a). Knowing 'what to watch for' and 'keeping alert' to possible dangers in mundane routines and public spaces is a task to which all good citizens are being urged to apply themselves. Bodywatching, then, can be seen as part of a generalised border apparatus and wider watchful terrain that constructs the targets of security via visual practice.

In *Abnormal*, Foucault discusses at length the way in which expert psychiatric opinion locates the motivation or cause of a criminal offence in an individual's 'parapathological' tendencies and moral faults (2003: 20). Expert opinion, argues Foucault (2003: 16), 'makes it possible to constitute a psychologico-ethical double of the offence' which 'allows one to pass from action to conduct, from an offence to a way of being, and to make this appear as nothing other than the offence itself'. In this 'doubling', the illegal offence is twinned with a subject's inherent delinquency and criminality evaluated from a 'psychologico-moral' point of view. Foucault (2003: 19) argues that in recounting an individual's misdeeds and faults (not in themselves punishable under law), 'the aim is to show how the individual already resembles his crime before he has committed it'. The 'author of a crime' thus becomes 'a delinquent who is the object of a specific technology' (2003: 21) and the expert assumes the authority to diagnose potential criminality.

At Locksdon, bodywatching was productive of a particular kind of visual expertise that was precisely concerned, in Foucault's words, to 'show how the individual resembles his crime before he has committed it'. A detainee would betray himself by suspicious movement or activity, or displaying the 'wrong attitude' or by being identified as 'a troublemaker'. Like Foucault's 'abnormal', the detainee and his dangerous potential could be diagnosed by noting and recounting 'a whole series of illegalities below the threshold' (2003: 19): watching a window, whispering in corners, moving away too quickly. The detainee was brought into view and literally made visible (Crary 1992) within the expert, diagnostic and authoritative gaze of the officers which sought out minor misdemeanours 'below the threshold', as Foucault puts it. As well as constituting the detainee as security body-object, then, the organisation of vision in Locksdon constituted the authoritative security subject – the Locksdon officer. The Enlightenment legacy posits vision as central to the unity, integrity and separateness of the rational individual (Cooley 2004; Crary 1992, 2001). At Locksdon, it was the professional officer whose careful eye would discern suspicious activity and avert the possible threat. It was the embodiment and performance of bodywatching that constituted the officer as an officer and as responsible citizen.

At the start of this chapter, I described Ed and the individual costs incurred by bodywatching: the feeling of 'having people in your face all the time'. The claim that the 'war on terror' has produced a novel and particular kind of affective politics – typically characterised by neurosis, or fear (see Isin 2004; Massumi 2005) – might be qualified by a more detailed account of the situated emergence and experience of particular emotions, whose effect might be discerned at particular sites of security. While pre-emption in the context of security decisions and the 'war on terror', then, is said to hinge on affective dispositions triggered by 'the looming uncertainty of ill-defined threat' (Massumi 2005: 8), much is taken for granted about the experiential manifestation of emotions.

It was certainly the case that officers saw 'ill-defined threats' to emanate from detainees – these were men 'who could be anyone'. It was the officers' concerns to 'keep the initiative' in the face of uncertainty that shaped pre-emptive moves within the regime – dispersing 'toxic' mixes of detainees, isolating men to 'cool off', removing men from Locksdon – but the 'mechanism of linkage', as Massumi (2005) describes it, was not only fear, but rather a subjective and embodied feeling of 'losing the initiative', of being disrespected, of having one's authority undermined. The distinctions between dangerous and safe, acceptable and risky, tolerable and intolerable, normal and 'trouble' in detention were not drawn up in advance and were not static. Rather they emerged from ongoing negotiation and vigilance, from observation on the move, from attentiveness to the minutiae of men's movement and interactions around the centre. The diagnosis of 'abnormal' emerged from the vigilant application of the attentive, expert eye of the officer. While never quite knowing what it was searching for, this expertise nevertheless sought to pre-emptively identify trouble in advance.

The next chapter examines the relationships among officers at Locksdon. It considers the detention centre as a gendered space, productive of masculine identifications, a place of loyalty, disagreement, friendship. If bodywatching as a kind of vigilance relied upon subjectively and socially negotiated meanings of threat and disorder, then understanding Locksdon's distinct working milieu becomes vital to grasping how the secure regime operated.

3
Being There: Social Life in the Centre

My first week [in a prison] I was shitting myself. Everyone told me it'd take six months before I felt on top of it. It takes ages to learn all the rules. I mean, some rules are hard and fast, they never change, like security rules, but learning how to … I mean there's no hard and set line, like in some jobs, where the answer can be yes or no. In the Prison Service, life is like that: wiggly [motions hand in an uneven line]. When you first start, you'll be on the landing and suddenly all these guys will be all around you – nasty guys. It's like going round all the worst pubs round here and rounding up the worst 300 [men] and sticking them all together. And they'll all know you're the new boy and they'll all make a beeline for you. 'All right guv? I wanna shower.' And you're not sure whether he can have a shower or not. So you go up to the SO [senior officer] and ask, and he says 'No way. He had his chance and he missed it.' So you go back to the con and tell him no, and so he starts kicking off and so someone else comes along and says 'What's the problem?', so you tell him and he just says, 'Give him a shower.' I mean, it's like that all the time. You have to learn what you can do, what they can have. It's happened loads of times that I'll be sorting out something for someone and another officer'll come along and say – 'Why're you bothering? He's an arsehole.' But you'll get on ok with him. Anyone can end up in prison. You'll get some people'll say they're all scum, but they're not. It just takes one bad mistake and you can wind up inside. Some of them are just like that – normal nice people. If someone is nice to me, then I'll be nice to them. When I first joined, someone told me, 'Don't leave your manners by the gate.' And I think that's right. Someone said to me that the best way to learn was to be yourself, but model yourself on someone who you thought was good. So I did. But you have to be yourself. And the way I worked was that I'd always work things out for people. If I said I'd do it, I would. Some people try and say they'll sort things out for people, but not have the chance. Cons want a yes or no answer. I carried a book of stuff to do and I'd always write it down. And I'd do it if I said

I would. There's nothing worse than saying you'll do something and then not doing it. These new officers [at Locksdon] haven't got a clue. They're moaning about this place? In a real nick, you'd never get the chance to sit down and have a cup of tea. It's constant – alarm bells going, confrontations, sorting stuff out, another alarm bell, writing reports, pre-sentence reports, personal officer reports ... You might have ten or more people to do that for. You never get a moment. And the confrontations ... You don't realise you're stressed, but I'd be going home knackered, exhausted. (Male officer)

Locksdon officers regularly argued that working with immigration detainees was like 'babysitting' in comparison to working with convicts. Despite key differences between prison and immigration detention, however, there were many similarities in the daily work, not least the difficulty of negotiating what the officer above described as 'wiggly lines' – acting on initiative while highly visible to other people. Despite the crude popular stereotypes that circulate about prison life and prison officers, good prison work is complex. In their book *The Prison Officer*, Liebling and Price (2001: 7) argue that '[r]esolving and avoiding conflict, avoiding the use of force, and under-enforcing some of the rules ... were acts requiring skill, foresight, diplomacy and humour'. The securing of a 'good day' (with no trouble) involves the application of finely tuned skills of people-management and the diffusion of pressurised situations through judgement, experience and sensitivity. Hay and Sparks (1991: 3) similarly argue that, 'prison officers sometimes exercise social skills of great refinement and complexity without dwelling upon or articulating what they are doing'. At the very core of prison work is what Liebling and Price (2001: 143) call 'flexible consistency'; 'the paradox which lies at the heart of keeping order and legitimacy in prison'. Prison officers must use their discretion in their dealings with prisoners, but must reconcile their actions with the presentation of a uniform front among staff and the achievement of 'the bigger picture'.

The unknown capabilities of the detainees, coupled with the frustrating conditions of detention, ensured decisions about 'wiggly lines' could have serious repercussions for individuals' physical safety. Given these conditions, the prison literature documents the emergence of unspoken 'rules' among prison staff. Kauffman (1988: ch. 6), in a study of a (troubled) US prison, produced a list of 'norms' which she felt constituted a 'code' for prison officers:

always go to the aid of an officer in distress; never smuggle drugs (or any items for inmates); never 'rat' on colleagues or make an officer look bad in front of prisoners; always support colleagues in disputes between prisoners and officers; always support officer sanctions against prisoners; maintain officer solidarity against outside groups (media, administration) and show positive concern for fellow officers. Liebling and Price (2001) agree with many of these 'norms', although their research at UK prisons revealed far less polarised atmospheres (see also Bennett et al. 2008). What these studies found, and what my own work at Locksdon IRC supported, was that the fraught conditions of life in a secure environment tended to produce a tight camaraderie between officers, who had to rely on one another not only in the ordinary running of the regime, but at its crisis moments. This, in turn, produced a strong boundary between 'them' (prisoners, detainees and management, media, outsiders) and 'us' (officers).

This chapter is about the demands and pleasures of working at Locksdon, about the sociality of the establishment and the relationships of affinity and responsibility in which officers were located. In the course of their work, officers at Locksdon had opportunities to see their friends and colleagues in times of considerable strain and physical demand, embroiled in scandals and personal crises, at their best and at their worst. There was an intimacy in the relations that officers had with one another that emerged from this forced closeness and the periodic physical trials they shared, and which shaped the detention centre routine.

DISCIPLINED SELVES

Locksdon was an overwhelmingly masculine place. All the detainees, and the majority of officers, were men.[1] Gender relations at Locksdon permeated the work practices of the regime, and also the centre's social life. I understand gender to be the categorisation of persons within socio-cultural discourses related to the materiality of bodies marked as different through the discourses of 'sex', as well as the contextual embodied social performance of identity in relation to these discourses, in intersection with sexuality, age, occupation, class, race and religion. Gendered discourse delimits what is contextually understood as proper, correct or 'natural' physical, emotional and social behaviour for a man and a woman, though the dominant discourses are constantly contested (see Connell 1995; Cowan 1992; Herzfeld 1985; Moore 1994). Judith Butler's (after

Foucault) insistence that 'materialisation is never quite complete [and] bodies never quite comply with the norms by which their materialisation is impelled' (1993: 1–2) is a prominent theme in the study of gender. Gender identity, for Butler, is a matter of performance, not in the sense of feigned action, but emerging from repeated 'stylised repetition of acts through time' that are relationally constituted with sex and sexuality and through which 'discourse produces the effects that it names' (Butler 1988: 520–3; 1993: 2).

'The masculine', particularly, has been understood as a contingent and performative identification – 'an uncertain and provisional project' (McDowell 2001: 182) within a set of contested masculine ideals. What Connell (1987, 1995) calls 'hegemonic masculinity' in the West makes appeals to male physical bodies in (violent, aggressive, powerful, heterosexual) action (see also Kimmel 2001; Whitehead 2002). That is, the ideal western male body – hard, bounded, active and forceful – finds its opposition in the softer, vulnerable and passive feminine body (Bordo 1999; Grosz 1994). Masculine power in the West also draws upon post-Enlightenment divisions between nature and culture, and between bodies and intellect. Intellect, rationalism and culture are associated with masculine forms, while the feminine is associated with the body, emotionality and nature (MacCormack and Strathern 1980; Moore 1994; Ortner 1996). More specifically, 'the affective' becomes mapped across a gendered terrain, with certain emotional experiences and displays being gendered and gendering in turn.

At Locksdon, 'work' and 'the workplace' were key terrains for the performance and experience of gendered personhood. Work, historically, is bound up in the West with distinctions between 'public' and 'private', and with the association of masculinity with the public and femininity with the private, and with the differential valuation of types of labour. Work practices allow for articulations of what Whitehead (2002: 118–19) has called the 'heroic male project', through which men make their mark on a 'public world' through skill, acumen, or physical strength and courage, or a combination of these traits. Particular kinds of occupation and labour, tasks and expertise have thus become become gendered (Baigent 2001; Cockburn 1983; Cooper 1995; McDowell 2001). 'Emotional labour' in the workplace, for example, is gendered and genders in turn (Hochschild 1983; Walby 1988). So too does the allocation and performance of even the most mundane tasks and expertise.

For male officers at Locksdon, work in a prison establishment enabled the articulation of a distinctive kind of masculine identity.

First, the general engagement in paid employment was understood as a moralised and masculine endeavour, allied to notions of gendered 'self-respect', personal responsibility and self-sufficiency. The very act of coming to Locksdon (being in work, turning up on time, assuming the responsibilities of work) was a gendered achievement allied to the idea of masculine provision (many of the officers at Locksdon were the main earners for their families). Prison work, second, was described as a 'proper job': it was seen as a public and community service; it was safe and secure; it privileged commonsense proficiency and practical skill (associated with traditional physical proletarian masculinity) rather than academic and intellectual prowess.[2] It was also associated with classically 'male virtues' of strength, 'hardness', judgement, 'character' and control. Prison work, like other 'traditionally male' occupations, draws on cultural narratives and images of hands-on, practical masculinity (see Baigent 2001; Cooper 1995). Officers would frequently contrast their work (at Locksdon, but also their 'fiddle' manual trades) with 'namby-pamby' (feminised) 'office labour'. Individual officers would sarcastically remark on their professed inability to 'do book learning' and scoffed at 'over-educated' and 'scrounging' students or 'out of touch' managers.

Participation in waged work in the public sphere, then, has been termed a key characteristic in 'the social definition of successful masculinity' (McDowell 2001). More than this, the increased responsibility that is borne by the individual citizen in what Miller and Rose (2008) call contemporary 'post-social' regimes of governance has configured work as part of a 'relentless imperative of risk management not simply in relation to contracting for insurance, but also through daily lifestyle management'. With the erosion of the welfare state, life's risks are increasingly the responsibility of individuals and civility is increasingly a matter of making 'correct' choices in relation to consumption and lifestyle to mitigate risk (Dean 1999; Rose 1996, 1999). As Rose and Miller (1992: 174) put it, governmental power is 'not so much a matter of imposing constraints upon citizens as of "making up" citizens capable of bearing a kind of regulated freedom'. The moral citizen is contrasted with 'problematic' populations through dividing practices within populations: between responsible citizenship and irresponsible 'others'; between civility and incivility; between genuine and bogus; between legality and illegality; between deserving and undeserving (see Coutin 2007, 2010a, 2011; Heyman and Smart 1999). Work becomes an ever more moralised (and gendered) life 'choice', an individual responsibility linked to a concern to 'keep the world in moral order' (see Lamont 2000): a way of ensuring that environments and society were safe and predictable for everyone.

Officers' sense of self and identity was an embodiment of this individualised responsibility.

> I left school at sixteen and joined up [the Army] and I sometimes wish I had done things differently, that I could go back [to college] … But then, you know, I'd argue that I've done pretty well for myself, better than a lot of people. I'm doing all right. I've got a good job, I've got plans … I've never had any handouts from anyone. I just got on with it, what else was I supposed to do? I've got a family to support. (Male SO)

> I've done it all on my own. Anything I've got, I've got it through me. Nobody ever gave me anything. (Male officer)

For the officers, cultivating the 'disciplined self' was vital for the moral reproduction of society. Those who were incapable or unwilling of making the 'right choices' became denigrated. In general discussions, social ills such as crime, unemployment, poverty, drug dependency and failure in life were generally blamed on an individual's lack of personal integrity and application. Applying oneself, working hard to make something of one's life (whatever the circumstances) and taking responsibility for oneself and one's family were choices available to everyone, the officers implied. Not making those choices and settling for a career in crime, or drugs, or dependency was a sign of weakness:

> There was a time when I could've ended up on the other side [criminality? dependency?]. I was a tearaway when I was younger. But I didn't, and now I'm here. I fucking hate dole scroungers. We used to have some live over the road from us and they used to make everyone's life a misery … they had a disabled parking place outside their house and there was nothing wrong with any of them … whingeing to the council, their kids up and down the bloody road. And the worst kind of con is a junkie – it's pathetic watching them skulking around the landings, selling their arses. (Male officer)

The notion of the disciplined self indicated a commitment to the moral imperative of work, and a division from other 'undeserving' people who were happy to be dependent and 'take handouts'. Howe's (1990) study of unemployment in Northern Ireland has shown that 'deservingness' is related to evaluative criteria that people apply to other people and imagined groups as strategies of impression management. The 'deserving' unemployed or poor are those who are out of work through no fault of their own, keen to return to work and willing to accept any reasonable job offer. These 'deserving' people share the value placed on work, independence and individual responsibility and are part of the same moral community. Howe (1990) argues that the moral discourse of work is linked to reciprocity; people exchange their labour for wages and use this to buy goods and services. Through work, people engage in reciprocal relations within society and achieve independence in relation to their peers. Work gives a person status in the family, community, polity and economy, but working also involves costs and sacrifices, and it demands moral strength. The officers at Locksdon displayed generalised resentment against 'the undisciplined other' (unwilling or unable to assume the moral responsibilities of work) that was given salience by the officers' personal experience of career criminals and fraudsters in prisons. Important for the purposes of this discussion was the way that criticisms of this 'type' came to include the detainees.

Officers performed the disciplined self in everyday movements and encounters. In the visible spaces of Locksdon, the officers' movements were efficient, formal and measured, their bodily posture rigid, their professional façade and 'presentation of self' (Goffman 1969) were expected to be detached, controlled and steady. Their concern with self-control and rigid physicality was bound up with a desire to project authority and strength, and contrasted with the detainees' enforced vulnerability. Young (1991: 113) has argued that policemen contrast their own physical hardness, strength and kempt cleanliness with the dirt, disorder and loose, sloppy 'animality' of criminals. Similar contrasts were tacitly drawn by the male Locksdon officers: their physical 'hardness' and discipline contrasted with the detainees' enforced inactivity, vulnerability and dependence.

MILITARY METAPHORS

The disciplined self was a masculine endeavour that was related to the military experience of the majority of the older officers at Locksdon. When I arrived at Locksdon, I was told: 'You're not going to find a typical prison officer here, you're only going to find out about typical ex-army.' Military metaphors permeated life at Locksdon. The idioms and slang which were used to talk about work – the references to 'not jacking' (giving up), the emphasis on 'taking the lead', 'taking the initiative' and 'getting on with it' – referred backwards in time to the periods that many officers had spent in the armed forces. Officers making mistakes with the roll check were jokingly given 'dog-watches',[3] for example, and those with military experience would recount youthful military escapades. Locksdon officers would always be interested to find out whether new members of staff 'had served'. The military experience often forms a defining chapter of many ex-service personnel's lives (see Morgan 1994; Woodward 1998). The masculine power associated with traditional theatres of war – described as 'the quintessential proving ground for masculinity' – is related to the requirement for courage, strength and judgement (Dowler 2001: 55). Military life is associated with a particular 'heroic male project', in Whitehead's (2002) terms: one of conquest and discipline, privileging physical perseverance, team work, as well as calm competence, technical rationality and nerve in the face of danger. The experience of military life distinguished those men (and women) who had experienced it from those who had not.

The stories, anecdotes and reminiscences shared by those Locksdon officers who had served in the forces, however, tended not to recall conflict situations, but instead invoked the (male) sociality of the barracks, pubs and training grounds of forces life. One man told me that he had enjoyed the army because 'people looked out for one another – we looked after our own. They were all local boys in our regiment and you felt part of it y'know?' He noted that he had not felt anything similar since joining 'civvy street' and still missed it. The nostalgia associated with the military, then, was for a highly structured and ordered existence, but also for the affinity of forces life. These relationships among 'men who have worked together, fought together and played together' (Messner 1992: 215; see also Dowler 2001; Morgan 1994) tended to bind men to other men in the military context while often separating them from 'civvy' men, and from women.

Prison work – with its formal structures, its emphasis on discipline and 'rank', its uniform and the co-presence of other ex-forces personnel – produced congruencies with military life. Like the military, the prison is also viewed as a 'key institutional site for the expression and reproduction of hegemonic masculinity [accentuating] male dominance, heterosexism, whiteness, violence and ruthless competition' (Sabo et al. 2001: 5). The military gave Locksdon officers a way of thinking about personal discipline and responsibility within a team. Individuals who had a military history made sense of the demands of Locksdon through their experience, and also made efforts to recreate a military ethos in their relations with others. Yet, like Cohen's (1985) discussion of the symbolic community, where a 'shared' icon can hold a multitude of meanings for individuals, the variety of personal military experiences (some of them very brief) and the nostalgia with which military life was recalled occluded a diversity of individual experiences.

In this way, the references to military life were not in reality a sharing of a common experience. Rather, ideals of militarism were used to make a provisional statement about life at Locksdon, and to build some kind of shared understanding of the obligations and duties of centre life. Shared reminiscences of military life were attempts to recreate the ideals of order, stability and constancy that many officers associated with 'having served'. Officers sought to place their own experience within a common meaningful framework, and to provoke a response from others about the social world of Locksdon. As Josephides (2008: xx) argues, 'the activity of making social knowledge explicit is simultaneously the activity that modifies that knowledge ... Eliciting talk is thus always a line with a hook, fishing for responses.' What officers sought to elicit in their recollections of military life in the everyday chat of the centre was only partly to do with appeals to the hypermasculinity of the armed forces. Anecdotes about military experience were more concerned with testing colleagues and friends about the vision of life at Locksdon and the kinds of obligations that were thought to adhere to 'being there' for colleagues and friends.

The broad, generalised values of work, discipline and responsibility crystallised into (tacit) codes of work practice of which every officer at Locksdon became aware: never 'shirk', 'do things properly', pull your weight in the team. These generally valued principles for working life were not specific to Locksdon, of course, but the officers' criticism of those who were seen to be shirking was upfront. Officers often engaged in ongoing vocal commentaries on colleagues' performance that indicated a high level of scrutiny in line with the vigilant environment. Being accused of 'malingering' or being 'lazy' (usually in 'jest' but meant to be taken seriously) was a sure sign that people had noticed an officer not pulling his or her weight:

Y has started letting me down a bit recently. I mean, he's usually good, but he's been leaving things for me to do, letting me start things off, letting me take the lead all the time rather than sharing it. (Male officer)

R is a fat, lazy, whingeing slug. He's fucking useless. If I see his miserable face once more today ... Moping and whining, self-pitying arse ... there's always a bloody excuse for him, always a reason why not. I'd never give anyone a hard time if I thought they were doing their best, y'know? Take W. I know guys that would've jacked on that job. But she just keeps going, she isn't whingeing. (Male officer)

Allied to their concerns for moral discipline was the officers' ideal of the kind of working relations that they believed should exist among them. These models drew on larger discourses of work as a moralised imperative, and in turn become generalised into models for social relations and the kind of persons with whom the officers wanted to deal.

TRUST AND FRIENDSHIP

The more you go on, the more you realise that you're just a little man, that you're never going to make a scrap of difference to anything in this life. All you can do is just watch out for yourself, your little bit, your family, your corner. What matters to me most now are my friends. I think a lot of my friends, and I expect a lot from them too. Some of the people [officers] in here [Locksdon], I wouldn't trust them with anything ... I wouldn't let them babysit my kids, y'know? But I'd trust R and F. I'd trust them with anything, my life. My kid is fiercely loyal to his friends ... I'm proud of him for that. (Drew, Locksdon officer)

Locksdon was understood by those who worked there as a capricious context. The fallibility of human nature meant that imprudent officers and staff members were vulnerable to being influenced by manipulative and desperate detainees. The worst kind of officer (at Locksdon, or a prison) was an officer whose lack of judgement threatened to ignore the boundaries on which a secure environment relied. These boundaries (between officer and detainee, officer and management, Locksdon and 'outside') had to be upheld in every encounter. In relation to the detainees, the officers needed to 'keep the initiative', but daily life and the 'wiggly lines' of decision-making meant that the ideals of the regime were always being dissolved. It was because of this that trust and loyalty were such highly valued qualities, and vital to good discipline. Trust is a 'tentative and fragile' response arising from future contingency and uncertainty about the future (Dasgupta 1988; Gambetta 1988: 218; Misztal 1996). Trust occupies the gap between our knowledge of the here and now, and our anticipation of the future. Loyalty is linked to trust. The *New Oxford English Dictionary* defines loyalty as, 'the quality of giving or showing a firm and constant support or allegiance to a person or institution'. Loyalty implies acknowledgement of valued social relationships, constancy in fulfilling obligations emerging from these relationships and the ability to live up to the extension of trust.

At Locksdon, trust and loyalty in working relationships were understood as a sense of prioritisation of others over self. This prioritisation was not altruism, exactly. Rather, the idea of placing others before 'self' delineated a requirement that officers were not 'selfish' (the ultimate failing in many officers' eyes): that they thought about the context in which they were operating, that they thought about the consequences of their decisions for others, that they acknowledged their place among colleagues. A good officer (and a good person) should show dependability, reliability and a sense of duty to others. In an emergency situation, officers had to rely on one another to act 'properly', that is, to look out for one another. Given the visibility of the social arena in which they acted, officers had plenty of opportunity to witness their colleagues in action, and praised examples of incidents when others acted well (or badly). Locksdon officers often expressed feelings of solidarity in terms of 'being able to count on someone' in a crisis. By this they meant a violent incident, a dangerous detainee or some emergency where people's welfare was on the line. A 'good' person and a good officer was someone they could get along with in the mundane routines of centre life, but also someone who they felt confident standing next to in some imagined emergency:

> If things kicked off, and I looked round and saw T by my side, I'd think 'Yes! All right!' There's some officers you'd be glad to have there, you'd be pleased it was them. And it doesn't come down to women or anything. I mean … if I had B there, I'd be glad. I'd think we had a good chance. But some of the wankers in here … I mean, you just wouldn't want to depend on them. (Male officer)

He's a good guy, O. I mean, if I called him up in the middle of the night, saying, 'Sorry mate, I'm in Glasgow and I need some help', he's the kind of guy who'd drive through the night to get to you. He'd be there. He'd do what he could. (Male officer)

At the start of this section Drew talked about friendship, and the importance loyalty had for him. I often heard Drew refer to fellow officers as 'mates' but he explicitly singled out two officers, Mandy and Bob, as friends. Drew made a qualitative difference between these two categories. Mates were those with whom he enjoyed working:

I think of Joe as a mate ... But we'd never go out drinking together, we'd never meet up outside, but we get on ... we're all right with one another. I only see him here. We've just kind of accepted that it's never going to be anything more but it's ok.

Friendship, on the other hand, was a deeper type of relationship and he placed it, theoretically, in a higher position than the relationships he had with his family.[4] Friendship, for Drew, involved sharing experiences (pub nights out, trips, holidays), sharing problems and doing favours for one another ('that's what friends are for'). Friendship was a way of thinking about being a good person, a way, as Carrier (1999) puts it, of thinking about moral selfhood and norms. Being a loyal friend, standing by friends and offering them help were all ways in which Drew saw himself reflected back in his best light. I once witnessed Drew become angry with his friend Mandy for accusing him of helping a female friend 'because you want to sleep with her'. Drew's anger centred on the accusation of a nefarious motive behind an act of friendliness: 'It wasn't like that ... I did it because I'm a nice guy,' he insisted.

Despite its idealised character, friendship is built on 'shifting sands' and involves 'strategic revelation', and loyalties are always accompanied by betrayals and treasons (Paine 1999: 44). For example, Drew considered Mandy to be a great friend but Mandy appeared to privilege other relationships (see below). Far from being a relationship characterised by acceptance, freedom and honesty, with no compulsion of reciprocity (see Pahl 2000: 163–4), friendship and 'being mates' at Locksdon involved pressure and conformity, and structured a whole series of obligations. Amity at Locksdon involved dilemmas about loyalty and trust and juggling hierarchical obligations. Drew declared that he expected a lot from himself within friendship, and that he also expected a lot from those he considered to be his friends. Drew expected and demanded an active, balanced reciprocity. He was concerned not to be 'let down'. For instance, he described the way he had fallen out with an officer Frank (once a good friend) because Frank had 'wimped out' on him. He had invited Frank on a walking holiday with several ex-army friends, and Frank had given up on a tough day's walking, insisting they turn back, embarrassing Drew. Frank had demonstrated several contemptible qualities: lack of perseverance, lack of loyalty (to Drew in front of his other friends) and laziness. As far as Drew was concerned, the friendship was dissolved.

At Locksdon, I was most friendly with a set of officers (mostly younger officers with families) who would socialise, exchange favours, help each other with DIY jobs and go on holidays together. This set had a satellite group of older family men who did not participate in the drinking and socialising of the younger officers. Members of this group considered themselves (and those they approved of) to be 'switched on' about the job, conscientious, modern and professional. Most officers were aware of the rough split within the staff. One officer (not a member of the set) told me:

> There's some officers here, I'll call it a clique, who think they're it. They think they know the best way of doing things, think they've got it all worked out. You're not allowed to question them, argue with them. You're either in or you're out.

The ties among the officers within the set structured mundane sociable acts – tea-making, going to the gym to train together at lunchtime, after-work trips to the pub or stadium to watch football, arranging to be on nights together – which were manifestations of conviviality. I have described this set because within it I became familiar with the cross-cutting loyalties involved in 'being mates' at Locksdon:

> Vic and Mandy have known each other for years. Mandy jokes that she and Vic are like spouses, despite the fact that Vic is happily married. Many people at Locksdon believe they are having an affair. Mandy and Vic know people will gossip about them. Loyalty between them is absolute; no-one at Locksdon can come between them. Drew and Mandy are firm friends. Drew lived with Mandy for a while during a difficult time at home and she is a confidante for him. Drew refers to Mandy and Greg as his

only real friends at Locksdon. Mandy, however, will gossip about Drew to Vic (and me), though she does so with affection and in the knowledge that we will keep the confidences. Greg is admired by Drew, who thinks of him as a great friend with fine qualities. However, Greg and Mandy often appear to be closer. Greg shares secrets (usually involving liaisons with women) with Mandy, who passes them swiftly on to Vic (and me on occasions). Drew is not included in this gossip about Greg. Frank used to be a firm friend of Drew's, but Drew has written him off, unbeknownst to Frank. Drew often mocks Frank behind his back. Frank's lazy lifestyle has caused him to go down in the estimations of his former allies. Mandy reportedly once had a brief affair with him. I am friendly with Frank and there is speculation about whether we are having an affair. Drew is, according to reports, very protective of me. He resents Frank, and Mandy says he's jealous. Frank will not talk about Drew behind his back, stating that this would be wrong as Drew is his friend. Drew does not reciprocate this esteem. While Mandy unleashes her sharp tongue over Frank's failings, he fondly imagines that she would like to resume their attachment. Frank tells me this, but I am careful not to let Mandy know. Frank and Vic are also friendly. Vic is more loyal to Frank than Mandy. No-one gossips about Vic – 'I'm as pure as the driven snow'. Mandy agrees. 'That's what it's like at Locksdon,' she tells me. 'Everyone's got shit on everyone else. But you'd never tell.' Vic concurs: 'You'd never tell, ever. If you think it's happening, if you could possibly imagine something happening, then it probably is. You can just assume that it is.'

This is just a small snapshot of some of the relationships to which I was privy: there were probably more tangled histories than people admitted to me and to one another. Locksdon was an environment where everybody became linked in some way to everyone else (through affairs, friendships, shared experiences), and although it was possible to 'keep oneself apart' to a certain extent, the nature of the working environment meant that everyone became entangled in the close-knit atmosphere.

EXPERIENCING THE INSTITUTION

The good officer and good colleague was a professional who would 'be there' and act well in a crisis, but was also someone with whom officers could enjoy spending time in the confined centre. The detention centre was a temporary and unwanted 'home' for detainees, but it also became a kind of homeplace for officers, who had to 'fit in' with one another. The cramped working environment, the enforced visibility and sociability, and the shift work, meant that Locksdon was constantly transformed into something more than just a workplace. Like the military barracks or the firefighters' station, the prison was a quasi-domestic zone that blurred traditional separations between 'public' and 'private' (see Crawley 2004: 129; Hall et al. 2007). Rapport (forthcoming) argues that home should not be considered simply a physical place. Rather, he argues (citing Berger [1984: 64]) home is located in 'words, jokes, opinions, gestures, actions, even the way one wears a hat'. Home is 'a subjective space of body-plus-habitus, encompassing world-views, bodily routines and "life-projects"' (Rapport 2003: 215–39, 2009). This idea of home as comprised of habits and routines captures perfectly the way in which Locksdon became a place of familiarity and comfort, but also frustration and irritation. On night shifts, particularly, the establishment became 'like home'. Four officers were locked up together in charge of the regime and they had to occupy themselves during extended periods of boredom and inactivity. The night was punctuated by obligatory checks on the establishment and the detainees, but officers passed the rest of the time by dozing, watching TV, chatting and visiting the gym. Officers would organise nights on with friends if they could and, if successful, the evening would become a cheerful occasion of shared meals, DVDs and banter. In contrast to the active, moving, alert body of the day shift, the night shift produced the body as relaxed and exhausted. The shared experience of the exhaustion, tedium and passivity of the night shift was a crucial part of work at Locksdon among officers: a form of forced intimacy that was a pleasure with friends, but an unwelcome trial with others.

In a highly visible, monitored environment, there was pleasure to be had in exerting control over the possibility of being seen, and to readjusting the scopic and temporal regime to escape attention and conduct another kind of life at Locksdon. Certeau (1984) used the term '*la perruque*' to capture the way in which time and resources are 'borrowed' from the workplace for personal uses – for making a social phone call, for example, or arranging and conducting other work. For Certeau, '*la perruque*' was an example of a creative, tactical diversion of time that is 'free, creative, and precisely not directed toward profit' (1984: xiv–xv, 25). Certeau was concerned to 'undo' what he saw as the 'managing, differentiating, classifying and hierarchising' tendencies of Foucault's disciplinary society (1984: 96). He placed great importance on the possibility of the subject being a 'poet of his own affairs' and the way in which the spatial, political and social order could be 'tricked by an art' (1984: 26, 34). The spatio-temporal regularity that the regime strove towards was interwoven with other routines: staff would leave their newspaper in the same place every day, would meet for cigarettes with colleagues at the same time, would laugh at the same jokes, would 'wind up' colleagues on each meeting.

Drew Smith is immigration liaison officer for the morning. The detainees have had their breakfast and education, the exercise yard and the gym are all open. As men mill up and down the corridors, Drew shuts himself off in the ILO office and sorts through the paperwork, grumbling that yesterday's ILO has left him too much to do as usual: distributing movements documentation, giving detainees faxes from solicitors, and faxing solicitors in turn. Drew has a cup of tea that one of his mates made for him in the centre office and he sips it as he despatches the paperwork. He calls over the tannoy to a detainee who has an interview with an immigration officer. When the man turns up, Drew accompanies him past the dormitories and through several gates to the appropriate office. The immigration office is interesting these days as there is a new member of staff over there, a single woman. This could be the start of a flirtation, a new 'project'.

Over at the office, the woman is not in, but Drew stops for tea with the other immigration officers while the detainee is being interviewed. The conversation is well-rehearsed: the immigration officers (IOs) bemoan the immigration service and the work at Locksdon. Drew stays a while, eats a few biscuits and has another cup of tea, before the detainee has finished and is accompanied back to the centre. On the way back, Drew tells me that he is sick of being a lackey for the IOs and that they are scared of coming over to the centre because they get inundated with questions and requests by detainees. Although these guys visiting Locksdon are 'all right' the immigration authorities are generally 'fucking useless', he claims.

Now, with an hour to go before lunch and enough work finished for the morning, Drew moves on to the main business of the day. He retreats to a hidden office on the other side of the establishment, where most people never routinely have cause to venture. This room has a telephone line, and he spends the next half hour on calls related to a bit of work he is doing on his rest days; Drew is a skilled craftsman and is not alone in 'doing the double' on his time away from Locksdon. Then he rings up about a motor bike he had seen advertised; nice-looking, good price but it turns out not to be quite what he was looking for. He spends some time flicking through a tool catalogue, lazily teasing me about being a student; when am I going to start working and paying taxes? Suddenly, the door opens and several members of the works staff come in to collect some storage boxes. This is unlucky; no-one usually comes into the room. The works men smirk to see me and Drew sitting together – more gossip for the centre – but Drew simply carries on flicking through his catalogue. The men leave, one of them warning me about 'being careful about lusty old screws', and Drew shakes his head at them, rolling his eyes to me.

The bell rings over in the centre and we make our way back to the centre for roll check. There then follows a bit of banter with the other officers who have drifted back to the centre – some are old friends, others are tolerated colleagues. A nurse pops her head round the door with a query and Drew fondly 'winds her up', accusing her of being work-shy and stalking him: will she stop following him for once? It is getting embarrassing; everyone's noticed. The nurse makes the requisite sarcastic reply. After roll check, it's time for lunch and Drew decides not to go for a run as he normally does, but to pop out into town to run some errands and to 'get away from that shithole' for a while. Back in the afternoon, Drew reports to a friend that he saw an officer and an admin girl together in town; a new liaison perhaps? These sorts of sightings are never innocent and Drew chuckles to himself as he checks the staff detail for the afternoon. He is on exercise yard duties, so he gets a pen and paper to note the movements of detainees round his patch and settles down for the duration in the exercise yard. It's a sunny day. He scans the yard, keeping an eye on the detainees, and starts to doodle a design for a gate he is making. He gets several visitors – a good day – and one of them brings a cup of tea and sits for a while and they chat about this and that, gossip about colleagues, criticisms of lazy officers. Finally, after a long and boring afternoon – 'something happen, something happen, something happen', Drew mutters at one stage, drumming his pen against the hut window – the bell sounds again and it is almost time for home. Another round of tea back at the centre office and some more banter. There is a night out planned for the weekend, but Drew isn't around, or else he doesn't feel like it; these events aren't as much fun as they used to be. Someone gets the roll check wrong – the centre officer has miscounted the new arrivals – and there are exasperated re-counts and much pointed 'joking' about incompetence before Drew is finally able to collect his bag and head off home.

Drew's day, read via Certeau, was a series of diversions conducted in pockets of time and hidden spaces 'borrowed' from the regime and enabled by it, 'rewriting' Locksdon's regime, introducing the 'guileless ruses of different interests and desires' by selecting 'fragments … in order to create new stories' (1984: 34). The spatio-temporal order of Locksdon, as a total or 'austere' institution, was constantly doubled up by Drew and his colleagues, and by the detainees too, who claimed space and time within the regime to live another kind of life.

The secret places of the establishment (cupboards, store rooms, offices, tea rooms, the gym at night) became spaces where the officers' collective imagination took hold. As people sought to utilise them to escape the 'public' life of the IRC, so they also took great enjoyment in piecing together the movements of their colleagues – other people's relationships, habits, movements, friendships and romantic dalliances (admitted and secret). Officers took delight in this alternative practice of 'bodywatching': speculating about colleagues through half-glimpsed shadows, emerging from darkened rooms, following each other down corridors, or alone in the gym at night. Gossip, everyone acknowledged, was rampant in Locksdon, and was a way of turning what was seen or imagined into social and political currency. Gossip, the ongoing narrative of Locksdon, was experienced by individuals as a parochial imposition and a visceral feeling of being judged by others: 'People here have nothing better to do than sit around and judge you. Everything gets noticed. If it's not interesting enough, they'll make it up.'

Gossip constantly linked and divided people, exploring the limits of what was tolerable and desirable. It was a way of people testing loyalties and staking claims. Gossip was a speculation about the nature of people's lives and the world, 'an activity through which individuals examine and discuss together the rules and conventions by which they commonly live' (Rapport and Overing 2000: 154). Gossip was also a way of negotiating position, or furthering individual aims and cementing relationships (see Paine 1967). People shared and withheld information as part of their social manoeuvres, expressing and marking social affiliations and new allegiances. It was a way of reflecting, or claiming, or forcing intimacy with others. Gossip and teasing at Locksdon was concerned with creating a sense of 'what is going on here'. An officer would tell a friend that a new female colleague had been sunbathing at lunchtime with her blouse open; irresponsible or titillating? Another officer would report that a reception officer had missed a concealed razor blade during a body search: an understandable mistake or evidence of ineptitude? Someone would report that a mischievous colleague had been reprimanded by the governor for pinning up a postcard of a naked woman: unacceptable childishness or evidence of the governor's humourlessness? Gossip was concerned with shaping a vision of 'what we are like here'.

Life at Locksdon, with its periodic crises, familiar routines and dreary lulls, produced an intimacy among colleagues in the sense described by Berlant (1998: 281):

To intimate is to communicate with the sparest of signs and gestures, and at its root intimacy has the quality of eloquence and brevity. But intimacy also involves an aspiration for a narrative about something shared, a story about oneself and others that will turn out in a particular way.

The 'brevity' of social life at Locksdon was to be found in the one-liner that perfectly captured common feeling, the single word that harked back to an infamous or hilarious event that took place the previous week, a comment that demonstrated a person's conceits had been recognised. 'Intimacy' captures the way in which this 'something shared' designated warmth, familiarity and affection, but also oppression. People felt uncomfortable that colleagues claimed to know them – they contested other's version of themselves, or were irritated by the reputations attributed to them. Yet they also revelled in the satisfaction that could be gained from being part of this ongoing narrative, by being known to the group and by knowing others in turn, however objectionable many colleagues found one another.[5] As Mandy put it: 'Everyone's got shit on everyone else. But you'd never tell.' When people said 'that's what it's like at Locksdon', it was with a certain rueful pleasure and pride. There was satisfaction to be gained from belonging as part of the group and the camaraderie that people felt with colleagues was a central source of job satisfaction.

I think I'd miss it [Locksdon] the routine of it. Y'know, coming in … the same faces, seeing your mates … the wind-ups… I've laughed 'til I've cried in this place, I mean, we've been *paralytic* with laughter. I just don't know if I'd get that if I moved on. (Male officer)

I stopped Harry at the gate just now [Harry had had a row with another officer, lost his temper and was preparing to storm out, for which he would have been disciplined]. I mean, I'd like to think someone would have done the same for me. Whatever's happened, it's not worth losing your job … That's what people would miss if they just had a quick look at Locksdon, that sense of looking out for one another. (Female officer)

'SHE'S DANGEROUS'

In the overwhelmingly masculine environment of Locksdon, women were frequently seen as a 'problem' by their male colleagues. Studies of gendered relations within the Prison Service show that the increase in the number of female officers has threatened the traditionally male domain, with men resenting the 'positive discrimination' women are perceived to receive (Farnworth 1992). The literature about women in traditionally male occupations has consistently demonstrated that women bring ambiguity, danger and uncertainty. The literature also attests to the limited subject positions that are available to women: they are viewed as weak and needing protection, or as ugly, 'de-feminised' pseudo-males, or as dangerously sexualised objects and sources of temptation (Crawley 2004: 195; Young 1991: 191–220). While women's 'natural' skills of diplomacy are generally viewed as a calming influence on prison establishments, female officers are ultimately seen to be doing a 'man's job' (Crawley 2004: 123).

Locksdon's female officers could certainly be regarded by their male colleagues as 'good officers': reliable, hard-working, 'switched on'. Male Locksdon officers generally 'valued' female colleagues. In fact, several men professed to prefer them – 'I like working with women. There's none of that macho stuff you get with men. And they can make really good officers. They know how to calm things down.' Paradoxically, the stereotypical physicality (indeed, brutality) popularly associated with prison work was understood by officers themselves to require balancing by skills more usually associated with 'the feminine': the ability to negotiate, to demonstrate understanding and empathy. The 'good officer' (male or female) was not to be 'soft' in dealings with detainees, but did have to appreciate the difficulties of being incarcerated. Despite the valuing of empathy, the use of physical force at crisis points in the regime privileged physical strength and (masculine) corporeal vigour. The officers ultimately had to be prepared to engage in physical struggles with detainees when necessary, to secure the regime and stave off the threat of an out-of-control detainee (see chapter 5). 'The girls' (inexperienced and unskilled female officers) at Locksdon were separable from the expert, respected and admired female colleagues, but women in general (female officers and other female staff) were associated (by their male colleagues) with weakness, both in the sense of physical vulnerability and also in the sense of being 'more emotional'. More specifically, gendered understandings of 'emotion' did not link women with anger, pride or 'machismo', but to 'sympathy' and 'kindness'. This rendered them more susceptible to manipulation by detainees, but also more suited to the work of 'care'. As one female officer put it, 'they [male officers] just don't have a clue. When a detainee starts crying, they just freeze and call a nurse.'

The task of securing the detainee body via bodywatching and the use of force was the job of the *officers*, while tasks associated with the 'care' of detainees were seen by (male and female officers) to be the prime responsibility of others – education, nursing and religious staff. The pastoral concern extended to the detainees by nurses in the health care department, for example, or by teachers in the education department (both predominantly female), or by visiting religious leaders, became understood within a gendered framework. Nurses constantly complained that the officers were over-protective and patronising towards them, as well as expecting them to bear the brunt of the 'emotional work' of the establishment. Officers were concerned with the detainees within a visual regime of security and control. When a senior male health care professional was appointed to the establishment, nurses were angered by officers telling them that 'Now we won't have to look after you' and that 'You'll feel safer now, won't you?' Officers, on the other hand, constantly complained that the detainees would manipulate the nurses.

On one occasion, for instance, a detainee with a history of self-harm threatened to kill himself on hearing he was about to be deported. For officers, a threat of self-harm or suicide was met with a protocol response: the opening of a SH2052, the allocation of regular visual checks and the removal of the man to '3 dorm' (which was nearest to the centre office) for ease of observation. Nick, a senior officer, was in charge for the day and called the detainee in question to the centre office to tell him to move his belongings to the new dormitory. The detainee was upset and angry at having to move away from his friends:

> *Nick*: You've told us you feel you want to kill yourself, so we have to keep an eye on you and make sure you don't hurt yourself. We have to move you to 3 dorm so we can do that more easily.
> *Detainee*: But I don't want to hurt myself now.
> *Nick*: So why did you say it? Why did you say you would kill yourself? Go and get your stuff, and we can review the situation tomorrow. If you feel happier, we can see about moving you back.

The detainee left, unhappy, and Nick immediately shook his head and turned to a colleague: 'He'll go straight to the nurses now, go crying to them.'

A few minutes later, Jenny, a nurse, popped her head round the centre door and asked for a word with Joe, the other senior officer in charge: she wanted to talk about the detainee. Joe promised to go along in a moment. Once she had left, Nick exploded with anger.

> *Nick*: You go Joe, I'll only get wound up. He's just gone crying to her. She'll say that he shouldn't be moved. She set up the policy of moving them for observation! So we implement it and then she undermines us! It makes us look stupid, undermines us!

Later in the day, Nick told me that he had 'a word' with Jenny, and the detainee had been moved to 3 dorm, probably to return to his original dormitory the following day. This, he told me, was a long-running battle between health care and the centre. Another officer, overhearing the conversation, remarked sarcastically, 'I don't know. Why do these nurses always have to show understanding?'

On another occasion, Sharon, a nurse, was in charge of the health checks at reception when a young North African detainee was brought in. Once placed in the 'dirty room', he became agitated and started kicking the door. The reception officer simply stood at the door and told him in a low voice: 'Don't kick the door.' The man continued to protest and was eventually brought out, and suddenly he was crying. The reception officers were bewildered, and immediately turned to Sharon, who had only just remarked to me that she was exhausted from 'taking on everyone's problems' and that she was sick of 'having to step in with these guys all the time'. The new detainee spoke little English and he appeared to be ashamed to be in what he thought was a prison. The reception officers wanted to place the man in the special accommodation unit (that is, in isolation), but eventually phoned the principal officer, who advised getting an immigration officer and native speaker to talk to the man. He was taken to health care, his situation was explained to him, and he was placed in a dormitory. A few days later, Sharon remarked that the man had been 'no trouble' and was 'as good as gold'.

These examples demonstrate the division of labour between 'security' and 'care' that existed at Locksdon. The work of the officers, as they saw it, was the secure orderly maintenance of the regime. As one officer put it:

> When I first joined the service ... an SO asked me what I thought my job was. I gave him the old 'stop them reoffending, spend their time constructively, addressing offending behaviour' stuff. And he turned round to me and said 'Bullshit. You're here to make sure they don't escape. That's it.'

The proper 'masculine' work of protecting the regime (keeping the initiative, retaining control of the detainees) thus tended to preclude the more 'feminine' work of 'caring' for the men. For the officers, the enactment of 'care' by other staff often undermined the imperative to keep control of the secure establishment. Yet, importantly, the presence of 'caring' female staff at Locksdon was necessary for the production of meaningful boundaries around the (male) officers' own (more important) tasks of security and protection. Women – both female officers and other female staff – frequently drew forth protective and paternal styles from male officers. More specifically, women officers, especially those perceived to be inexperienced, vulnerable or weak, produced a new set of boundaries that male officers felt they had to secure: female officers had to be relied upon as colleagues, but their presence, for many male colleagues, threatened the regime by constituting vulnerable points.

The presence of women in Locksdon was also necessary for the articulation of a particular kind of sexualised masculine identification among male officers. Female bodies at Locksdon became objectified and sexualised within certain groups of male friends and colleagues: women's bodies were noticed, commented upon, discussed and evaluated. Discourses of masculinity often focus on the achievement of successful sexual performances with women, construed as *objects* for the pleasure of men (see Itzin 1992; Young 1991: 190–220). These 'reputational' masculine forms are distinct from more 'respectable' forms of masculine identity, which draw on loyalty and fidelity to wife and family, for example, with individuals contextually moving between these discourses. At Locksdon, the casual pursuance of available females (married or not) was a matter of competition among some men: one of life's pleasures, a 'natural' way for men to behave. A small cohort of officers would brag and share details of their sexual exploits with trusted friends and colleagues as a way of expressing, performing and accentuating a certain kind of masculine identity among peers. Women were tacitly assumed to be ultimately responsible for the maintenance of boundaries with predatory male colleagues, having a lot more to lose in terms of reputation. Men could gain only kudos from their male peers from sexual liaisons. Women had to carefully monitor male colleague's advances and expressions of their own sexuality in order to protect their reputation, among (male and female) colleagues.

One officer, for example, spoke to me in detail about the way he successfully seduced a new female clerical staff member. He admitted he did it as 'an ego-boost' rather than out of genuine affection for, or strong attraction to, the woman, 'though I like her – I'd never do it with anyone I didn't like'. He was ambivalent about his actions: while apparently conforming to his own masculine expectations and those of several of the peers to whom he bragged, he also expressed rueful admiration for more family-oriented men. He told me, 'Listen, I'll shag anything. I'm the least moral guy you'll meet. But you know, it's the least imaginative form of escapism there is ...' There was ambiguity here between an acknowledgement of the 'badness' of casual sex and the inherent worth of more respectable, less 'reputation-oriented' masculinities, coupled with an unapologetic celebration of the 'natural' masculine pleasures of chasing women.

Halfway through my year, the arrival of six new female officers in quick succession at Locksdon prompted a series of minor crises around femininity. One senior officer told me that he was having trouble making sure that staff rotas were arranged so that there would never be an all-female group 'on nights'. This was because women could not strip search detainees in case of a suspected weapon find, and were seen to be less physically capable of restraining violent detainees on their own:

Now that the girls are here, there are more reports of sexual harassment. The detainees can wind the girls up more and the girls can claim that sexual stuff has happened. Emma has had comments about her trousers being too tight, the Jamaicans have tried to put their arms around the new ones. There have been lots of complaints about the Turkish detainees. (Male officer)

The bodies of these female officers became the terrain for struggles between and among (male) detainees and (male) officers. These new officers became, for many male colleagues, the target of 'jokes' of sexual innuendo, comments on physical appearance, 'avuncular' arms around the shoulders and 'humorous' pats on the backside, with a comment about a 'great ass' and winks to male colleagues. Newly arrived women simultaneously became objects to be protected from similar actions from detainees, with officers roundly condemning detainee's wolf-whistles, for instance. 'Jokey' comments made by male colleagues and detainees were a double test for female staff. Would 'the girls' report 'harmless fun' to management? Or would they 'give as good as they got' and stand up for themselves? More importantly, would they adequately police the boundaries of propriety with detainees? Detainees would frequently hiss or comment as women staff members passed. A woman's lack of response to this disrespect for authority was criticised by experienced (male and female) staff. Women, then, embodied a sexuality that could be pleasurable, and a vulnerability that had to be protected, and in drawing forth or accepting this protection, women risked their place as 'equals' with male officers.

Mandy, as a well-respected and experienced officer, was the harshest critic of her new female colleagues. She labelled one young female officer as 'a tart' shortly after this woman's arrival, and accused her of giving sexual favours to a male officer. Furthermore, this female officer had been spotted pat-down searching a detainee, who had jokingly put his arm around her, at which the female officer had simply giggled. Another female officer was criticised for her 'prima donna' behaviour when she had made a complaint about a senior member of staff's 'attitude' towards her. Mandy's gossip pretended to demonstrate concern about the suitability of these women for life in the Prison Service. She intoned the importance of maintaining proper boundaries, of the dangers that emerged when 'weak' officers became embroiled in inappropriate relationships with inmates and detainees, and the necessity of putting up with the established hierarchy of officers in order to win a position for yourself; complaining (as the second woman had done) that a grumpy older officer had not treated you as you wished was no way to 'fit in'. Yet Mandy's gossip was mostly concerned with protecting her own hard-won position among her male colleagues. Experienced, respected and 'a good officer', Mandy had negotiated a position for herself as a valued and accepted confidante and friend to a small circle of the most popular younger officers. She gained a kind of prestige from her close relationships with these men that came from being accepted by her colleagues as a woman, but not of the category of woman that the majority of those men associated with sex and its pursuit. She condemned the new females because they threatened to undermine her own position (men's sexual weakness meant that other women could make claims to loyalty that would undermine her own position). By making accusations about these women's willingness to succumb to male advances or to make those advances themselves to win acceptance or satisfaction, Mandy highlighted the way her own relationships with her male colleagues transcended such morally ambivalent terms. She and her chosen few were friends, and equals, and this was a qualitatively different kind of relationship than mere sexual affiliations.

SILENCING DETAINEES

One day I am standing near an African detainee who is leaning against the centre corridor wall. An older officer, Fred, passes this man and asks whether he is feeling ok, meaning why isn't he engaged in regime activities? The man replies that he hates Locksdon and that it is why he is miserable. How would he like it if he [Fred] had travelled to his country of origin and had been imprisoned? Fred retorts that he had no intention of visiting Africa and sarcastically asked whether, given the awful conditions here in England, the man had considered going home. I am called by another officer, my attention is distracted and I turn to see the detainee wander off.

The following day, I am asked by Susan, Locksdon's diversity officer[6] in charge of race complaints at Locksdon, to see her in her office. Several officers tell me to 'watch out' when I proceed to her office because Susan is 'dangerous'. Susan tells me that the detainee has put in a race incident complaint against Fred and has cited me as a witness. I am uncomfortable to be asked to speak against an officer, my informant, and I briefly consider pretending I do not recall the conversation before telling her that

I remember overhearing part of the conversation, but I am not sure about a charge of racism. Susan tells me that she has known Fred for years and she knew he 'would never do anything like that'. Would I mind writing down what I had seen and heard? I immediately approach Mandy and ask her advice, safe in the knowledge that she will circulate the story (and my concern to be open) around the establishment. She initially tells me that I should just pretend I heard nothing. When I explain that I am planning to write I overheard the conversation, but would not want this to be used as a charge of racism, Mandy doubtfully agrees this would probably be ok. I write a brief report, submit it to Susan, and worry all evening.

The next morning I decide that I will talk with Fred (who had been on a rest day). On arriving at Locksdon, I am surprised to see his car (I had believed that he was on a rest day again) and take the letter I had been planning to leave in his pigeonhole down to the gym, where he is on the rowing machine. At the gym, Fred listens carefully when I explain the situation. He is still rowing, and there is a short silence.

'Well, I would have preferred it if you had said that you had heard nothing. If you say that you heard something, then things get tangled. Sometimes less is more.'

I wait for Fred to finish and we walk out together. I tell Fred that I feel uncomfortable for having become involved, and that, if presented with the opportunity again, I would not be drawn into the situation. It is awkward for me, I tell him, as I am an observer at Locksdon. Fred softens and tells me not to worry.

'She's sly [Susan]. She'd love to drop someone in it. It'd be great for her if she hooked someone. She's failed promotion twice and this is the only way she'll ever get promotion. She's only doing it for herself.'

Over the next few days, I am separately approached by five officers who give their interpretation of events. Their views on the matter all coalesce around the fact that Susan is using her role as diversity officer for her own purposes in general, and in this particular case. I was told 'she doesn't count dorms any more [meaning she thought herself above the boring mundane aspects of the job, despite being a normal grade officer]. One of the officers tells me, 'She's so keen, that she would probably love to see someone sacked after an investigation by her. It would be a great coup.' Another officer told me:

She's doing it all for herself. She's not doing it for the good of the service, not for anyone else but herself. If you feel you were coerced into it Alex, you can just withdraw your statement. She should never have gone to you. She's evil. And she's self-serving.

I bump into Fred a week later, and learn from him that 'there is no case to answer'. Fred thanks me, and when I tell him, 'Next time I'll know better than get involved', he grabs my arms and bounces me up and down affectionately, grinning, 'Ah Alex, you'll see nothing and hear nothing, eh?'

This example demonstrates how relationships among officers 'silenced' the voices of detainees. The first point to draw out from this example is how, on this occasion, the detainee's protest was ignored. His accusation of racism was a protest at the insensitivity, ignorance and offensiveness of Fred's remark. Given the limited resources available to the detainees, it was in the language of 'the race complaint' that protests against officers were formally made at Locksdon. The collapsing of generalised insensitivity and ignorance into 'racism' (understood by officers as a blanket prejudice based on skin colour, blatantly unequal treatment relating to this prejudice or the use of explicitly racial language) meant the officers were able to easily dismiss detainees' accusations by claiming they were not racist and 'would never do anything like that'. The officers 'knew' that Fred was not racist (by this they meant that they knew Fred was not stupid enough to say anything that could place him in danger of being accused of racism). Any legitimate claim the detainees had was immediately undermined by the protocols made available to the detainees to 'be heard'. One officer, impatient with my soul-searching in this case, told me:

Listen, if I saw someone with his hand around some guy's neck yelling 'you nigger' in his face ... stuff like that. Well, that would be stupid of him and I would have to say something, whether he was my friend or not. That's not acceptable.'

The implication was that only in extreme cases like this would the issue of 'acceptable behaviour' arise.

Second, I gained a good reputation (from the officers) from this incident: I could be 'trusted' and I had demonstrated 'loyalty' to Fred. Also, I had 'fronted' Fred, that is, I had been open with him, had sought him out to explain myself. The whole incident, though, filled me with unease, crystallising as it did the moral dilemmas of long-term ethnographic research. With six months of fieldwork yet to go, I was concerned to save face with the officers with whom I had developed good relations, to ensure my fieldwork was not jeopardised. Fred's comment took no account of the detainee as a person worthy of respect, but neither did my response. I would not have been prepared to speak against an officer, whatever Fred had done.

Third, the incident crystallised many of the themes about the social life of Locksdon that this chapter has discussed. Particularly, the criticisms of Susan brought into relief the way in which certain individuals were seen to transgress the 'moral equilibrium' (Parkin 1985: 6) at Locksdon, throwing into relief the kinds of expectations that people had of one another. Susan's 'evilness' and 'dangerousness' seemed at first to be over-expressed, but the strength of feeling surrounding her was related to the fact that fellow officers could not rely on her to place the group above herself. She did not conform to the ideals of trust and loyalty that were supposed to be upheld among officers, neither was she seen to privilege others over her individual aims. Other officers *felt* they could not trust her to do the right thing for them, whether this was true or not. Worse still, she was seen to be keen to use her position as diversity officer to *disrupt ties of loyalties*, engineering conditions when staff and officers had to speak against one another rather than maintaining a united front. In short, she confused the proper boundaries of Locksdon.

I acknowledge that this whole episode was an experience of mine, and my position within Locksdon at that time was unique. Yet my personal unease offered an insight into the social world that was inhabited by the officers. In her discussion about the emergence of empathy within social relationships, Josephides calls the ability to make one's way in an environment 'social knowledge'; 'the ability to judge situations and what they called for' (2003a: 62). This, she argues, is linked to morality; 'relationships create intricate situations in which we have to act beyond the breviary of general rules' (2003a: 56, 57). In the context of Locksdon, successfully 'feeling one's way' (acquiring and using social knowledge) among friends and colleagues involved the careful negotiation of clashing loyalties within hierarchies of obligation and reciprocity. I had stumbled across the vital 'social knowledge' of Locksdon and had reproduced the moral boundaries between those who 'counted' and those who did not. Several occasions proved that my experience was shared. For example, one officer told me that he had been in the room when a senior officer had lost his temper with a detainee: 'He had him pinned against the wall. I mean ... that puts us in a very awkward position. We become involved then, it's our problem too. We cover for him.' Another told me that he kept his mouth shut when he witnessed a fellow officer 'lose it' with a detainee: 'He could have been sacked for that ... I told him to get a grip of himself.'

In the last chapter, I discussed the way in which the visual regime at Locksdon objectified detainees within technologies of control. The individual detainee was registered in Locksdon's scopic regime as an abstracted body-object rather than as a person. There was a violence to this visual regime, not in the sense of 'directly visible, "subjective" violence ... performed by a clearly identifiable agent' (Žižek 2008: 1), but in a symbolic and systemic sense. Žižek (2008: 2) sees symbolic violence to be enacted through the 'imposition of a certain universe of meaning', and he calls 'systemic violence' the violence that adheres to a '"normal" state of things'. It is the violence of everyday exclusions, he argues, that is necessary to 'the smooth running of our economic and political systems' (2008: 1). In this chapter, I have described another facet of the hidden violence that adhered to the normal state of things at Locksdon. In the social and moral relationships developed between officers – which I have argued were a product and cause of the fraught working environment and the shared view of the detainee as a potential threat – a detainee's complaint for better treatment was silenced. His claim to be recognised and treated as a person was frequently dismissed or sidelined as officers strove to maintain their moral and social obligations to colleagues.

This chapter has argued that Locksdon was an environment where there emerged, despite a seething social complexity, a sense of egalitarianism, a strong imperative to display loyalty to the group, and a pressure to acknowledge the multiplicity of relationships in which one was entangled at any one time. 'Being a good officer' at Locksdon was relational, contextual and emerged from the specific milieu of fraught centre life. The officers' concern to respond to the demands of their friends and colleagues emerged from their reliance on one another, as I have argued, and also on the emphasis on 'fitting in' and the friendly relationships that existed between people. One of the products of this milieu was the imperative to 'see nothing, hear nothing' as Fred described it. Moral life at Locksdon became a matter of weighing obligations to certain valued relationships, and exacerbated the position of the detainees as outsiders.

4
Compliance and Defiance: Contesting the Regime

It is just after lunch in the centre office. Sam, an SO, is duty officer for the afternoon and is responsible for the overall running of the regime. He is also centre officer and must deal with detainee queries in the afternoon period – requests to send faxes to solicitors, appointments to see Locksdon's manager. As Sam settles behind the desk, a few detainees enter the office. One man comes in holding his detainee card. 'I want to make a hole in my card,' he announces (many detainees kept their cards on strings or chains round their neck). Sam eyes him earnestly, 'Go on then Lofty' (the man is short). The other officer in the room smiles indulgently at this joke. The detainee stands with his card, uncertain. 'I want to make a hole in my card', he repeats. 'That's great! Good idea!' answers Sam, grinning encouragingly. The detainee realises he is involved in some joke but does not understand. He smiles resolutely, holding up his card hopefully. Sam grins, takes the card and punches a hole in it. The detainee takes his card and wanders off, muttering to his friend.

Sam whistles and chats with the other officer: holiday plans, his kids, football. A group of detainees suddenly crowd into the centre office doorway. The men form a small arc round the desk. Sam tries to listen to the first request, but is distracted by the detainees blocking the entrance, their faces craning over each other's shoulders, gently jostling each other for a better view and talking with one another in several different languages. He suddenly stands up and tells them to get in line. 'Go and wait outside until it's your turn,' he tells them, gesturing them back with his hand. The men stare at him. He comes from behind the desk and spends a moment organising them into some kind of queue, then returns to the desk to deal with their requests. Before long, new detainees pile into the office to drop off 'Apps',[1] and the queue dissolves into a cluster of restless bodies again.

After the rush, there is a lull for a few moments while Sam leans back and sips at a cup of tea. At the doorway appears an Albanian detainee. This man has recently been the subject of a security report following the discovery of a hole in the ceiling above his bed. He has a history and reputation at Locksdon. Sam sits up. The detainee enters abruptly, as if in the middle of a conversation he has put on hold in the corridor. He stands in front of the desk with his arms by his sides and distractedly, as if thinking about something else, gestures with his chin to the pool balls (which are kept on top of a filing cabinet) with a toss of his chin. Sam, with a slow, deliberate turn of the head, follows the direction of the detainee's chin and immediately knows what the man wants. He turns to the detainee and feigns ignorance. 'What?' he asks. The man, slightly impatient, points with his arm to the pool balls, then folds his arms. 'Balls', he says. Sam leans back slowly, folding his arms behind his head, scrutinising the detainee. The man stares back. Sam leans forward, arms crossed, head extended forward slightly, retaining his aggressive eye contact. 'Give me pool balls!', the detainee demands, arms crossed, half confused at his lack of success, half defiant at Sam's eye contact. Sam snaps. 'Don't shout at me', he shouts. 'Don't come in here like that. Don't tell me what to do.' For a moment, the detainee and Sam stare at each other. Sam's jaw is clenched tightly. Then the detainee unfolds his hands, and relaxes his body. He opens his arms outwards, palms upturned, shoulders slightly shrugged, in a gesture of innocence, bowing almost imperceptibly and lowering his head slightly, still maintaining his eye contact. 'Sorry, sorry', he mutters rapidly. His posture is stylised, and slightly mocking. Sam eyes him suspiciously. After a pause, he stands up and gets the pool balls, handing them to the detainee. The Albanian man takes them, saying nothing, and walks from the room with a barely audible comment, at which his friend in the corridor can be heard laughing loudly. It obviously wasn't a thank you. Sam, irritated, wanting to get the last word, somehow knowing the detainee has gained the upper hand, shouts sarcastically after him, 'Thank you for coming!'

*   *   *

Sam's encounter with the detainee crystallised the way in which the placement of the body in time and space was crucial to Locksdon's regime. Time and space, as I have described, were divided into blocks and zones in the regime with associated norms and routines: orderly procession to the canteen at lunchtime, quiet activity in the education centre, brisk processing at reception. The detainees, however, did not embody docility and conformity in accordance with the demands of the regime. The detainee's visibility and temporal organisation within the regime did not make him 'the principle of his own subjection' (Foucault 1977: 202–3). This chapter is about the ways in which the detainee's body became a locus of resistance and disruption at Locksdon. It was through battles over compliance – the 'proper' way to queue, the 'acceptable' way to make a request, the 'right' way to move around the centre – that control and its loss were co-produced in everyday life, as Sam's struggle shows. Far from exerting a totalising grip upon detainees and officers, the detention regime held in tension a series of relationships between discipline and indiscipline, order and disarray.

'Keeping the initiative' was on one hand about upholding the rules of the centre. Some of these rules were never to be broken (keep keys in a belt pouch, always lock gates and doors, never handle items for detainees) but other rules were indistinct and were constantly tested by detainees and officers alike, such as the objects detainees were allowed to have 'in possession', the kind of footwear and clothes detainees were allowed to wear to the canteen, the designated places men could smoke. Gaps in detention centre protocol were filled with the norms of penal practice and the 'wriggly lines' of discretion that the officer in chapter 3 described. Disagreements over 'doing things properly' among the officers were disagreements about good prison work – between rule-bound 'dinosaurs' overly concerned with minutiae and 'switched on' officers who could use 'common sense' to secure a bigger vision.

On the other hand, 'keeping the initiative' was, for the officers, a nebulous feeling of control within mundane encounters like Sam's. Battles to elicit 'proper' subservience were part of an ongoing indistinct struggle to secure deference to the officers' authority and create the regime anew in everyday social interaction. Unruly bodies had to be organised in queues, personal bodily space had to be defended, insolent detainees needed to be kept in check. These practices of control were as important to the regime as the official rules. Yet the detention regime produced points of disorder as it strove for control: indeed, officers relied on points of irregularity (disobedient detainees, unruly movement, people out of place) to gain traction on the population at Locksdon. The 'agonistic' relationship between power and resistance that Foucault (2000: 324) identified, where there is 'no power without potential refusal or revolt', was experienced by officers as a physical sense of apprehension and irritation – about 'letting things slip' or 'losing the initiative'.

In Sam's case, the Albanian man's tone of familiarity and disrespect could not be tolerated. Sam could not allow himself to be ordered about in front of observers. If 'mind reading' is what people do when communicating with peers – attributing motives, ascertaining moods and desires, anticipating actions (Carrithers 1992) – then Sam's refusal to mind read (despite knowing what the man wanted) retained the detainee as 'other'. The detainee's bodily conformity – adopting a more 'appropriate' stance and somatic deference – only emulated docility. The man's subservience was feigned, his apology insincere, his conformity superficial. As Scott (1985, 1990: 19–20) argues, sly commentary and whispered subversions are 'neither empty posturing nor substitute for real resistance': these minor acts of sabotage and critique form 'weapons of the weak'. In the detainee's parting comment – an obscenity, perhaps, or insult, or joke – Sam was made an object of ridicule in front of another detainee and an officer. He had somehow lost the upper hand despite his best efforts to exact obedience from the detainee. Experiences like this were an intrinsic and difficult part of working at Locksdon.

THE RESISTING BODY IN TIME AND SPACE

The emphasis on bodywatching and the relentless timetable at Locksdon meant that the inhabitation of time and space, appearance and disappearance were always sites of struggle at Locksdon – what Herzfeld (1992: 170) calls 'social weapons'. Officers, for example, would retain control of time, not only in the sense of enforcing the timetable (with its roll checks, visit times and so on). They would generate small delays in everyday interaction to make the detainees wait for their attention: they would postpone a response to a request, or impose a queue like Sam, or feign deafness to 'impolite' demands. A common complaint from the officers was that, as one SO put it, 'Some of the detainees have been here too long, they get too familiar, start demanding too much. Get too friendly with staff.' One of the ways in which 'too friendly' detainees demonstrated their lack of proper respect for the regime and the authority of the officers was through using 'familiar' forms of address, and through playing with the temporal organisation of the centre. Detainees would enter the centre office and ask for 'favours' (like retrieving items from stored luggage, or a last-minute appointment with an immigration officer, or an envelope) outside their allocated time. They would arrive late back from the gym or education. On one occasion, a detainee came into the centre office, tapped an officer on the arm and asked him for a favour, calling the officer 'mate'. The officer, like Sam, had to reassert the boundary between him and the detainee in front of his colleagues, and he snapped irritably, 'Don't call me mate! I am not your mate. I am Officer T to you!'

Detainees constantly manipulated their visibility within the regime. Men would hide at roll check (behind curtains, in the toilets), or would generate small delays themselves. Moreover, they would use their 'exchangeability' to disrupt the numerical logging of subjects, one of the key ways of knowing and controlling the detainee population. This numerical logging (via the roll check, for instance) as I have argued, was part of the means through which the establishment administered identical treatment for all men, through which detainees became indistinguishable, one 'body' among many. Detainees who ignored the roll call bell and remained with friends in neighbouring dormitories, or who kept talking on the phone, would stall the progress of the timetable and the correct 'tally'. Mismatched roll calls forced officers to delay their own lunch and tea breaks to re-count the dormitories. More specifically, officers would have to engage with every man individually. If a dormitory number failed to tally with the official roll number, officers would be forced to check off each of the men in a dormitory against their detainee ID cards. The hidden detainee would disturb both the numerical coding of the establishment and the abstracted methods of governing the detainee population, but this disruption, in turn, would invigorate the regime by giving the officers 'targets' of attention. On one occasion, when the dormitories would not tally and officers had made several re-counts, losing about ten minutes of their break, one detainee eventually emerged from the 'wrong' dormitory and asked to be let out. The centre officer was furious, 'Why, when you saw all these officers chasing up and down did you stay on the phone talking? Why didn't you get back to your dormitory? I know you can understand English, don't pretend you don't understand. If you're late again, you're for it!'

Detainee exchangeability was inscribed via the Locksdon uniform (a tracksuit). Feldman (1991: 156) argues that the uniform of the prison is 'the apparatus through which the prison regime comes into direct physical contact with the inmate … a stigmatic action upon the body' which is crucial to 'visual serialisation and training'. At Locksdon, detainees did not have to wear uniform, but reception officers frequently encouraged it when men first arrived, arguing that it was a way of the detainees 'saving' their own clothes. The uniform was part of the way in which the detainee's body became coded as belonging to the IRC as a prison-like space. The uniform rendered men equivalent, easily recognisable and immediately distinguishable from visitors and staff. It denoted detention as a liminal place where the detainees' lives and identities were suspended. Some detainees, however, chose to wear their own clothes, so maintaining a gap between the intimate grip of the detention regime and their bodily self. Other men became creative with their uniform: they wore their tracksuit inside out, or rolled up one trouser leg, or wore both legs rolled up, or slung low on their waists with their underpants showing. The uniform here became a mark of individual difference and rebellion.

A man hiding behind a curtain, delaying the officers' lunch break, rudely muttering in languages incomprehensible to the officers: these were tactics, in Certeau's terms, diversions and 'clandestine forms' adopted by those 'caught in the nets of "discipline"' (1984: xiv–xv, 25). Tactics, Certeau argued, are 'scattered practices' and 'arts': 'multiform ... tricky and stubborn procedures that elude discipline without being outside the field in which it is exercised' (1984: 48, 96). Notably, tactics are a 'clever *utilisation of time*, of the opportunities it presents and also of the play that it introduces into the foundations of power' (1984: 38–9; emphasis in original). Tactics are opportunistic: they take place in the space of 'the other' – they are not separable from the systems and organisation they 'undo'. They take on 'indeterminate trajectories' to form a 'diachronic succession of points' rather than forming a logical sequence of events that might be clearly defined as coherent 'resistance' (see Bleiker 2000). Detainees, then, tactically took advantage of opportunities in the ordering of space and time at Locksdon to refuse the demands that the regime made of them, and to unravel the tight control of the timetable. They would use quiet, secluded spaces (dormitory rooms, behind the shelves in libraries) to escape the oppressive visibility of Locksdon. It was not only detainees, of course, who appropriated Locksdon's routines for other ends. Locksdon officers and other staff also used the offices, rooms and corridors of Locksdon for another kind of life (see chapter 3).

When appearance and disappearance were contested, and when the officers' prime duty was to visually track and account for detainees, an escape constituted the ultimate breakdown of bodywatching and the detention regime. There was one successful escape during my time at Locksdon. On this occasion, a Saturday, the lunchtime roll check revealed a 'body' had disappeared since the morning check. There was a standing roll check, a full search of the establishment and a lock-up, with extra staff drafted in and a tracker dog team. Staff had to stand round the perimeter fence in case the detainee was still hidden in the establishment. Despite their efforts, the detainee was never found. The escape looked very bad for the establishment and its protocols: someone, staff muttered, was not doing their job properly. A theory sprang up among officers about the bread van that had made a delivery that morning: kitchen staff saw a detainee watching the van, but only reported this after the escape had taken place, which infuriated the security officer (this was knowledge that should have been shared). 'They'll try and blame someone', one officer told me. Sure enough, the OSG on gate duty that morning came under scrutiny. It was she who was in control of vehicle searches, including a mirror search underneath the van. Ultimately, however, there was no way of proving how the detainee escaped.

The officers' expressed dismay and embarrassment at the escape. The embarrassment came from other establishments discovering Locksdon's failure (made even worse by the population at Locksdon not even being hardened 'cons'). An investigation team from the prison estate conducted a local enquiry and annoyed officers like Mandy, who scoffed, 'They are treating us like idiots, asking whether we think he is still inside the establishment about four days after he went: do they think we haven't checked?' There was also a collective sense of humiliation in front of the detainees, one of whom had managed to find a gap in the vigilant regime. The placement, distribution and accounting of bodies in space were basic aspects of the officers' work and the professionalism and reputation of the establishment and of the officers was measured in part by adherence to these basics. Several officers reflected after the event that 'he never came to our attention', meaning that the detainee had not distinguished himself in any way. Bodywatching had not successfully brought his intentions into focus (although clues had been there in retrospect). There was grudging respect for the escapee and intrigued speculation about how, exactly, he had managed to escape.

BODILY STRUGGLES

At a basic level, the officers' work and the establishment's responsibility was to administer the needs of the detainee's body as physical entity. Their job was to fulfil a detainee's physiological requirements for food, exercise, 'association' and sleep. The detainee was reduced to a set of biological elements: a mouth to be fed, a set of energies to train, a physiological being whose health and fitness became the target of interventions and procedures. In Agamben's (1998) sense, the detainees embodied 'bare life', in that their banned political status and identity gave way to another 'form of life', a biological life to be administered. Meeting the requirements of the different elements of this bare life became a means of securing the 'humane' regime.

Food was one of the most fraught relationships between the detainees and the detention centre. It bound detainees to the detention centre not as social persons, but as 'bodies'. Foucault argued that locating points of resistance can shed light on the way power invests and circulates through bodies (1982: 211; see also Abu-Lughod 1990). The centrality of food to detainee resistance revealed the way that sustenance was a relationship of dependence but also control within the regime. Detainees could buy snacks and food from the detainee shop, but the provision of food was otherwise tightly controlled: when and what a detainee ate was dictated by the centre. The kitchen at Locksdon had to cater for an array of dietary needs of a constantly changing population of men with a very small budget. The kitchen manager held regular meetings within the Detainee Consultative Committee to get suggestions from detainees, and collected new recipes and ideas. There was a varied menu, explained in various languages and menu pictures around the dining hall. Despite these efforts, detainees would frequently complain about the quality and quantity of food. The canteen was the site of several violent clashes between detainees and staff during my fieldwork. On one occasion, for instance, a detainee demanded more rice, but was refused by kitchen staff. He would not move from the hotplate, and became angry. When officers tried to forcibly remove him, after having tried to persuade him to move, the detainee resisted, and other detainees tried to drag the officers away from the man, throwing cutlery, trays and plates. The situation 'boiled over' as one officer reported: 'It was the most scared I have ever felt in here. I mean, there were fifty of them, and five of us.' All available staff were called to the canteen and peace was eventually restored when officers, and other detainees, persuaded the 'ringleaders' to return to their dormitories.

Refusing food was a significant method of protest. Food refusal disrupted a core task of the 'secure but humane' detention regime – to physically sustain the detainee in good health. For the officers, food refusal was part of a broader set of 'self-harm' activities. News of a food refusal could come through a friend or dorm-mate of the man in question. At the time of my fieldwork, food refusal, like a threat of self-harm would involve an SH2052 form being 'opened' on a man and an officer being designated to check on the detainee regularly during his or her shift, usually every hour or so, and make notes on the detainee (what he was doing at the time of the check, how he was feeling, whether he was eating, how he appeared). The SH2052 would be reviewed regularly with the detainee by senior officers and the health care department to ascertain whether the man 'felt better' and whether the file could be closed.

Food refusal would be used by a detainee to protest about the immigration authorities, an impending deportation, or the very act of being detained. The officers – 'we're just doing our job' – were unable to alter the course of men's immigration cases, or their detention, and became frustrated at having to deal with food refusal, which was generally seen as 'attention-seeking' and 'holding us to ransom'. Refusing food was seen as an inappropriate act of manipulating the regime by a detainee. It was a way of 'taking the initiative'. Food refusal (and other self-harm incidents) was not generally perceived by officers to be an expression of the traumas of persecution for asylum seekers, for instance, or the existential insecurity generated by interminable detention times and impending deportations, all of which created and exacerbated mental health problems.[2] Rather, food refusal became an issue of power and control. As one officer put it:

> This is what we're up against everyday. How do we really know if he is refusing food? He may not be going to the dining hall, but his friends may be getting him food from the canteen. And to send them out to other IRCs is sending out the wrong message. (Male officer)

The problem, as the officers saw it, was that food refusal and suicide attempts often precipitated a transfer to another IRC, one that was seen to have better-equipped and more specialist medical facilities – Harmondsworth, for instance. The probable outcome of food refusal, then, became understood as the motivation for refusing food: via food refusal, a man could secure a transfer to a 'better', more modern and comfortable IRC. Incidents of food refusal, or self-harm attempts, were seen by officers to disrupt the ideal of detainee equivalence. Officers frequently declared that 'everyone is treated the same at Locksdon'. This 'egalitarianism' meant indistinguishable treatment for all men; treatment that removed all acknowledgement of the detainees' individual circumstances, experiences or needs. It was an 'egalitarianism' that hid the production of an interchangeable detainee. Tactics to gain *non-identical* treatment – food refusal to secure a transfer, for instance – became construed as a morally dubious demand for 'special treatment', to become something other than one detainee among many.

As Ortner (2006) argues, resistance is frequently a struggle first to be recognised *as a subject*, capable of action and speech. The segregation and isolation of detention populations, as Isin and Rygiel argue, produce populations held within 'inexistent states of transient permanence in which they are made inaudible and invisible' (2007: 198). The 'invisibility' produced by detention is not simply via the spatial isolation of detention centres, which literally 'hide' detained populations, but also via the everyday practices of the secure detention regime. In the terms provided by Agamben (1998), the detainees became the embodiment of 'bare life' in detention: they were visually produced as 'objects', they were abstracted into biological elements to be administered, they were stripped of other means of identification and status, and were, for many aspects of the regime, rendered simply 'bodies'. Nyers (2003: 1078) argues that those who find themselves subject to technologies that 'make abject' (in this case, the detainees) have to 'interrupt the dominant political (speaking) in order not just to be heard, but to be recognised as a speaking being as such'. For Edkins and Pin-Fat (2004), paradoxically, it is precisely by 'taking on' the bareness of life – by using the body as a site and means of protest, for instance – that banned, excluded people can gain a political voice and visibility. As the biopolitical control and reduction of the detainee pervaded all aspects of men's life in Locksdon, so the detainee sought to use his abstracted and biopolitically invested body to resist the regime and the grip it had over him. Through food refusal, or protests about food, or manipulating visibility or placement within the regime, detainees captured in the 'inclusive exclusion' (Agamben 1998) of the detention centre used their bodies to become more than 'bare life'.

UNREASONABLE OTHERS

Detainees' resistance to the disciplinary, biopolitical mastery of their bodies became caught up in a 'grid of intelligibility' (Foucault 1977) at Locksdon which constituted them as 'unreasonable'. The discourse of the unreasonable detainee combined several aspects.

First, the detainee was compared to the hardened and reasonable 'con' of a 'proper prison':

> These ones are so unreasonable. Take this lunch time, when the power went off [there was a power cut]. In a prison, there wouldn't be all that whingeing and complaining, the cons'd understand it was a power cut and there isn't a thing we can do about it. We don't carry screwdrivers round with us, do we? Cons'd understand. This lot are so unreasonable. You just can't talk to them. They're so demanding. They're like kids, especially the Jamaicans. You have to entertain them, else they get moody. And they just won't be reasonable. (Male officer)

> I'm so sick of it. You can reason with cons. You can explain why they can't have what they want. With them [detainees] they just expect everything to happen right now. (Male officer)

The con in a 'proper prison' was reasonable because he was able to 'get on with it'. The con could suffer the penalty and consequences of his actions (crime), he was realistic in his expectations of prison life and he was pragmatic in his approach to his incarceration. He had simply to 'keep his head down' and 'do his time'. The detainee, on the other hand, did not accept the conditions in which he found himself, and the consequences of his actions (falling foul of immigration law). He did not 'get on with it' or 'keep his head down'. Rather, he complained, made demands and protested about his confinement. Because he did not, or could not, 'keep his head down', the detainee was unreasonable. Jamaican detainees, for instance, were frequently accused of 'being unreasonable'. The 'style' of masculine performance of some Jamaican detainees – drawing as it did on anti-authoritarianism and non-conformity – was in direct conflict with the concerns of the officers to maintain fragile power hierarchies and a compliant detainee population. The officers became irritated by the Jamaicans' 'confrontational' behaviour, their 'whingeing', their 'toxic' effect on the regime and their 'inability' to behave well.

Second, the unreasonableness of the detainee was productive of, and shaped by, the detainees' general emotionality. In chapter 3 I discussed the relationship between gender and 'emotion' in relation to 'securing the regime' and 'caring for the detainees' – I argued that the establishment's emotional work was gendered and that gender relations at Locksdon tended to reproduce, and were organised by, a division between masculine discipline, control and rationality, and feminine physical vulnerability and emotion. Emotions in western discourse generally tend to be opposed to 'the rational' and are associated with powerlessness rather than control and choice. Emotions are seen as capricious, unreliable and inconsistent, associated with 'base' animal-like physicality and sensation (see Blum 1980: 2; Lutz 1998: 56–64; Nussbaum 2001: 26; Parkinson 1984: 116).

'Being emotional', or rather experiencing and displaying certain kinds of emotion, produced divisions between men and women staff, but also between officers and detainees. That is, the expression and performance of emotion was productive of masculine hierarchies as well as hierarchies between men and women. Being a good officer, as I have described it, ideally was to embody cool judgement, stoicism and self-discipline. While (male) officers were supposed to be controlled in their expression and revelation of 'emotion' (like anger, sadness, distress, sorrow), detainees were understood to be 'overcome' by their emotions. This was especially the case when emotion was manifested in culturally 'other' physical displays. 'African' detainees, for instance, were known to be liable to go into trances, or 'have fits' or become hysterical or express anger or frustration via irregular and unfamiliar (to the officers) movements. On one occasion, I observed a detainee complaining about the establishment to the manager after having made an 'App'. The detainee was angry at his detention: he was from a good family, he had never committed any crime or been a terrorist. Why had he been detained? In his country, the detainee shouted at the manager, many English people visited every year and they were treated well – why had he been subjected to such bad treatment? The man claimed to have been living in Manchester for years, and he had a girlfriend there, and it was only because he had had a fight with her that the police had come and he had found himself at Locksdon. The detainee complained about the staff's attitude: they were rude to him, they shouted and did not treat him with respect. The manager was concerned to pinpoint a specific member of staff who had committed wrongdoing, but the detainee became visibly upset. He started to breathe very heavily, panting, tutting repetitively and shaking his head distractedly. He seemed unable to speak, and was almost hyperventilating with frustration. The manager told him that getting upset was counterproductive, and to return with a specific officer's name. After the detainee had left, the manager flicked through the detainee's history sheet and the Obs book and questioned several officers (who had been waiting outside): 'I don't think he is all there,' he noted, 'we'll have to keep an eye on him.'

Detainees' complaints or expressions of frustration, anger or desperation, then, were always at risk of being entangled with discourses that posited this behaviour as evidence of 'unreasonableness' or 'not being all there'. That is, the 'otherness' of the detainees was manifested through their emotional outbursts, which were performative of different (and denigrated) 'ways' of embodying male gender identity. Detainees' 'histrionics' (as one nurse called them) was when the hysterical and uncontrolled body revealed its generalised difference and indiscipline. Like the detainee above, men who were unable to accept the conditions of their detention were not framed as protesting subjects, but were accused of lacking reason. It is important to note here that health care staff at Locksdon did take seriously the traumatised detainees who passed through the centre. It was through their efforts, largely, that troubled and disturbed men would be referred to mental health specialists. It was also not the case that all officers at all times were indifferent to the misery of the men in their control: officers regularly found themselves acting as 'social workers', as one officer put it – listening to and sympathising with detainees. Yet in 2002–3, the detention regime at Locksdon, concerned as it was with security and control, was simply not able to cope with the complexity of detainees' health issues, especially when these issues produced threats to the secure regime.

Bodywatching, for the officers, was not only concerned with managing bodies in time and space as a means of producing security and predictability within the regime. It was also intertwined with an ongoing and critical assessment of detainees' moral character, which was understood to be revealed via everyday behaviour and interaction. In her discussion of the cultural and literary history of the 'willful subject', Sara Ahmed (2011: 232) argues that character has a 'because of' logic. The character in a text is attributed with character in a deterministic sense – character shapes acts and through these he or she is characterised. The 'because of' logic 'creates the illusion of a behind (a character appears behind an action, or as what is behind an action)' (2011: 232). A character, in this sense, 'is a glimpse, what creates an impression that there is someone being glimpsed'. Moreover, the 'problematic' character draws our attention. Ahmed argues (2011: 233) that 'when someone becomes a problem, we tend to question their character. We might be concerned more with what is behind an action when this action is not one we are behind'. In particular, the wilful subject – Ahmed specifically discusses the wilful child and the wilful woman – 'is one who poses a problem for a community of characters, such that willfulness becomes that which must be resolved and even eliminated' (2011: 233). The wilful subject combines moral danger with stubborn obstinacy:

> the willful character insists on willing their own way, without reference to reason or command. Willfulness could be described as a character perversion: to be willful is to deviate, to will one's own way is to will the wrong way. (2011: 240)

The character as 'glimpse' and 'as a system for creating distinctions between things' (Ahmed 2011: 232) resonates with the social world of Locksdon. It captures the way in which detainees' mundane action and actions within the detention centre became windows onto a problematic 'behind':

> One Wednesday afternoon, a time usually reserved for staff training, Mandy tells me that there is a five-a-side football tournament being organised by the officers in the gym for detainees. Extra officers are being asked to watch as support for the PEIs in case of trouble and she has volunteered. Would I like to watch the games? As I walk with her down to the sports field, we pass a Nigerian detainee. Mandy scoffs to me as we walk on that he 'was a real pain in the arse'. The man has been 'making a name for himself' since his arrival a week before and he is already unpopular with the officers. He has demanded to be sent to another immigration removal centre and he had 'staged' a suicide attempt the previous night. 'It was pathetic', Mandy proclaims. 'He got his roommate to go and call us and when we got there he was lying on the bed with a sheet wrapped round his neck. When we got there, he rolled off the bed with the sheet tied to the bed post.' The man had been placed in the Seg Unit to be monitored, where he had complained all night.
>
> When we reach the sports field, detainees have gathered into teams based on dorm affiliations and nationalities. There is a team of 'Eastern Europeans', another of 'Africans' and an Algerian team. Mandy and I settle to watch the short games in the winter sunshine. Mandy cheers the players when the need arises. Before too long, it is the 'African' team's turn to play. Mandy nudges me when the Nigerian man appears. 'He looks really suicidal now,

doesn't he?' she remarks as the man runs up the pitch. Before long, there is trouble among 'the Africans'. They begin shouting at one another, and the Nigerian man seems to be accusing his team mates of some wrong against him. He claims the ball for himself and begins an elaborate display of ballmanship, bouncing it off his chest and dribbling it excessively, ignoring the cries of his team mates. He is eventually tackled and falls over. Amidst gestures of despair and ridicule from the other players, the game continues, and the Nigerian man appears to sulk, cursing his team mates. Mandy turns to me and says:

> They're like that, the Africans. They just can't play in a team, they always end up screaming at each other. They're like bloody children. He couldn't wait to get the ball to himself and show off. Look at them – they're all over the place. Hopeless.

It was because the detainee was 'unreasonable' (in the sense of not being able to accept his detention and in the sense of being overcome by emotions) that he became 'like a child' and a 'wilful' character in Ahmed's sense. The detainees' struggles to become more than a detainee and more than a body – to change the course of their detention, to register a protest, to speak against the conditions under which they were kept, to make themselves visible – were annulled by a response from officers which construed their actions as over-emotionality and 'childishness'. In mobilising the bareness of their life in Agamben's terms for political contestation, they were confronted by interpretations of their actions which denigrated their bodily actions as evidence of out-of-control emotions, petty childish tactics and unreasonableness.

EXPERIENCING THE BORDER, IMAGINING THE NATION

Officers frequently invoked national citizenship and 'Britishness' in their everyday talk in the centre. The 'national order of things' (Malkki 1995a) was salient in moral and political life: for the officers, it 'naturally' organised loyalties, economic resources, morals and political obligation. 'Nation-ness' (Anderson 1983; Billig 1995; Edensor 2002) was used for thinking about a sense of community, self and identity.

(a) I think it's human nature to want to stick with your own kind. When people here club together and officers start saying, 'Oh, the

Algerians are causing trouble', I always say to them that if you were in a strange country, you'd stick with the English people too, wouldn't you? (Male SO)

(b) I know British history – the empire and everything – I know there were atrocities. But a lot of good came from it too. India wouldn't be where it was today if England ... you know ... a civilised country hadn't been there. We did some good too. I'm proud of England – history and that, what people have done in England.

(c) I tell my daughters they should be proud to be English. When they put on a stupid American or Australian accent, I tell them, 'Don't do that. You should be proud to be British. We gave English to the world. Don't lose it. Speak properly.' (Male officer)

(d) England has historically led the British Isles, so if Scotland and Wales want their independence, good for them ... I'd like to think we don't need them. I'd like to think we're superior. I think in the future, English national identity will be important again – it'll take the forefront, but I've no doubt that if it ever came to it ... then England, Scotland and Wales would stick together. We have nothing in common with Europe, with the Mediterranean – France, Spain and Greece. We seem to have more in common with the Germans. And we don't have that much in common with America. We are an island nation, and that makes us unique. (Male officer)

(e) I feel English. I like the English way of life. I couldn't live abroad. The French – we've got nothing in common with them. It all goes back to the war. We still hate them, don't we? I mean, I've got nothing against them personally, as individuals, but our culture's different, isn't it? We've got more in common with America. I've been to the US and – language, culture, shops, McDonald's ... I mean, it looks the same as here ... We're optimistic ... Take sport, football. It's so English, that optimism. Telling ourselves we're going to win each time, that this time'll be it, then losing ... [laughs]. And we're tolerant, and the weather, we're always saying it'll be nice. (Male SO)

These comments reveal a spectrum of beliefs concerning the nation and 'Britishness' and 'Englishness', but an unequivocal attachment to, and pride in, a national community. Nationalism is 'natural' (a) and orders people into groups of others 'like them' against other groups. History is used by several of the officers (b, c) to express a national distinctiveness (and superiority), as is language (c). The shifting loyalties produced by regional devolution have generated an increased awareness of Englishness as distinct from other British nationalities (d). The officer (d) uses the image of an island to explain Britain's uniqueness. The image of Britain as an island is a powerful one, often invoked by officers as an explanation of why Britain could not take the 'strain' of immigration. The final officer (e) uses Britain's old 'other', the French, to assert a cultural distinctiveness from Europe, maintaining that Britain has more in common with America. He uses popular culture – fast food restaurants, shops and 'appearance' to link the two countries, generalising from popular culture, urban-scapes and media images to assumptions about a shared culture (see Edensor 2002).

The arguments made by Anthony Cohen (1985, 1996, 2000) and Jean-Klein (2001), combined with those made by Billig (1995) and Edensor (2002), have highlighted how individuals recast the discourses and images presented by political and media rhetoric, and how local experiences become entangled with broader, more abstract discourses of belonging. For example, the officer above (e) draws on personal experiences to talk about the feelings he most associates with being English. He focuses on English optimism as a defining, stereotypical (clichéd) characteristic. He uses the example of football to show what he means. He switches from a 'national characteristic' to his own experience of being a football fan and his experiences of the performance of 'optimism', from which he then generalises back into things 'we', as English people, do. This officer is viewing the nation and its characteristics through his own experience. The officer above (d) talks about the affiliations between the countries and regions of the British Isles in terms of what would happen in 'trouble'. In conversation, the officers at Locksdon often expressed feelings of solidarity in terms of 'being able to count on someone' in a crisis. In volatile prison environments, this metaphor of solidarity in a crisis was a meaningful way of thinking about obligations and connections between colleagues and friends. The officer (d) is using similar models to express connections on a larger scale, between nations. The shared history of the British Isles would mean that the regions would unite and stand by each other in times of crisis, despite their differences.

The officers' choice of 'incontestable' symbolic forms was tinged with uncertainty: if Britishness is not history, language, 'tradition', then what was left? Their tone was often defiant when discussing history and loyalties (see b, d above), and their accounts and reflections held a sense of fragility and loss. The officers were arguing against an imagined 'other', who they saw to be criticising their 'natural' love of their country. This 'other' was generally understood to be the 'soft' liberal lobby, the urban elite and 'chattering classes'. These groups, it was understood, have power and influence in British society and do not share the officers' 'proper' pride in Britain. The officers' ideas about the nation combined with metaphors of defence and solidarity to become mobilised in ideas about detainees and immigration more broadly. The constant movement of new detainees through Locksdon gave fleshy reality to the media reports in 2002–3 that Britain was being 'overrun' and 'swamped' by 'bogus' entrants. Just as local personal experiences infused officers' ideas about 'the nation', their lived experience at Locksdon infused their ideas about 'the border'.

EMBODYING ILLEGALITY

The detainees' apparent inability to 'be reasonable' and 'get on with it' exposed the antagonistic relationship between the officers' penal understanding of Locksdon as a place of punishment and the detainees' resentment at their confinement.

> What lots of people don't understand is that the people being held here have broken the law. All these do-gooders saying they have done nothing wrong. They've all broken immigration law. Immigration law isn't different from other kinds of law. If you come to the country with an illegal passport, then that's against the law. If you've overstayed your visa and have claimed asylum five years after you came here, that's bullshit ... I think the way they behave in here is a fair measure of how they are going to behave outside. If they are willing to accept that the system is there, and to accept that they have broken the law, and to just accept that they are being detained for having broken the law, and wait, abide by the rules and get on with it, then maybe that should be taken into consideration. (Male officer)

The detainees had broken the national law via fraudulent entry, or an 'inauthentic' asylum claim, or visa deceit, this officer argued. This rendered them legally liable and morally culpable. The officers showed little appreciation or knowledge of the complex, historical relationships between illegality and statecraft.[3] For the officers, the detainees' illegal acts induced detention as a consequence and penalty. In this sense, the detention centre was like a prison. The detainees' detainable status was a result of, and evidence of, their illegality and their illegality justified their detention in turn. As De Genova (2007: 435 2002) argues, the border 'enforcement spectacle' of detention 'involves a staging of presumptive "guilt" that, in effect, produces culprits' (see also Bashford and Strange 2002; Malloch and Stanley 2005). Goffman (1961: 81) similarly notes that the 'logic' of the institution often generates circular arguments and interpretive schemas which make sense of the inmates; people in secure institutions 'warrant' their seclusion or else 'they would not be here'. At Locksdon, also, detention produced detainees as illegal and 'detainable'.

Officers at Locksdon frequently commented on the 'different types' of detainee passing through the centre, particularly the rise in the numbers of foreign national ex-offenders:

> It used to be that when I first came, you'd never get any confrontation, nowadays they're all like petty criminals coming through. I hardly ever got involved in C&R [control and restraint], since Christmas, we've had at least one a month. They're like the short-term sentencers at a prison – mouthy, lippy, real whingers, they'd cause trouble for everyone. We've noticed a real difference in the guys coming through. There is a stronger criminal element. Do you know why there are so many Algerian guys here for months? Because the Algerian government don't want them back! They stall on passports. They know these guys are just criminals, the scum. They think, well, they [Britain] can take care of them. We give them education, a gym, they see a doctor whenever they like, which is more than I can do. And they still whine! (Male officer)

> I didn't have any idea about immigration when I first came here, and when I first started working with them [detainees], I felt a bit sorry for them. But after a while that goes, you've seen it all before, heard all the stories. (Male officer)

The 'problem' with ex-prisoner detainees was that, as one officer put it, they 'knew the system', meaning that they would be overly demanding and 'trouble'. The knowledgeable and experienced ex-offender introduced a dangerous kind of penal expertise to Locksdon that would be in confrontation with officers' authority and at odds with the ideal docile, compliant detainee. At Locksdon, the constant stream of people passing through the centre became intertwined with the 'provable' criminal histories of a small proportion of the detainees to produce a moralised culpability for the whole group.

Moreover, the officers viewed the detainees' 'illegality' as an *individual choice*. The illegality of the detainees, attributed to them via their illegal acts in gaining entry to Britain, was because of their morally compromised and weak character rather than desperation and necessity. Media reports about asylum seekers and benefit scams, housing fraud and criminality crystallised around certain criminalised individual detainees at Locksdon and produced a moral culpability for the detainees. The legal and moral status of the 'typical detainee' thus rendered him 'undeserving' (of protection as an asylum seeker, of inclusion as future citizen). Howe (1990, 1998) notes that discourses of 'the undeserving' (his case is unemployment) tend to invoke an individual who is jobless through *choice* or *weakness*. It is a discourse that privileges the atomised individual-citizen and his or her responsibility for making 'correct' life choices (see chapter 3).

Unwilling or unable to engage in proper reciprocal relationships with society, the undeserving chose to 'take' but did not 'contribute'. At Locksdon in 2002–3, detainees were not allowed to work and could not demonstrate their conformity with the ideals of work espoused by the officers.[4] As I have discussed, officers understood work, provision, self-sufficiency and individual responsibility to be integral aspects of moral worth as a person, and also of demonstrating conformity to masculine ideals. Denied the right to work, the detainees became 'burdensome'. They were being supported by 'tax payers' money' but were giving nothing in return.

> I overheard these two guys in the corridor one day, from Jamaica. One of them said he was thinking about signing to go back home [that is, officially withdrawing his claim for asylum or his application for immigration status]. The other guy went to him, 'What do you want to leave here [Britain] for? It's all free here … housing, everything. Stay on and it's all free.' (Male officer)

The view that the detainees were exemplars of a larger category of people attempting to infiltrate Britain and 'milk the system' contrasts with Heyman's (2000) study of US immigration officers at the Mexican border. These US officers demanded respect for the US law but also respected the illegal Mexican *peon* trying to better his or her life. As long as the hierarchy between US citizen and outsider was maintained, those in lower positions were given sympathy, although this sympathy dissolved when migrants did not display 'correct' deference and when they demonstrated 'complex volition' (see Walzer 1994). The US immigration officers used the market as a means of understanding inequalities between people: people must sell their labour on the market and this produces a morally acceptable form of inequality; market success could make people equal, but markets also structure 'natural' hierarchies and inequalities among people (Heyman 2000: 644; and see Lamont 2000). The Locksdon officers were similarly affronted when faced with displays of 'complex volition' among detainees, but they did not see detainees as entrepreneurial people seeking entry to Britain to work and to better themselves. On the contrary, detainees were, as a general group, entering Britain to *escape* work or fraudulently claim benefits, or to work illegally and escape paying taxes.

EMBODYING INAUTHENTICITY

Detainees' complaints about their detention were perceived as a manifestation of their 'undeservingness' but also their 'inauthenticity'. As one officer put it, 'If I was being persecuted and tortured in my country, I wouldn't complain. I'd be grateful to have somewhere safe. They get fed, they're looked after. If things are so bad back home, they should be grateful.' If the men were truly 'deserving' (that is, authentic asylum seekers escaping persecution and in fear of their lives), then their temporary accommodation in Locksdon would induce gratitude, not resentment:

It really winds me up, the way they go on about their country being so bloody brilliant – my country's beautiful, we don't do that in my country, I love my country, all that crap. If it's so bloody brilliant, why the hell are they here? Why don't they go back? (Male officer)

They say they want to come here, so why aren't they down there [Education] learning English? Most of them can't speak a word, and if they want to get on, get working when they get out, they should be doing all they can, not lounging round the bloody dorms whingeing. (Male officer)

At issue here is not only the 'undeserving' jobless subject as social burden, but the figure of the 'genuine' and 'authentic' asylum seeker or refugee. This iconic and imaginary cultural figure – characterised by pure victimhood, passivity and helplessness – has shaped the international legal categories through which humanitarian protection is administered and allows the 'correct' objects of compassion, aid and pity to be recognised (see Malkki 1992; Nyers 2006). Legislative developments within asylum and immigration systems are underpinned by moral distinctions between the 'undeserving' asylum seeker and the 'deserving' genuine refugee (see Sales 2002, 2005). Displaying 'complex volition', or attempting to resist detention (the consequence of a man's choice to break the law), or complaining were all ways in which the detainee betrayed his inauthenticity.

Detainees' resistance to the regime was an affront to the norms of hospitality which officers understood to shape the relationship between detainees (as uninvited 'guests') and the host sovereign nation, Britain. Hospitality implies a welcome, within which 'home' is transformed into a 'sanctuary'. This welcome, however, contains internal contradictions. Hospitality as a stance to the other maintains the host as a sovereign authority, able to define the conditions and temporal limits of welcome. In this way, hospitality recognises the guest *as guest*, keeping him or her at a distance and imposing obligations of reciprocity and moral indebtedness (Herzfeld 1992). Derrida (2001: 53) argues that hospitality contains a risk, such that '[t]his other becomes a hostile subject, and I risk becoming their hostage'. There is, argues Derrida (2001: 55), 'No hospitality, in the classic sense, without sovereignty of oneself over one's home, but since there is also no hospitality without finitude, sovereignty can only be exercised by filtering, choosing, and thus by excluding and doing violence.' The notion of hospitality captured perfectly the way officers understood the dynamics of life at Locksdon, where detainees' bad behaviour became a violation of moral obligations to the host (Dikeç 2002; Herzfeld 1992: 171–5; Werbner 2005). A detainee's illegal act (on the basis of which he was detained) was thus understood as a disrespectful subversion of the rules governing hospitality: his illegal entry breached the border, his claims for status threatened the sovereignty of 'the host', the 'gift' of protection was violated by detainees' illegality and criticism of detention. It was not only that the detainees' mode of entry into Britain constituted a culpable breach, but that their 'ungrateful' behaviour in Locksdon exacerbated this breach, and was evidence of their 'undeservingness'.

It was those detainees who understood their position in the UK as tenuous and conditional, and who confirmed in their behaviour the officers' understandings of their position, who were most likely to be labelled as 'acceptable'. Those who did not espouse such a view of their position (and perhaps asserted their *right* to be in Britain, to claim asylum or seek a secure life) were those most likely to be labelled as 'undeserving'. Just as work and personal responsibility were mobilised to condemn detainee populations, so they provided means through which certain individuals became includable within the officers' imagined moral community. For example, one detainee had been running a shop in a local town for years before being arrested and detained by immigration authorities. He was fighting deportation on human rights grounds. Several officers argued that he had been 'getting on with it' when he was arrested; he was contributing to society, supporting himself and his family and should have been left to his life, whatever his legal status. Another detainee proved himself popular with officers:

> We were talking the other day and we all agreed we'd let Mr X in. I mean, he's on our side, he's one of us. He speaks English, he's polite. He'd make an effort to integrate, help himself, get a job. He's always clean and smart. Whenever he goes over to Visits, he's got a clean shirt on, has a shave. He spends his whole life in the ironing room! Why on earth they're keeping him in and letting some of the scumbags out, I'll never know. (Female officer)

The officers viewed this man as being able and willing to 'integrate'. 'Integrating' was something that the officers often spoke about in relation to the detainees. 'Integrating', in the officers' eyes, amounted to gaining fluency in the language and 'the British way of life'. It involved 'fitting in' with the existing status quo and contributing to society by means of working hard. Locksdon officers were concerned to maintain boundaries and hierarchies that emerged from locally produced notions of 'deservingness' and 'undeservingness', which were often distinguishable from legal categories of rights and belonging. In short, the type of person who the officers believed would 'fit in' was someone who shared their own particular moral vision.

mundanity

CONCERTED INDISCIPLINE

One day in spring 2003, when the midday bell sounded for roll check, the usual routine was disrupted. Rather than returning to their dormitories before lunch, a group of detainees remained

Susan - power shapes discourse
Ls gossip shaping role of power

milling around the corridor outside the centre office. The detainees were staging a peaceful protest, they collectively announced. They offered staff a list of demands; they wanted to speak to the governor about their immigration cases, their detention and their treatment at Locksdon. The staff in the centre office made a quick call to the manager, who refused to speak to all the detainees together, but offered to meet a few. The detainees were not happy with this, and an afternoon of 'concerted indiscipline' began.

A sense of occasion immediately descended on the centre. The officers had trained for events exactly like these and were relaxed. A senior officer, Sam, and Gareth, a PO, were now in charge of 'on the scene' 'bronze command' in the centre and 'silver command' was set up in the administrative building, comprising the managers, a member of the Visiting Committee, local immigration officers, officers trained in C&R and several administrative staff. At the centre, officers walked about the corridor, talking with detainees, keen to 'play it down' and 'keep things calm'. They suggested that the detainees 'elect' a spokesman to 'make their voice heard' to the managers. The detainees made it clear their problem was not with the officers, who they knew were 'just doing their job'. Rather, they wanted their grievances about being detained, and the violation of their human rights that their detention constituted, to be heard by the governor and 'immigration' *en masse*. The manager, however, refused to see all ten men together. Settling down for the duration, the officers at the centre called in extra staff on overtime, brought out magazines to read, set out plans so staff could take breaks, and arranged for sandwiches to be brought in from the canteen.

There were communications between silver and bronze every ten minutes or so. A general feeling soon emerged at the centre that silver command's instructions were not coming through quickly enough. A long, protracted discussion broke out between bronze and silver about how to get food to the detainees who were not participating in the protest. Should the food be passed directly to the detainees in sight of the protesters, and so risk inflaming the situation? Several detainees gave up the protest after an hour or so and headed back to their dormitories, perhaps hoping for something to eat. A few men were let into the locked dorms to go to the toilet and then let out again to rejoin the protest.

Over in silver command in the administration suite, there was more tension in the atmosphere, reputations being made (and lost) through handling of incidents such as these. The office was abuzz with muted, urgent conversations, ringing phones, coffee being drunk. People pored over plans of the establishment and made notes about the ringleader detainees on a large whiteboard. It emerged that the key protest organisers 'had nothing to lose', being near the end of their immigration appeal process and soon to be deported. Every ten minutes or so an update from the centre arrived – how many detainees were in the corridor, how many had gone back to the dormitories, the mood of the protest. There were regular updates made to the area manager. The detainees could not decide on representatives and the manager refused to talk to more than a dozen in one go: stalemate. The afternoon wore on. To complicate matters, a call arrived from an officer at home on a rest day who reported that a member of Locksdon's volunteer visiting group was on the local TV talking about the protest, and there was a demonstration by anti-detention campaigners supporters outside the centre. To what extent was this group involved in organising the protest?

After several hours of impasse, the Tornado Team arrived. The Tornado Team was a collective of officers from surrounding prisons who had been trained in advanced C&R techniques and who were experienced in dealing with riots. They wore protective clothing, helmets and carry staves and shields. Their arrival was a decisive moment. The team tactlessly started unloading their riot gear in full view of the centre and an officer rushed over to usher them into the Visits area, where they would not be seen by detainees. The discussion in silver centred on how many C&R teams might be required if the worse happened and all the detainees needed to be forcibly removed to their dormitories. Where would the detainees be strip-searched in case they had weapons? What area should they be removed to? In silver, the mood was stubborn. The manager at one point argued that, 'I won't let the tail wag the dog. We are in charge here and they should remember it.' In bronze, the view was more critical, with talk that the whole thing was being handled heavily, 'like a prison riot'.

Back in the centre, word from silver was that the three main 'ringleaders' (two Jamaican men and an African national) would be removed. Gareth, a popular, respected PO, argued that removing the African detainee would be disastrous:

> He's a good influence. You can talk to him and the things he is saying make sense. If we ship him out we are going to give the message that if you complain about something here, you just get moved on. We've spent all afternoon telling them that someone will listen to their complaints, to be reasonable, and now we're

going back on it. The whole thing will blow up. There'll be real trouble if he goes. He made his point, but he was ok about it. We asked him to listen to us, and he did listen and we listened to him. When we explained that we have to get everyone back in the dorms for everyone's sake, he understood that. If we send him off now, what kind of message is that? We asked him to be reasonable, so we could be reasonable with him, and he was, so we can't go and send him packing now. It wouldn't be right.'

The decision was made to remove the two other 'troublemaker' leaders, who had a 'reputation' and were unpopular with officers.

Suddenly, despite not having spoken to the manager, the detainees announced that they wanted to end the protest and return to their dormitories. Confusion ensued. There was no clear 'surrender plan' and there followed an odd ten-minute pause when it was uncertain whether silver actually wanted the detainees to be let back into their dorms at all, despite the men now queuing up to return. Then word finally came through to let everyone back in. The detainees drifted back to the dormitories and everyone was counted. The regime was back on course.

This was not the end of the matter though. After a short lull, all officers were called into the centre office where it was explained that the two 'troublemaker' leaders were to be removed to another establishment. In case of trouble there would be a Tornado Team presence in the corridors. An officer volunteered to go and tell the two men to pack – the idea was to get them to go peaceably without the use of force. He went to talk to the men, accompanied by several other officers. Within minutes, the door at the end of the corridor opened and the Tornado Team entered, about twenty men marching in pairs dressed identically in dark helmets, anonymous, faceless, carrying shields and batons. It was a menacing show of force. A few minutes later, the two detainees emerged from their dormitories, carrying their belongings in the establishment's large cardboard boxes, their eyes wide, glancing nervously around them. They filed silently along the corridor between two rows of Tornado Team officers, and Locksdon's own staff, who were lined up and watched them blankly, and then they were gone.

*   *   *

The concerted indiscipline exposed several long-running fractures at Locksdon. Centre officers 'on the ground' criticised managers, whose distance from the messy, complex and ambiguous everyday life of the centre rendered them ill-equipped to make swift, authoritative decisions: one officer summed up the mood, 'See what our management are like? They can't make a single bloody decision. Abysmal.' Educated, ambitious and immersed in bureaucratic policy, managers were removed from the difficulties of centre life, especially graduates who had been 'fast-tracked' and who did not have 'hands-on' prison experience. The best managers, according to the officers, would always engage (and defer to) the expert opinion of the officers. In 'overreacting' to the situation, and in stalling decisions, the managers in this case were accused of exacerbating the situation, making conditions more dangerous for the officers and detainees. Moreover, the role of the volunteer group in 'inciting' indiscipline in Locksdon was also a long-standing point of contention. Members of the group were admitted to Locksdon at the manager's discretion to befriend and support detainees, but the group was seen as overly politicised and its members as inappropriate advocates of the detainees (see chapter 5).

The unfolding of the concerted indiscipline revealed the inconsistency with which 'protest' and 'contestation' were viewed by the officers at Locksdon. The ringleaders had demonstrated an audacious politicisation: they had conferred with the volunteer group, they had organised themselves, they had 'taken on' and troubled their exchangeability by refusing to appoint a leader. It was this sudden visibility and audibility, coupled with media exposure 'outside' the walls, that transformed the submissive detainee population into a troublesome and active presence. Despite denying the 'right' of individual detainees to manipulate the system via 'unreasonable' petty disruptions, officers appeared to view the protest as a legible, even legitimate, protest. In part this was because the inevitable response that was drawn forth by this kind of indiscipline was the Tornado Team's physical display of overwhelming authority. Indiscipline of this kind was agonistically related to spectacular shows of physical power. Concerted indiscipline ultimately reinvigorated the regime.

Yet what to do with the main 'ringleader? In 'listening, and being listened to', and in 'understanding what had to happen' this man had distinguished himself from those other 'wilful' detainees who had simply wanted to cause chaos and disruption. His actions troubled the clear line between 'reasonable' officers and 'unreasonable' detainees that so often characterised officers' perceptions of their charges. What kind of response did this man deserve, having forced himself to be considered as a reasonable subject? This man had been *recognised* within the valued ideals of the centre and, having impressed himself upon the officers, his removal 'wouldn't be right'. It was the problem of what to do with this man that ultimately proved the real challenge to the entrenched divisions of centre life. I discuss the ethical encounter between detainees and officers in more detail in chapter 7.

CONCLUSION

At issue in the examples of indiscipline that I have described throughout this chapter is the way in which people subjected to modes of governance which prevent them from 'exercising political subjectivity by holding them in spaces of existential, social, political, and legal limbo' (Isin and Rygiel, 2007: 188–9) can become political subjects. In his question, 'Who is the subject of the rights of man?' Jacques Rancière (2004) confronts this question directly. He examines Arendt's paradox: that 'inalienable' human rights that are supposed to protect those who have nothing left but their bare humanity are 'enjoyed only by citizens of the most prosperous and civilised countries' (2004 [1951]: 273). He argues that Agamben's view of the camp and reading of Arendt too quickly conflates abjection and being without rights with the condition of being political. Rights and the condition of being political do not adhere or '*belong* to definite or permanent subjects'; rather, the important political space is 'shaped in the very gap between the abstract literalness of the rights and the polemic about their verification' (Rancière 2004: 306, 307). So, for Rancière, it is in the act of *taking the rights one does not have* that subjects engage that gap and stage a 'dissensus'. A dissensus is 'a division in "the common sense"; a dispute about what is given, about the frame within which we see something as given' (Rancière 2004: 304). This political 'taking' can be enacted by subjects made abject (like refugees) as well as by 'citizen subjects' with status because it constitutes political action as materialising 'through interruption' (Rancière 1999: 12–13).[5]

The 'concerted indiscipline' at Locksdon can be understood as an 'interruption' in these terms, a means through which detainees engaged the gap and sought to be recognised as something other than bodies to be administered, and to claim the rights (of protest, complaint, audibility, visibility). The incident was a 'taking subjectivity', where the *taking* of political subjectivity is the enactment of political equality and a political act of citizenship

(Nyers 2003: 1077, citing Honig 2001). The detainees at Locksdon, then, enacted the political capacities that 'were not theirs': they challenged their atomised and abstracted organisation, they demanded to be heard, they refused to be ignored, they repudiated the norms of the afternoon regime, they seized the initiative. In so doing, they not only interrupted the afternoon regime, they also undermined the deferential, docile condition that was associated with the category of detainee.

The 'taking subjectivity' of the protesting refugee is a difficult moment for the state, argues Nyers (2003), because it threatens to subvert the entire framework of the authoritarian, speaking, visible citizen versus the passive, invisible and 'victimlike' refugee. Indeed, the kinds of resistance that are associated with refugees and asylum seekers as 'bare life' frequently invoke either the acceptance by subjects of their bodily reduction (Edkins and Pin-Fat 2004) or else the assumption of a 'warrior' subjectivity (Nyers 2003, 2006). Nyers (2006) argues that the 'warrior' refugee (who has objectives and demands, who acts violently) troubles the categorisation of the refugee as a subject characterised by passivity, non-violence and compliance. The notion of 'warrior-hood', I would argue, frames resistance as a matter of responding to force with force, violence with violence. It demands that for resistance to 'register' as resistance, or for a subject to be political, he or she must be as active and forceful (even violent) as the forms of control and exclusion he or she seeks to contest.

In the case of Locksdon, I have shown that the 'taking on of bare life' by detainees (via food refusal for instance) contests the biopolitical grip that the regime has on detainees. Yet I have also shown that detainees using their bodies to contest the regime were always at risk of being reduced anew, via discourses of unreasonableness and emotionality. Moreover, the actions of detainees and officers alike were understood within a gendered grid of intelligibility that tended to privilege forceful, antagonistic and aggressive (masculine) action as the kind of action that 'counted' (to secure the regime, for instance). So, the violent, 'taking', proactive warrior detainee (to borrow Nyers' terms) was certainly recognised at Locksdon – this kind of action was a 'natural' and 'understandable' masculine reaction to detention. However, a detainee's demanding, aggressive and proactive action was met with violence in turn. I shall discuss in detail in the next chapter, how violent suppression of indiscipline was one of the ways in which control was reinvigorated at Locksdon, and through which officers embodied sovereign authority and performed their masculinity. Demonstrations such as arson attacks, riots, violence and so on became part of a 'reciprocity of violence' between officer and detainees that was comfortably accommodated within the penal culture of detention. So, while the vocal, organised and protesting detainee at Locksdon altered the distribution of active agency, initiative and audibility within the regime, events of concerted indiscipline like that described above did not trouble the fundamental divisions and boundaries that gave Locksdon its sense. In many ways, it simply strengthened them.

Perhaps it was the African ringleader and the dilemmas that he posed for the officers that were more problematic for the detention regime. I will argue in chapter 7 that conditions of uncertainty in everyday social life at Locksdon were part of the fostering of an ethical stance of respect and recognition between detainees and officers. This chapter has argued that the multiple challenges, refusals and disruptions that featured in detention point to a kind of resistance that was frequently ambiguous and incoherent. As Ortner (2006: 44–5) argues, there are questions regarding what actions 'count' as resistance. She argues that resistance is characterised by 'psychological ambivalence and social complexity' and calls attention to 'the presence and play of power in most forms of relationship and activity' (2006: 44). Rather than being associated with force and counter-force, a more troublesome form of resistance might well be located in uncomfortable and disconcerting moments when subjects suddenly find themselves in doubt over their prior assumptions and judgements (see Amoore and Hall 2010). I will argue in chapter 6 that the recognition of detainees not as detainees but as persons was related to a form of disruption that was not easily captured by notions of resistance as a 'great refusal' (see Amoore 2007b), or resistance as 'counter' to or 'outside' oppressive situations (see Bleiker 2000), or as warrior-hood (Nyers 2006). Before looking in more detail at the ethical encounters between officers and detainees at Locksdon, however, the next chapter looks at the use of physical control in response to the unruly detainee.

5
Drawing the Line: Discretion and Power

The Locksdon alarm bell could sound at any moment of the day or night. Its loud ringing indicated a crisis in the regime: a detainee or staff member in danger, a medical emergency, or a fire. Alarm buzzers were positioned around the establishment so that officers or detainees could call for help from every zone. For officers, the alarm bell signalled an emergency where life itself could be at stake. When it rang, the establishment appeared to freeze for a second before bursting into action. Available officers would drop what they were doing and run to the illuminated plan near the centre office to find out where the alarm had been raised. They would sprint to the call, with other officers emerging to follow from side offices. The response had to be quick.

When officers arrived on the scene, one of the worst case scenarios was an outbreak of violence. A detainee could have 'kicked off' and become physically unruly, threatening his own safety, or that of a staff member or fellow detainee. In escalating situations, officers were authorised to use physical force against detainees. Prison officers at Locksdon were all trained in control and restraint (C&R) procedures. Basic C&R consisted of a range of techniques for controlling a disruptive, violent person by isolating and applying pressure to parts of the body – limbs, fingers, nose and thumbs. C&R techniques were ideally used by teams of two or three officers. The techniques in deployment during 2002/3 were as follows: one officer would grab a man's arm, twisting the limb behind the detainee's back and applying pressure to the thumb by bending it back. Another officer would do the same with the other arm. When he or she had secured a limb, the officer shouted 'lock on' to his or her colleagues. In extreme cases, a third officer would apply pressure to a man's nose, pulling upwards and backwards to gain compliance, or else he would push a man's head down from behind, while the other officers kept up their hold on the restrained man's arms so that he was forced to walk forwards. The lead officer would constantly communicate with the restrained man so he knew what was expected of him (walk forwards, keep calm, stop struggling) and that the restraint holds would be stopped when the man complied and was calm.

If a restrained man continued to struggle and had to be moved to another location, he was walked in a 'bent up' position, with officers on either side of him. He was then instructed to lie face down on the floor, with his arms still twisted behind him. His legs were bent up to meet his arms behind his back, and the officer who had previously taken his head and had been communicating with the man would place his foot on the detainee's hand and foot while the officers on either side retreated. The final officer would then release his foot and move backwards. C&R techniques are not meant to cause the restrained person lasting physical harm – they are designed to secure compliance by applying short-term pain and pressure only. Nevertheless, their use in prisons, care and police custody is contentious, and is especially controversial in the immigration detention estate.[1]

During 2002/3, C&R was used at Locksdon in at least four incidents that I witnessed or discussed with officers. One new arrival had become distressed and physically disruptive on his way to Locksdon in the escort van and was restrained on arrival. Another detainee became angry and violent when he was confronted by officers about allegations of bullying made against him by other detainees at Locksdon. He lashed out at staff and was restrained by two officers. Another detainee became involved in an altercation about food in the canteen and officers used C&R on him. On another occasion, a detainee became hysterical in health care and went into a trance-like fit, smashing furniture and hurling himself against a wall. Officers used C&R to place him in the special accommodation unit to 'cool off', and the nursing staff tried to talk to him. He had become furious, distressed and violent, threatening to kill himself and staff members, and tearing off his clothes. Staff intervened four times with C&R techniques when he had tried to make a ligature out of paper clothing that had been given to him. Staff finally decided to transfer him to another IRC when he started to rip up the plastic skirting boards and destroy the room.

In the UK detention estate, the authority to use force is conferred by the *Detention Centre Rules* (2001). These rules state that 'a detainee custody officer dealing with a detained person shall not use force unnecessarily and, when the application of force to a detained

person is necessary, no more force than is necessary shall be used'.[2]
Paragraphs 43.1–43.2 state that:

> The Secretary of State (in the case of a contracted-out detention centre) or the manager (in the case of a directly managed detention centre) may order a detained person to be put under special control and restraint where this is necessary to prevent the detained person from injuring himself or others, damaging property or creating a disturbance ... In cases of urgency, the manager of a contracted-out detention centre may assume the responsibility of the Secretary of State ... but shall notify the Secretary of State without delay after giving the relevant order.

The decision to use force, then, is ultimately devolved to staff at the frontline – people like officers at Locksdon. Paragraph 65 of the *Detention Centre Rules* (2001) explicitly states that the manager of an IRC may, with the leave of the Secretary of State, 'delegate any of the powers and duties under these Rules to another officer of that detention centre'.

The *Detention Centre Rules* make clear that the legitimacy of the use of necessary force rests on the separation of a normal situation in detention from an emergency situation, where life and the good order of the establishment are at stake. At Locksdon, the designation of such a situation occurred within split-second judgements by officers. An officer could suddenly resort to force to move a recalcitrant detainee, for example, or he or she could use a 'personal safety technique or defensive strike' – what PSO 1600 describes as 'an exceptional measure'[3] – when he or she perceived a threat from a detainee. C&R techniques were not used lightly within the regime at Locksdon, but they were frequently justified to managers after or during their occurrence. This was particularly the case on night shifts, where four ordinary level prison officers were in charge of the establishment and managers were on call.

This chapter is concerned with the C&R incident at Locksdon from the perspective of officers, and the relations of power which manifested themselves in physical struggles. Why did officers use force? What kind of experience was the C&R incident? What did it achieve? I will argue that the C&R incident was the moment at which the disciplinary control and biopolitical investment of the detainee's body within Locksdon reached its height. The C&R incident also, I argue, brings into focus the importance of 'the decision' at Locksdon – the officers' decision to use force, in what circumstances it was taken, and in response to what kinds of situation.

'WRAPPING HIM UP'

Locksdon officers referred to C&R as 'wrapping up' or 'bending up'. Officers talked about the processes of C&R as actions upon the detainee as physical entity: they used phrases such as 'when you bend a body up' and 'we wrapped him up and moved him away'. These terms captured the way that a restrained detainee body became contorted and twisted, with his limbs wrapped or bent securely behind his body, and his head bent forward or back. The training drills for C&R emphasised the individual techniques and their safe but effective application, but the reality of C&R was chaotic. Officers used the term 'rolling round on the floor' to indicate the confused task of securing the disruptive body as it thrashed and struggled. 'Rolling around on the floor' captured the individual experience of C&R, but also referred to the requirement of officers to engage in force as part of their everyday work. That is, 'rolling round on the floor' was an infrequent, but core, part of the work at a prison and at an IRC. As one officer summarised it: 'they [management] want us to be social workers, but then, suddenly, we're expected to roll around on the floor with them. You can't have it both ways.' On the one hand, using force signalled a failure of good prison work – 'if we're always rolling round on the floor with them, it means we're not doing our job well'. On the other hand, engaging in periodic violent struggles with detainees was seen as an essential and inevitable means of securing the regime. The capacity to unleash physical force in the face of crisis (however irregularly) was a vital requirement of working in any secure environment.

Violence was much more frequent and regularised in mainstream prisons than in a detention centre. Experienced officers would frequently trade stories of dealing with convict aggression:

Violence is the only way they [some convicted prisoners] can settle things. The only way they can feel better. I've seen it loads of times. Some guy will just go berserk, swearing, screaming and so on. If someone hits them, they're happy with it. He kicks off, we bend him up, he gets a bit hurt, he ends up in the block. Next day he's up before the governor and he's all, 'I deserve everything, I would like to apologise to Officer Smith, blah, blah, blah.' Then often as not you'll be walking him back to his cell. The day before he wanted to kill you, but now he's all chatty, saying, 'Sorry guv, got a bad letter' and so on. For some people a punch up is the only way out of it all. (Male officer)

Another officer recounted how he had become involved in a fight with a convicted prisoner:

He just egged me on and I rolled around with him. The cons on the landing were saying the guy should report me, but the cleaner, who was the landing hard man, warned them off. As far as he was concerned, it was a fair fight, one-on-one, y'know, and the guy was begging for it. (Male officer)

The violent encounter between a male prison officer and a male prisoner was seen as a normalised type of masculine engagement and communication. First, 'kicking off' was understood as a standard response by (some) men to (some) fraught situations. That is, within the prison context, the embodiment and performance of emotion via violent bodily action was understood within a gendered discourse which posited such performances as 'normal'. Men like 'cons' are not 'unemotional' (Hearn 1993; Williams 2001). Rather, their emotion is 'naturally' expressed via aggressive, violent and destructive physical outbursts. While this violent display of emotion is 'recognisable as masculine' within penal discourses, alternative embodied expressions of anger, frustration or distress (such as detainees' 'fits' or 'trances' at Locksdon) registered outside the norm. Second, the violent tussle between officer and disruptive subject in a prison was understood to be a standard outcome of confrontation. Officers like the one above described being 'egged on' by convicts and succumbing to a physical altercation that was seen as almost inevitable. Violence signalled a crisis in the regime – the break down of good prison work – but also its proper resolution between men. A good prison officer should be self-disciplined, but the 'answer' to the violent con was sometimes to 'give in' to the normal (masculine) expression of feelings of anger or disrespect and become violent in turn.

The normalised economy of violence that officers described at the prison did not exist at Locksdon, but for the officers, the response to the alarm bell nevertheless crystallised the physical dangers of work inside the IRC, when the indefinite capacities of the detainee were manifested as physical aggression. The race to the alarm call was always a race to an unknown and uncertain scenario – a violent attack, a self-harm incident, a hostage situation, a colleague or detainee in distress. The C&R incident was when dependability, loyalty, and obligation to 'the group' materialised in physical action. When things 'kicked off' was when officers came to tangibly experience being (and being next to) a good officer, a good colleague and a good friend. It was when notions of professionalism distilled into action. This was when officers became aware of 'being glad to have X there', of being 'pleased it was them' (see chapter 3). Locksdon officers saw the alarm bell as distinguishing individuals (men and women) who were willing or able to risk their bodily safety for their colleagues. More particularly, officers who considered themselves quick to respond to a call (brave, loyal, willing, able, fit) would draw attention to their own performance by recounting which colleagues joined them in the rush towards the crisis and which colleagues were slow to respond. In one of the examples described above, officers discussing the C&R incident described seeing a senior officer 'excusing himself and muttering that he was needed in the centre office' when the alarm bell rang. As a result, a principal officer 'from works' (building maintenance) had to oversee the incident, despite the fact he had little operational experience.

The gendered dynamics of the C&R incident in detention were central to its operation and effect. The C&R incident, I argue, was the site of production of hierarchically ordered gendered subjects and subjectivities. The C&R incident was performative in the sense that Judith Butler described, when gender becomes materialised in action. If, as she argues, the body is a 'set of possibilities to be constantly realised' (1988: 521), then the C&R incident provided the conditions of possibility for the emergence of a particular gendered masculine form of action and experience. As I outlined in chapter 3, gender is a 'social practice that constantly refers to bodies and what bodies do ... [though] not social practice reduced to the body' (Connell 2005: 71). Connell (2005: 71) notes that 'true' masculinity frequently invokes the male body in action, although there are multiple 'ways' of performing a masculine identity (Cornwall and Lindisfarne 1994). The C&R incident as a site of gendered practice tended to prioritise the male body in action. More specifically, it prioritised the youthful, strong and able male body, although all officers (male and female) would engage in the use of force if necessary. C&R incidents, especially planned and major ones, assembled a core set of younger, physically fit male officers at Locksdon, reinforcing the ideal-type masculine hardness perceived as necessary to prison work. To be clear, being a good officer was not in any way equated with brute force; in fact, nothing was worse than a needlessly aggressive officer. Staff were clear that any secure environment required different 'types' of officers, with a range of qualities and skills (kindly, tough, easy-going, 'hard'). Nevertheless, crises in the regime were ultimately seen to require a tough physical response to restore discipline and proper order. When diplomacy, negotiation and 'understanding' failed, force was necessary. This force was most effectively deployed via the strong, brave and vigorous body. This body was usually male. The response to the alarm call and the C&R event privileged a certain kind of 'usefulness' among officers within a spectacular and highly visible event that eclipsed more mundane and less visible skills involved in being an officer at Locksdon.

The C&R incident was a test of officers' (men and women's) bravery and physical capacity – when an individual's reputation as a friend and colleague was at stake. The actual tussle was a confused, chaotic affair, and (apart from the dangers to detainees) officers could be injured. It was a close, even intimate, engagement with the body of the detainee and the body of a colleague, with risks of contamination and infection for everyone. The C&R event produced an embodied uncertainty, fear and vulnerability among officers. The notion of embodiment – what Csordas (1994: 6, 10) calls the existential ground of culture and self – emphasises the meanings that the body assumes in the context of lived experience, and the way the body constantly materialises cultural, social, historical potentialities. Embodiment captures the existential immediacy of the lived body – an experiential 'being in the world' which is 'through and through compounded of relationships with the world' (Merleau-Ponty 2004: 70). As Csordas (1994: 137) argues, the textual, representative, discursive aspects of the body are always accompanied by embodiment – 'an indeterminate methodological field defined by perceptual experience and mode of presence and engagement in the world' (Csordas 1994: 12). The body 'as object' and 'object of study' is inscribed and produced within relations of power and possibility, but is also, via its embodiment, generative, experiential and expressive (Harrison 2000: 503). The notion of embodiment highlights individuals' experience and action within (and between) dominant discourses of gender, for instance, and the 'subject positions' created within these discourses.

The C&R incident was a terrorising and overwhelming experience for the person who was restrained. At Locksdon, the disorientation of detainees and the difficulties of communication with men who could not speak fluent English, as well as possible prior experiences of police or prison brutality in their countries of origin, made the C&R event traumatic, frightening and physically dangerous. Locksdon officers also viewed C&R with trepidation. Officers could find themselves having to respond quickly to a call, or to a colleague in need, but they could also find themselves preparing for a planned and orchestrated C&R incident. The way in which the C&R incident privileged youthful masculine toughness meant that younger men on duty would find themselves under pressure to volunteer themselves on these occasions, though women and older men would also be expected to 'kit up' if required. The planned C&R incident produced an embodied nervous apprehension. On one occasion, when officers were waiting for a distressed and violent man who was being escorted to Locksdon, I witnessed two of the four 'kitted up' officers become quiet and withdrawn. One was visibly pale and trembling, and started to noticeably sweat. The other two officers became loud, over-excited and boisterous. Three officers confessed separately to me on different occasions that they hated 'rolling round on the floor'. As one officer told me:

> It's a big thing. Even when you've got your helmet on and you're all kitted up, you get scared. You don't know what's going to happen and it's scary. Everyone knows who's good in a fight. (Male senior officer)

While the C&R incident could be painful, dangerous and risky, 'rolling round on the floor' could also be experienced with something like excitement, even pleasure. One officer, for example, recounted a C&R incident at a prison when he had been concentrating on securing a flailing leg, gripping it as it slipped and kicked around. He was so bent on his task that he had struggled to hear what his colleagues were saying in the confusion, until he suddenly heard his colleague crying out, 'That's my leg Jack! Let go of my bloody leg!' The officer in this case confessed that he missed the 'good honest fights' with cons and the chance to 'roll around' with colleagues. The C&R incident crystallised a sense of (masculine) camaraderie and 'release' expressed and experienced through the body.

Jackson (1998) describes the relationship between embodied social practices and intersubjectivity, when the self emerges from, and is shaped within, interactions between object and subject, self and other in life as it is lived. Jackson argues (after Merleau-Ponty) that at 'every stage and moment of our lives, our interactions with others involve ... a "wild" logos of carnality, emotion and sensation that the mind does not constitute yet informs the way we think' (2005: 36). As Sigrid Grønseth (forthcoming) argues, this phenomenological approach to embodiment and intersubjectivity understands bodily 'being' and 'experience' not as 'fixed and closed' but as 'an open and flexible cluster that is ready to connect with its environment and other people' (see Csordas 1994). Intersubjectivity is a way of thinking about reciprocal bodily experiences that are experienced within the self, but also between self and others. As Sigfrid Grønseth (forthcoming) explains, 'in moments of rupture and "out of the ordinary", one can experience an empathetic and bodily connection ...'. The C&R incident, I argue, was an inter-subjective physical experience for officers. It was when individuals embodied sensations of excitement, fear, struggle and pain alongside others. 'Rolling around on the floor' produced shared experiences and connections that were lived, expressed and felt within individual bodies, but also between bodies in action. When officers said, 'There's some officers you'd be glad to have there, you'd be pleased it was them', it was in the sense that the C&R event was a physical distillation and bodily sensation of ideals of solidarity, camaraderie and loyalty. Moreover, metaphors of what would happen if 'things kicked off' were used to think about and express the kinds of social relationships of loyalty that ideally pertained to being an officer at Locksdon (see chapter 3).

The aftermath of the C&R incident elaborated and extended this shared physicality. A formal debrief after an incident would usually be accompanied by a more sociable dissection of events at the local pub. Officers who had participated in a crisis, or who had been on duty, would drink, reflect about the event, make jokes and recount other stories. With the threat averted and good order restored, the post-incident drink was a pleasurable occasion where the anxieties of the event could be diffused within the group. Rapport (2002: 299) uses the term 'reciprocity of physical relations' to capture a local sense of belonging that emerges from, and cements, sociality and cohesion among local people in his village context. 'Reciprocal physicality' involved the bodily routines of local work and living but also included shared drunken social activities at the pub: drinking and dancing, playing games and sharing gossip, which 'extends and ramifies past physicalities into the future' (Rapport 2002: 314–15). Outsiders were excluded from the physicality of events and from their creation and recreation in gossip, and people could not gain full acceptance into local life without finding a way into this reciprocal physicality. He concludes that people who kept themselves apart – who never *did* with villagers (Rapport 2002: 315) – would always be out of place.

At Locksdon, similarly, the C&R incident – its shared sensations and emotions, its physical reciprocity and its aftermath – bound together a tight circle of colleagues and excluded those who did not 'do'. Officers who had experienced the embodied chaos and mutuality of the C&R incident were separated in the incident. The group would be re-assembled and re-differentiated at the sociable get-together, which would in turn shape the next C&R response in terms of designating who was 'good in a fight'. The shared physicality of the C&R incident frequently led on to an evening of rowdy drunkenness, also full of shared physical experiences of dancing, play fights, flirting and staggering around pubs. These convivial and sociable events, then, tended to recreate boundaries between a set of youthful, fit, willing and strong male officers and older colleagues and female counterparts, and these boundaries were brought forward into the next C&R event. These boisterous social events tended to revolve around typically 'male' interests and pursuits (watching football, for instance). Ad hoc social events after a hard shift or stressful discipline incident – usually involving 'the usual suspects' from the officer cohort – were distinct from other more inclusive and organised staff gatherings (at Christmas, for example) when all staff members were invited along.

'GHOSTING OUT' AND THE 'SEG UNIT'

Understood as a productive site of gendering and gendered power, the C&R incident hierarchically ordered masculine subjects within the physical scuffle. More particularly, the C&R incident manifested and reproduced the boundary between the active officer and the passive detainee. The performance of masculine physicality within the C&R incident produced, and depended upon, the forced submission of the detainee. As Feldman has argued in his discussions of Northern Ireland internment and Abu Ghraib (1991, 2005), modes of control under conditions of incarceration achieve mastery through various means, including the enforced passivity and feminisation of confined male bodies. The cultural association of passivity with 'the feminine' and with denigrated forms of masculinity meant that the C&R incident at Locksdon was always a way of 'correcting' disarrayed gendered organisation of the centre. The 'taking', 'protesting' and 'active' detainee – who used his body to contest the regime and to shape his trajectory in detention – was at odds with the ideal grateful and passive detainee. Moreover, it was a contravention of the gendered hierarchies of the centre – it was the officers (especially male officers), not the detainees, who were supposed to embody 'action' via their probing visual habits, their 'initiative' and their use of force.

'Bending up' the detainee was thus a reinstatement of the proper order – proper gendered order – of the detention centre, in the sense of forcibly containing the wilful and disruptive detainee. The containment of the disruptive detainee was also always bound up with the realignment of gender hierarchies. The violent detainee could not be allowed to 'gain the initiative': his rebelliousness had to be 'bent' and 'wrapped up'. As the male officer's masculine identity was performatively brought into being (Butler 1990) within the physical enactment of C&R techniques, the detainee's capacity for action was annulled. As the officer asserted his strength among colleagues in an intersubjective application of force, the detainee's physicality was suppressed. As the officer found himself alongside friends, the force of his or her body amplified within a physical mutuality, the detainee was isolated from others and divided from himself. If, after Foucault (2000: 340), power is relational, productive and contingent and also resisted – 'an action upon an action, on possible or actual future or present actions' – then the C&R incident was where Locksdon's regime dissolved into pure violence. Violence, as Foucault argues (2000: 340) 'acts upon a body or upon things, it forces, it bends, it breaks … it closes off all possibilities'. During a restraint incident, the antagonistic power relationships between officer and detainee dissolved and 'power, at its zenith, disappears and becomes pure administration' (Edkins and Pin-Fat 2004: 9). In this way, the C&R incident was when biopolitical and disciplinary mastery of the detainee's body was complete, when the detainee's body was reduced to an inert, contorted and 'wrapped up' body. It was also when the masculine energy of the recalcitrant detainee was annulled, when he was made passive, just as the officer's body was materialised as 'male' in its force and vigour.

The C&R incident, then, was the symbolic and material restoration of the masculine and disciplinary order of the detention centre. As I described in the previous chapter, the most spectacular expression of physical and symbolic power at Locksdon was the deployment of the Tornado Team. These teams of specially trained officers were drilled in the suppression of violent disturbances. They wore riot gear – helmets, boots, black uniform – and were armed with batons and carried shields. The Tornado Teams were visually impressive: ominous, disciplined and anonymous. They moved in disciplined formation and fought as a team, in stark contrast to the isolated detainee. The Tornado Team was the ultimate weapon in the officers' ongoing battles to 'maintain the initiative', and left no doubt about who was ultimately in control of Locksdon. The mere presence of the Tornado Teams could reassert 'proper' order: an unmistakable demonstration and show of violent force.

In most instances, a detainee who had been C&R-ed (like the man at the start of this chapter) would be placed alone in the 'special accommodation unit'. This unit was informally referred to by officers as the 'Seg Unit' (segregation unit), reflecting prison jargon. The Seg Unit was a room where detainees could be isolated and 'removed from association' within the regime. The Seg Unit was designed to offer the officers constant visibility of the isolated man through a viewing hatch in the door. According to the *Detention Centre Rules* (2001: para. 40) detainees can be 'removed from association' when 'it appears necessary in the interests of security or safety that a detained person should not associate with other detained persons, either generally or for particular purposes'. Again, the *Rules* state that 'the Secretary of State (in the case of a contracted-out detention centre) or the manager (in the case of a directly managed detention centre) may arrange for the detained person's removal from association accordingly' and stipulate that managers and ordinary officers may wield this devolved power. Like the use of force within C&R incidents, removing a detainee from association was often a quick judgement. A detainee would be isolated in the unit to 'cool down' after becoming distressed or angry, or men who were considered a suicide risk would be placed in the unit for monitoring. The Seg Unit was a place for controlling the 'contagion' of disorder (see Bashford and Hooker 2001). It was also the place where the detainee was completely alone – individualised, isolated – and the officers' control over him became most focused.

In certain situations, an 'unruly' or 'disruptive' detainee could also be 'ghosted out' of Locksdon. 'Ghosting out' referred to the removal (swift, often with no warning, and by force if necessary) of a detainee to another establishment. For example, in early 2003 there was a spate of minor discipline incidents involving two detainees from Turkey. These 'ringleader' men refused to obey orders from officers (to return to dorms at roll check, to stop smoking in certain areas). Officers found a weapon concealed in the bedpost of one of the men – a piece of wire from a coat hanger embedded in what looked like a portion of wooden broom handle. These events were coupled with a series of self-harm incidents. The issue of securing access to a 'better IRC' came to the fore. At a regular staff meeting, the manager of the establishment explained to staff that the Turkish detainees in question would be 'ghosted out'. The practice of 'crying self-harm' and 'causing trouble to work the system' and get transferred to another IRC had to stop, he argued. He had made a special arrangement: detainees who caused trouble at Locksdon would temporarily be sent to a nearby prison establishment where they would be accommodated alongside prisoners. They would then be sent back to Locksdon to 'report' to fellow detainees the new outcome of indiscipline. The manager summed up: 'We will maintain control and have the initiative. We will not allow anyone to take the initiative from us. We will show them we have control and being ghosted out of here is not the easy option'. Later on, one officer summed up the new temporary rules to a colleague: 'We're going to show them that we is the daddy.'

The use of the Seg Unit and 'ghosting out' in cases like these reflected a paradoxical sense of powerlessness on the part of officers. Staff resented the dearth of punitive techniques available to them when confronted with 'troublemaker' detainees who 'worked the system'. As one officer told me:

> With cons, you've got more control. If a con doesn't want to do something, you can nick him, send him to the block. But here, if you tell them something, and they don't want to do it, what can you do? They could turn round and say, fuck off, and you've got no way to answer back.

Locksdon officers lamented the general erosion of prison powers over convicted prisoners, but also the lack of 'ways to answer back' to insubordination in immigration detention. The kinds of punitive power that are traditionally wielded by prison officers in a prison – to remove privileges from prisoners, for example, to 'send [them] to the block' – are supposed to form part of a disciplinary reshaping and readjustment of the convict. The work of a prison officer with prisoners – producing sentence plans and reports, organising training, education and therapy to address offending behaviour, engaging with convicts – is still harnessed to ideals of reformatory modification of the incarcerated subject, despite the increased 'risk containment' and retaliatory strategies of contemporary penal contexts (Garland 1990, 2001). In immigration detention, the 'correction' of detainees cannot take the same form as the 'correction' of prisoners. Yet Locksdon officers still craved the kind of authority that they wielded over prison populations, notably the power to punish infractions and disobedience. The case of the Turkish detainees being 'ghosted out' demonstrated the officers' desire to 'show the detainees who's daddy' (reassert the hierarchies of the centre, which were gendered) and punish the detainees (for the officers' loss of initiative). The transferral of the detainees to a proper prison establishment was a *punishment* for insubordination, a method of 'correcting' the unruly and wilful detainee, inculcating a more disciplined detainee population and as well as a means of reinstating an orderly regime.

In the case above, the manager's arrangement with nearby prison establishments to temporarily accommodate Locksdon detainees reflected the liminal position of Locksdon at that time – still making the transition to full IRC, the centre was uneasily situated between the mainstream prison estate and the detention estate. Indeed, one of the major problems for staff at the time of my fieldwork was inexact procedural guidance for the management of detainees, especially in emergency or crisis situations. When the *Detention Centre Rules* (2001) did not specify a particular point, staff reverted to 'default' Prison Service rules. The effects of this were problematic in the sense that the meaning of rules was negotiated in action and practice. At Locksdon, the power to use force was lawfully conferred on officers in order to 'prevent the detained person from injuring himself or others, damaging property or creating a disturbance'. Yet this lawful embodiment of power was transformed in its moment of enactment and experience into a punitive reassertion of the boundaries of detention as the officers understood and experienced them: to reassert the 'correct' gendered hierarchy, to realign the distribution of 'initiative', to 'show who's daddy'. The legitimate securing of an orderly regime, as designated by the *Detention Centre Rules*, became entangled with forms of retaliation and retribution against detainees who thought they could 'work the system' and 'wag the dog'.

THE 'DO-GOODERS'

Officers at Locksdon had a tense and ambivalent relationship with the volunteer visitors' group that visited detainees to befriend them. On one occasion in late 2002, officers discovered that a man who had been taken from Locksdon to the airport for removal had 'kicked off' on the plane and had not been allowed to fly. Security staff at the airport had searched the man and had found a handwritten note from a woman, Mary, which read 'I hope you haven't had to use the bag yet'. Staff at Locksdon's security office were concerned that this woman had given the detainee something to 'get out of' flying. What was in the bag? What had she meant by the note? Was she a member of the Locksdon volunteer group? The SO in charge of security complained to his colleagues that the volunteer website posted advice about how detainees could avoid removal by feigning illness, becoming violent and so on. He said: 'That's incitement, that is. That's not what they're here for. That's not their remit. The governor lets them in with the understanding they'll just chat about the weather, not get given tips on how to get off flights.' The SO and his fellow security officers traced a paper trail of Visits records back to people who had met with the detainee in question. They looked up the detainee 'prop' (property) card to find out whether he had received anything from outside or from a visitor. The man, it transpired, had received a package several weeks earlier, which had been opened, searched and logged appropriately. The officers who had opened the package were consulted: could they remember what it was? Yes, they could. It was an expandable holdall. Excitement over. The volunteer's details were passed to the police liaison officer and the conversation turned to the 'do-gooders'. The security SO summed up the general feelings:

> They're so misinformed, these people. They have an idea about what the detainees are like and it's only part of the picture. I mean, I think a handful of people here deserve asylum, I really do, but only a handful. Not the majority of them. I don't know what they think should happen. I mean, we've had terrorists, criminals, really nasty pieces of work through here. What do they want to happen: just let them out?

The 'do-gooders' represented a threat to the officers' authority at Locksdon. The perimeter fence at Locksdon delimited a domain of control and power for the officers, where they had the power to search, constrain, monitor and forcibly move detainees. Relationships which spanned the perimeter fence and linked the detainees to 'outside' presented a challenge to officers' initiative. Group members were seen to 'incite' indiscipline (see chapter 4) among the detainees. This incitement was seen as a deliberate and wilful attempt to subvert the officers' control over the detainees, and thus to threaten the bodily safety of staff and detained men alike. Moreover, those in the volunteer group were seen as overly politicised and active advocates of the detainees: group representatives made periodic appearances on local television and radio, protesting against immigration detention in general and about Locksdon in particular. The officers claimed the group lied about conditions at Locksdon; staff would pin newspaper cuttings with media reports about supposed 'bad treatment' on the centre notice board. The officers resented the fact that the group members cast aspersions of their professionalism; they complained that the 'do-gooders' 'treat us like animals' and 'make us sound like barbarians'. One officer said: 'I overheard one of them asking the detainee if he was beaten. I mean, what do they think we are?'

The officers also mocked the group's 'naivety', recalling with glee an instance where a bailed detainee staying with a volunteer had absconded, losing the man a good deal of money. The group members were derogatorily referred to as 'middle-class', part of the 'blue rinse brigade' or even nonces[4] with nefarious motives 'for wanting to befriend young boys … I mean, what's in it for them?' By 'middle-class' the officers meant educated, liberal, 'comfortably off', with cultural capital and influence to make their voices heard. One officer told me, on discovering another 'disruptive' plan by the group: 'It's the middle classes trying to screw us over again.' Another retorted: 'We don't ever get to put our side. But then what do we know? We're just oiks, right?'

The antipathy that the officers felt towards the 'do-gooders' was a moral and social critique about 'loyalty' in the context of their experience and investment in 'the nation' as a meaningful social and moral category. In officers' discussion about strengthening borders and the swift expulsion of those 'who do not deserve asylum', they invoked a vision of citizenship and belonging within a politics of nationalism that was also a moral order. The officers' ideas about the nation were related to efforts to clearly delineate loyalty and obligation within and across national borders. Extrapolating from their own conceptualisation of moral selfhood in terms of fulfilling obligations to relevant others, loyalty and friendship (see chapter 3), the 'national order of things' (Malkki 1995a), for them, organised a 'moral cartography' (Shapiro 1999). Citizens as members of the national community should demonstrate loyalty to one another and the state before 'outsiders'. The officers' appeals to the nation were appeals to a vision of citizenship that could 'stick together' and place the needs of 'insiders' before 'others'.

The detainees at Locksdon became symbols of the fractures and fissures contained in experience of 'the nation'. Officers perceived 'traditional' certainties about jobs, houses and pensions to be shifting, the welfare state and the national distribution of resources to be altering, and the 'traditional' loyalties of fellow citizens to be eroding. The officers' assertions about 'what we share' and why 'we should stick together' invoked the solidity of a national political, economic and moral order within deteriorating, atomising and uncertain socio-economic terrains (see Bauman 2000, 2001). Lamont (2000) and Lamont and Aksartova (2002) have shown the way that working men (their cases are from America and France) make sense of social and political change by drawing boundaries between themselves and 'people above' and 'people below' them on an imagined social scale. The working men see 'people above' them to be selfish and morally insincere, working to further their own comfort rather than working for the good of the whole.

These points resonate with the views of Locksdon officers. For them, the overwhelmingly 'middle-class' character of the volunteer group invoked a broader swathe of British society uninterested in the kinds of social, economic and political problems that concerned the officers, as the self-defined 'working class'. The comfortable existence of the volunteers afforded them the luxury of championing the needs of 'outsiders' because, argued the officers, they were safe in the knowledge that they would never have to personally suffer the practical consequences that 'letting them [detainees] all in' would involve: losing jobs, divided communities, 'house devaluation'. The accusations levelled at the volunteer group, brought into play an imagined boundary between 'people like the officers' (with common-sense, down-to-earth, pragmatic ideas) and others (whose self-interest and naïve ideas threatened society). The group's prioritisation of the detainees was in direct contrast to the 'proper' loyalties that should exist between co-nationals. Their championing of 'difference' and 'change' by advocating an open, inclusive border, for example, challenged the traditional social and moral order of British society as the majority of officers understood it. The group showed a prioritisation of self over others, a despicable moral failing. The do-gooders disrupted proper moral boundaries between 'us' (national insiders) and 'them' (unknown outsiders), provoking feelings of betrayal. The proper moral, economic and political hierarchies of the nation were being slowly eroded, and privileged people were developing allegiances across borders, channelling resources, effort, time and goodwill into endeavours that apparently threatened the future integrity and prosperity of the national community, as understood by the officers.

'INCOMPETENT' IMMIGRATION

The officers' critiques of the 'do-gooders' were coupled with critiques of 'immigration', understood as the general bureaucratic system surrounding asylum and immigration processing and decision-making. Staff at Locksdon had first-hand experience of the apparently chaotic workings of the immigration system, and recounted stories of immigration authorities mislaying files, for example, of detainees being 'lost' in the system, of men waiting for months and years with no immigration decision, and of inefficient and 'pointless' movement of detainees between IRCs. On one occasion, for example, immigration authorities detained a French national for nine months before finally releasing him when 'lost' papers proving his right to be in Britain were uncovered. When detainees who had been living in Britain for years with no papers were brought into Locksdon, officers saw evidence of 'failures' of immigration officials to 'do their job properly'. The system, they concluded, was out of control.

> I think the immigration system is swamped and they can't cope. I've got no faith in it at all. There needs to be a system that will just be faster. They shouldn't be sat here for months on end. I mean ... how much is it costing to keep them here? Millions ... Send them all back to where they came from. No questions, no um-ing and ah-ing, just straight back at the airport. Are you telling me they're all in Britain for our human rights record? I don't think so. They look at this place as easy money. They shouldn't even be allowed in, just turn them all away. (Male officer)

> The IOs are swamped – it's all completely out of control. They haven't got a bloody clue. I mean DEPMU [detainee population co-ordinating body] will phone up and ask if we have so and so, and they're the ones with the bloody figures sending them to us! They're in charge. Fucking useless. Immigration don't know what they're doing. They're so disorganised they make us look good. (Male SO)

> I think there should be some kind of cut-off point. I mean, after ten years here, what the hell do they have in Africa? We've had guys through here who've been in England thirteen years, but there's

some plane chartered to Ghana and off he goes ... They've been working, getting on. It's daft, sending them back, and then letting in some Chinese guy in who can't speak a word of English. He'll disappear up to London, working in some takeaway somewhere. You'll never hear from him again. (Female officer)

The routine enactment of the decisions at the national border is one of the prime locations for the materialisation of 'the state' and 'state sovereignty'. It is through the promise of being able to make fair and expeditious decisions – on exclusions, exceptions and inclusions – that the state as sovereign authority is 'made real' and 'writes itself' (Campbell 1998). Indeed, the very idea of a 'political inside' comes into being through the notion of drawing and defending an existing border from a threatening 'outside'. Although the rules and criteria of immigration policy shift across time, reflecting changing socio-economic conditions and shifting international political terrains (see De Genova 2002), the promise of the sovereign state occludes these changes. Instead, the state claims to 'protect' a nation already constituted by recognising the clearly distinguishable lines between legality and illegality, between secure and risky, and between genuine and 'bogus'. While the idea of 'the sovereign state' and 'security' seems to be materialised through a promise to police a border already drawn, divisions between 'legal' and 'illegal', inclusion and exclusion, are not simply a matter of fairly enforcing rules. Decisions produce 'the rules': the 'state' and 'sovereign power' come into being through the everyday practices and interventions enacted in its name – from manifold claims to authority across dispersed fields, repetitions of bureaucratic rituals, everyday protocols applied by an aggregate of individuals, organisations and agencies.

Locksdon staff officers were daily confronted with the effects of these decisions about status, bail, deportation. The staff at Locksdon frequently considered these decisions to be 'wrong'. It was not simply that the processing of immigration and asylum claims was often a protracted process, or that the time men spend in detention was considered a waste of resources, or even that the application of the criteria for entry into Britain seemed inconsistent. Rather, it was frequently the case that the criteria themselves were considered faulty. The officers' ideal of a good detainee and worthy future citizen combined ambiguous elements of 'fitting in', working hard and 'getting on with it'. The decisions made by 'immigration' appeared to be letting people in who had no inclination to 'fit in' or respect 'the British way of life', or who had 'been trouble' at Locksdon. Like Gupta's (1995) notion of state corruption, the discourse of a 'failing system' which 'let in the wrong people' was a mechanism through which 'the state' and 'citizen' were visualised, constituted and contested. When officers referred to a swamped immigration system, they were also invoking its opposite: a 'strong', ordered and robust border, a mechanism for making quick and decisive judgements, an intolerance of 'trouble'.

DISCRETION AND DETENTION

Frustrated by 'immigration' and 'screwed over' by some imagined 'middle class', the officers' enactment of their duties at Locksdon became entangled with their frustrations about 'the system'. I want to draw out three points from the discussion in this chapter.

First, as discussed in the last chapter, officers were engaged in ongoing critiques of detainees' 'childishness' or 'unreasonableness' within the regime. The inability to 'get on with it' at Locksdon was 'evidence' of the detainees' inauthenticity and lack of moral worth. Being detain-able, the men at Locksdon had disrespected the law, but, more importantly, they showed through the most mundane actions their 'irregularity in relation to certain rules, which may be physiological, psychological, or moral ...' (Foucault 2003: 16). The expert eye that officers cast over the men in their control was, like the expert eye described by Foucault in *Abnormal*, concerned with a 'psychologico-ethical double of the offence' (2003: 16). The status of being detained was doubled with criminality and a reprehensible moral character, and this character revealed itself to the officers' expert bodywatching. The glimpses that officers captured revealed, in Ahmed's terms, the character behind the action – a wilful, troublesome subject. Ahmed (2011: 239) argues: 'willfulness arises as a diagnosis of the failure to comply with those whose authority is given'. As citizens of Britain (the 'host) and as guardians of the detention regime, the officer's authority 'was given'. The detainee's acts of protest and resistance constituted his wilfulness, that designated by the officers' own will (see Ahmed 2011: 240). It was the officers' embodied sense of 'keeping the initiative' that constituted the line between obedience and disobedience, security and insecurity. In the daily routine of detention this line was nothing other than the national border – the edge of a moral and political community over which the officers were designated protectors.

The resisting and complaining detainee was, like Ahmed's wilful subject, guilty of 'a character perversion' and an 'insistence on going against the flow': to be wilful is 'to deviate, to will one's own way is to will the wrong way' (2011: 240, 245). Wilfulness, she goes on, 'comes up' at the moment 'when an act of willing does not agree with what has receded' (2011: 245). At Locksdon, it was in the contravention of what had receded – the regime's production of the compliant, silent, passive detainee via officers' vigilance and action – that trouble was 'revealed' to the officers. The experts, as Foucault (2003: 20) argues, 'have always sought to reconstitute the dynasty of the extended series of ambiguities that lie just beneath the surface' and to show how 'the subject is present in the form of criminal desire in all these vile deeds and things that are not quite regular'. The reprehensible character of the detainee was revealed and diagnosed via the smallest acts of disobedience and wilfulness, that only the officers could see. Neither the do-gooders, nor 'immigration' had the knowledge or insight into the 'truth' of the detainees. The detention centre became, for the officers, a probationary zone, where their expertise and skill should hold sway:

> I think the way they behave in here should go into their immigration case. If they've done nothing but cause trouble, if they've broken the law, been a real pain in the arse, then that should go into a report and should be taken into account. We write reports about cons all the time in nick. (Male senior officer)

The 'things that are not quite regular' about the detainees formed the grounds for the visual enactment of security at Locksdon (pre-emptive dispersal of detainees, trained scrutiny of individuals). They also, importantly, formed the grounds for disciplinary acts which blurred the rational production of security (as an orderly, predictable, safe regime) with the desire for punishment and retribution. At stake in officers' decisions about the use of force, about using the Seg Unit or removing a detainee to another establishment was the understanding of 'proportionality', 'reasonableness' and 'necessity' as outlined in the lawful use of force. PSO 1600 argues that in prisons, the 'interpretation of reasonable is a key issue concerning a use of force' (1.1) and deciding 'whether force is "necessary"' is complicated, especially when risk to life or limb is not at stake, but rather the risk 'to the good order of the establishment'. In this situation the staff member must 'take into account the consequences of the prisoner not complying with his/her lawful instruction': it is 'not enough that a prisoner be given a "lawful order" to do something and has refused to do so'. At Locksdon, the use of force 'reasonable in the circumstances' and 'proportionate to the seriousness of the circumstances' were bound up in the officers' perception of their work with detainees as unknown, possibly dangerous, but also illegal and anomalous persons whose 'right' to be in Britain was under question.

At Locksdon, the ostensible maintenance of a rationalised regime and security was converted in the officers' experience and enactment of everyday practices into what Foucault (2003: 23) calls the 'sordid business of punishing'. At Locksdon, the application of what the *Detention Centre Rules* term 'special control and restraint where this is necessary to prevent the detained person from injuring himself or others, damaging property or creating a disturbance ...' was always entangled with a 'correction' or 'realignment' of the wilful, troublesome and irksome detainee. The C&R incident was the means through which a disturbance was averted, but it was also a chance for officers' to punish insolence, to regain a sense of masculine control ('show who's daddy').

Second, the decision to use force, to remove from association or 'ghost out' was a 'taking outside' in Agamben's (1998) terms. The idea that individuals' discretion shapes the way in which legalistic processes and categories are applied is well-developed in studies of the bureaucratic administration of national immigration work (see Fuglerud 2004; Gill 2009; Heyman 2000; Mountz 2010; Pratt 1999, 2010; Weber and Gelsthorpe 2001). Discretion, argue Pratt and Sossin (2009: 301) arises 'when an official is empowered to exercise public authority and afforded scope to decide how that authority should be exercised in particular circumstances'. At heart, they argue, discretion is 'about power and judgement'; that is, despite the widespread and traditional view that legal rules and discretion are separable and related in a binary manner, discretion is an integral aspect of legalistic systems and judgements. Discretion, as Pratt and Sossin (2009: 306) argue, is 'ultimately a political issue, not simply a legal one'; it is as much to do with the cultural norms, working protocols and social experience as it is about rule-based legalistic categories. Discretion, as Heyman (2009: 367) argues, involves 'decisions about when, on whom, and on what legal grounds to act but also decisions about when and on whom *not* to act'. Discretion, in this way, Heyman continues (2009: 367, 388), 'is not a formless domain of uncontrolled action, but ... an analysable domain of patterned actions that significantly affect law and administration';

these actions may 'draw on existing lines of social inequality and constitute and reinforce them'. Immigration and asylum law, for example (its interpretation and the effects of the application of legal categories) becomes shaped and inflected by subjective discretionary judgements that draw on multiple cultural norms and narratives – about appropriate behaviour associated with suffering and victimhood, for example (see Good 2007, 2008; Pratt 1999). Discretion is involved in everyday decisions about immigration at all sites of the border.

I would argue that discretion troubles 'the decision' that Agamben, after Schmitt, places centrally to sovereign power. Schmitt locates the decision in the moment of identifying the threat posed by the figure of the enemy: 'sovereign is he who decides on the state of exception' (Agamben 1998: 11). In being able to decide on the exception, sovereign power as a distinct form of power creates a 'zone of indistinction' where law is suspended. The biopolitical consequence of this suspension is to be found in the way certain people and lives continue to be included through their exclusion: subject to sovereign power, but without the full protection of the law (Agamben 2005: 2). For Butler, contemporary sovereign power is to be found in the moment of withdrawal of the law in the name of security and emergency by what she calls 'petty sovereigns' (2004: 54–5). The exception in Agamben's terms is a way of governing populations via an inclusive exclusion – a means of governing by 'taking outside'. In this inclusive exclusion, argues Agamben, law becomes suspended, and another kind of logic takes over. The detention of 'out-of-place' populations, then, can be seen as such a place of inclusive exclusion – where people do not enjoy the normal rights of citizens, yet are still vulnerable to sovereign power.

I have shown that inside the detention centre, there are spaces where the detainee may be 'taken outside' in a layered sense. The relegation to the Seg Unit, for instance, places detainees apart (literally and symbolically) and suspends for them the normal routines of detention. At Locksdon this isolation was a literal 'taking outside' by forcibly dissociating the detainee from the social world of Locksdon. Decisions taken by staff at Locksdon were also, I argue, sovereign decisions in the sense that Agamben argues. The manager's decision to 'ghost out' the Turkish detainees to a nearby prison, for instance, did not appear to be fully authorised by the *Detention Centre Rules*, and placed these men temporarily in a limbo between administrative detention and punishment. Treating the detainees in this way created a zone of ambiguity and flexibility around the official rules of the IRC. For the officers, measures like these were a way of maintaining authoritative control in Locksdon, especially in difficult and exceptional circumstances. In the decision to 'ghost out' was constituted the power inside and outside law that Agamben calls sovereign. One officer described to me how staff felt when Locksdon became an IRC: staff had found it hard, he told me, 'they lost their power ... no power is the wrong word. They lost control.' Decisions like the manager's above sought to protect and bolster officers' means of control, and so also bolstered their *sovereign* discretionary power in the border zone. It was a 'taking of sovereignty', an embodiment of the capacity to produce the biopolitical body, which, as Agamben (1998: 6) argues, is the 'original activity of sovereign power'. The isolated detainee was suspended in a zone where the officers' discretionary judgements constituted the norms and rules through which he was to be governed.

I have shown that 'the decision' at Locksdon was an embodied judgement made in contexts saturated by feelings of frustration, trepidation and irritation. More than this, it was a dispersed network of decisions, actions and judgements. The lawful rules of detention (about the use of force, for example) were always configured within discretionary complexes of officers' affective moods, contextual perceptions and shifting local agendas. I have shown that the decision to use force, to remove from association or 'ghost out' demonstrated a desire to punish, or rectify imbalances of initiative, or to regain control. In this way, I have shown officers at Locksdon to be not mere proxies of a sovereign power already constituted. Rather, the decisions they made in their everyday dealings with detainees manifested and demarcated a flexible zone of discretion and judgement that blurred the production of a 'secure and humane regime' with punitive, retaliatory and reactive practice.

[Handwritten annotations:]

Soft power - feminized

females - care takers - procemy - psychological
mind + body
erratic

daddy Albanian guy male - security

body controlling emotions

hard power - masculinized

gender is performed - Judith Butler
inculturated + constructed

6
Ethics and Encounters

One crisp morning in autumn 2002, I am in a classroom in the Locksdon education department. An Algerian student has written a story about a prisoner in a war camp in the English class. He describes his protagonist feeling like a shipwrecked vessel dashed upon rocks, alone. I ask him how long he has been at Locksdon, and he replies bitterly that he has been detained for many months 'for nothing ...' At that moment, Susan, Locksdon's diversity officer, enters with an announcement: she is organising a 'Festival of Faiths' at Locksdon. She tells the detainees that it will be 'their day' and she is inviting representatives from local organisations to visit the centre. She wants the detainees to enter a painting and writing competition, for which there will be prizes (biscuits, sweets, phone cards and personal stereos). She tells them:

> I want you to write a poem, paint me a picture, write me a story about your country or your religion. Some people have only heard bad things about asylum seekers and people at Locksdon. The fire department, police ... all they hear is trouble. This is your chance to show them another side.

The Algerian detainee next to me speaks up: 'You only want us to write good things about Locksdon, but I have many bad things to say about Locksdon.' Susan corrects him: 'No, no ... not about Locksdon. I don't want to hear about Locksdon, I only want to hear about your religion, your country, what's in your heart, what's in your mind.'

The majority of the other officers take a negative view of Susan's plans. Susan is regarded with suspicion by many officers: her championing of diversity issues is seen to disrupt the largely conformist working milieu and she is seen as 'dangerous' in her keenness to forge a career for herself and to place herself above 'the group'. The Festival of Faiths, several officers claim, is part of Susan's ongoing strategy to 'show her arse to everyone'. When

Susan bustles into the centre office a month later on the day of the Festival, the other officers on duty are indifferent. Sam, for instance, grumbles:

> I see Madam isn't wearing uniform today [Susan is dressed in a smart black suit]. She's on duty – she should be in uniform. She thinks she can just swan around as she likes. We don't know anything about this Festival thing.

As I make my way down to the gym, another officer quizzes me: 'Where are you going? What are you doing down there? Why'd you want to go there?' Shaking his head at me, another officer tells him: 'She's going down to cavort with the do-gooders.'

The Festival of Faiths is just getting under way when I arrive. Susan has invited representatives from the fire brigade, the police, local medical centres, members of religious groups affiliated to Locksdon, local council members and members of community groups, as well as the press. The manager of Locksdon is welcoming everyone. 'We have lots of different faiths here, and it's our job to look after them with humanity', he tells the crowd. Locksdon's on-site chaplain then steps up. 'We are all living in a multi-faith, multicultural society', she says, 'but here at Locksdon we live it everyday. We have many faiths here living side by side, and we must all get on together, in peace, and we are successful in doing so here at Locksdon.'

Susan then thanks everyone for coming and announces the first of the performances, a visiting troupe of Indian dancers clad in billowing trousers and sequinned tops. They perform a series of dances, accompanied by a portable stereo, before launching into an audience participation routine, inviting everyone to copy hand and arm mime movements. The next performance is a small group of detainees from Africa, who are to perform a gospel song. The men are invited onto the stage area and they start to sing and move around, shyly at first, but with gathering volume and enthusiasm, clapping their hands. After a while, they appear fully engrossed, eyes closed and bodies swaying to the rhythm. The leader calls his melodies and the chorus repeats, their voices rising higher and higher. The hymn is repetitive, and after ten minutes or so it appears the singing might continue indefinitely. The chaplain, after a nod from Susan, moves to end their performance. A member of the Locksdon nursing staff leans over to me and whispers, 'They're so much more expressive than we are, aren't they?'

I look around the room. The invited audience is seated on chairs in rows and are wearing name badges stating their name and organisation. There are twenty or so detainees sitting on several sports benches arranged at the front of the audience space. The detainees have no name badges. I am reminded of a school play where children must sit at the front and the parents sit on proper seats at the back. One of the detainees, an Indian national who has been in Locksdon for over a year, has his long legs uncomfortably curled up under him. He appears transfixed by the exotically dressed dancers. Around the edge of the gym hall, three officers are standing against the walls. With so many visitors present, any disturbance created by the detainees would be disastrous. One of the officers catches my eye and raises his eyebrows sarcastically. Around the edge of the hall are 'stalls' with displays about different religions and details about Locksdon (the regime, the routine, facilities such as the health centre and the education department). The detainees' competition art work and poems are displayed on a stall in the corner. At the far end of the gym I can see an officer standing by the door. The faces of several detainees are framed in the door window, straining for a view. The officer opens the door, shakes his head and quietly shoos them away.

Susan then invites everyone to a 'multi-faith' service at Locksdon's religious facility. Everyone wanders out of the gym and I become caught up in a conversation with an officer in the exercise yard. He views the group dispassionately:

> We've had loads of detainees asking if they could go along and we've had to say no. There's been nothing said about what's supposed to happen. It's supposed to be their day, isn't it? So how come just a handful get to go down? They all would have enjoyed that dancing. It's just Susan's day really.

I pass half an hour with him. I then return to the gym, where people are milling back into the hall after the service. Susan announces the next performance, 'Melodies to Unite'. An OSG and her partner are to sing a medley of easy listening tunes, accompanied by a staff member from the works department (building maintenance) on the keyboards. While they are playing, Susan invites us to visit the 'International Buffet' at the back of the hall, where plates of onion bhajis and other 'international' snacks await. The guests begin to move around. I watch the detainees. They move to the food and tuck in enthusiastically before wandering around uneasily, talking to one another or the religious leaders, whom they know. They do not interact with the other visitors, who have broken off into little groups and are making polite conversation.

Suddenly it is half past four and almost time for roll check at quarter to five. All at once, the officers swing into action and round up the detainees, asking them to return to their dormitories. The detainees slowly leave the hall. The visitors stay for another half an hour, the music still playing, and then slowly disperse. Susan looks visibly relieved and elated and is congratulated by several people. As I walk back up to the centre office, the officers are completing roll check, calling out the number of detainees in each dormitory along the corridor to the officer in charge of tallying the total. One smirks at me: 'Finished gallivanting with the do-gooders, Alex? How was it? Find out anything useful for your diss-er-ta-tion?' The officers achieve a satisfactory roll check – everyone is accounted for – and settle down for a cup of tea before dinnertime. Susan walks by. No-one says a word to her.

In the days following the Festival of Faiths, I speak to several people about the event. Susan felt it had gone well. I mentioned it had been a shame that the detainees had had to be herded off so abruptly. She agreed, saying the matter was not in her hands and the regime could not be disrupted. She was annoyed that the leftover food had not been put out for the other detainees and had been polished off by staff. She took this to be an indication of the other officers' insensitivity and selfishness. The majority of the officers showed supreme indifference. Whatever interest they mustered was for criticising Susan. They emphasised the hypocrisy of the event, to which only some detainees were admitted, and, by association, the hypocrisy of Susan and 'the do-gooders'. A teacher from the education department was most critical. She told me:

> I was absolutely furious, really angry. It was so badly organised. —— won a prize in the essay competition and he tried to get in, but he wasn't allowed. He was banging on the door, but they turned him away. He hadn't returned the consent form saying he could have his picture taken or something and he couldn't go in to collect his prize. I went down there myself to try to get him in. I think it's disgraceful. That day was supposed to be for them, he'd worked so hard, and then that happens.

*   *   *

This chapter is concerned with the ethical encounter at Locksdon, an encounter that is characterised by respect, recognition, generosity and responsibility. The previous chapters have discussed Locksdon as a divided social environment. I have argued that the central organising ethos of the detention regime was difference and division. The detainees – construed as 'illegal' outsiders, as security threats – were the subject of multiple forms of control and governance in the detention centre that inscribed and produced this difference and division in everyday routines. The regime was productive of 'symbolic' and 'systemic' kinds of violence, as well as physical violence, in Žižek's (2008) terms. The desire for security reduced the detainees to body-objects, and discourses of indiscipline and illegality produced the detainees as morally excludable. I have also described the way in which the resistant and politicised detainee was 'contained' by the regime, by force if need be. There were, however, other and qualitatively different kinds of encounter between officers and detainees within this divided environment, ones which were ethical in nature.

The Festival of Faiths demonstrated that even in apparently benign acts within Locksdon – Susan after all wanted the Festival to be 'their day' – the detainees were still subject to techniques of representation and power which reduced and excluded them. Susan intended the Festival of Faiths to be a celebration of cultural and religious diversity and Locksdon's success at accommodating the detainees' difference. The Festival of Faiths booklet (produced for visitors) drew attention to the establishment's catering, educational and religious facilities. Locksdon was presented as a modern, humane and inclusive establishment striving to ensure that the detainees' needs were met. The booklet stated:

> Locksdon is a truly multicultural environment where individuals are encouraged to worship in any way they wish. Today is a celebration of that diversity and opportunity for those who wish, to come together in an ecumenical service under the banner of 'one family' [sic].

'Multicultural' was associated with 'religious difference'. The booklet also had a definition of 'diversity': 'the mosaic of people who bring a variety of backgrounds, styles, perspectives, values and beliefs as assets to the groups and organisations with which they interact'. The booklet continued: 'Locksdon is a multi cultural [sic] centre and daily we all embrace the challenges that are created by the diversities of the many cultures, languages, religions, values and beliefs of the community at Locksdon'. Detainees and staff, the booklet suggested, were bearers of diversity of all kinds, and formed a community that actively 'embraced' differences.

Within the event, the detainees' alterity was a 'given', marked by religious beliefs and national origin. As Lavine and Karp (1991: 1) argue with reference to museum exhibitions, all displays draw on the cultural assumptions of the people who organise them, crafted for certain audiences. It is the alleged neutrality of displays that makes them efficacious instruments of power, through which moral statements are expressed and interpreted (Karp 1991: 14). When 'cultural others' are involved, exhibitions and displays become contested arenas for presentations of self and others, and for the narration of ideas about 'who we are' and 'who they are' (Karp 1991: 14–15). Using performance to 'display culture' assumes that there are specific ways in which the performers are different from the audience, and that this alterity can be presented in visual form (Stanley 1998: 173). Kirshenblatt-Gimblett (1991: 397–400) argues that using people as living signs of themselves steers exhibitions in the direction of spectacles.

The detainees' experiences in Britain and at Locksdon were excluded from their self-representations in their essays and art work.[1] The presentation of the detainees as 'religious' others, with different styles of worship (the African gospel singers) and different 'cultural traditions' (the Indian dancers and the 'International Buffet'), subsumed the detainees' unique individuality beneath banners of religion and 'culture'. Observers of the 'politics of multi-culturalism' have noted the way that categorising people according to 'cultural' identity reifies complex processes of belonging and identification (Appiah 1994; Modood and Werbner 1997). 'Culture' is reduced to a monolith and 'package' of behaviours and customs within which people are 'trapped' or 'determined' (Vertovec 2001; Wikan 1999, 2002). Within the Festival of Faiths, the audience were drawn towards what marked the detainees as different – more 'expressive' and religious than 'us'. The fact that many men at Locksdon were not at all religious, had varied personal histories and had travelled widely for complex political and economic reasons was ignored. Despite Susan's claim that the event was 'their day', the detainees did not play a large role in the Festival.[2] They were effectively infantilised. Many of the detainees were highly educated and skilled, yet they were asked to write poems and paint pictures like children. The detainees who attended the event were seated on benches like children and did not wear name badges like the visitors. They were 'detainees' rather than full persons.

In a discussion about the relationship between the border and theatre, Sophie Nield (2006) argues for a reformulation of cultural notions of 'the theatrical'. The theatrical, she argues, should not just invoke a sense of 'having properties like the theatre', conjuring ideas of illusion, pretence and pre-scripting (2006: 63). In contrast, the theatrical is related to 'a set of qualities, practices and forms of spatialisation' that are present in conventional theatre practices, but which are not confined to them (2006: 64). The theatrical, argues Nield, implies 'the production of a space in which "appearance" of a particular kind becomes possible; indeed, a space which is organised in such a way as to compel certain kinds of appearance' (2006: 64). At the border and the theatre alike, 'the question of who exactly is present – actor, performer, character, material body or representational figure – carries precisely the same sense of ambivalence' (2006: 54).

The Festival of Faiths crystallised the problem of appearance and identity that Nield places centrally in 'the theatrical' and 'the border'. As Nield (2006: 65) puts it, the border encounter raises the question of 'who is there?' – 'whether the person who is there is who they represent themselves to be and is, in fact, the legal/juridical object that legal/juridical mechanisms require them to be'. In the detention centre, the question of 'who is there?' is a central concern, as I have shown, and this question becomes elaborated and contested within social life. The majority of the Locksdon officers, for instance, were suspicious of the Festival's 'celebration of difference'. As I have argued, officers generally regarded their remit at Locksdon to be the provision of a secure environment. This certainly involved keeping the detainees occupied, but did not, as far as they saw, involve 'cultural' festivities. Officers generally saw differences in religion and culture not as sources of strength and celebration, but as possible bases for division and disunity. Celebrating the detainees' 'difference' (or 'difference' in general) was inappropriate: the detainees were 'guests' in Britain now and the onus was on them to 'fit in' with some nebulous idea of 'the British way of life'. Yet many officers and the teacher were annoyed on the detainees' behalf, recognising that many of the detainees who wanted to join in were excluded. The security requirements of having all the detainees in the gym area with visitors, however, would have involved altering the entire regime for the day.

The benign façade of the Festival of Faiths, then, highlighted the moralised discourses at Locksdon which variously recognised the men at Locksdon as 'other', as 'detainees', as 'victims', as 'security threats'. Nield (2006: 69, 65) argues that, like the theatrical performance, neither the border nor the border crosser, are ever 'quite "there"': just as the border materialises only in its bureaucratic production, so the border crosser is compelled to appear, to 'play [himself] and hope [he] is convincing'. Those who fail to convince, like the detainees at Locksdon, are condemned to inhabit the border – a 'thickened' space (Makaremi 2009) and a 'viscous spatio-temporal zone' where people experience 'waiting to live, a non-life' (Balibar 2002: 83). This book has discussed the life of this 'thickened space'. It has understood Locksdon as a border zone. Locksdon is, quite literally, the inhabited national border where status and political inclusion hang in the balance. The detention centre is a border zone in the sense of being inhabited by people whose identity is undecided and whose future is in doubt. I have described the other borders that come into play in the border zone of detention – moral boundaries between deserving and undeserving, lines between security and insecurity, gendered boundaries. This chapter is concerned with moral boundaries at Locksdon – their maintenance and reinscription – but also with what happens when borders momentarily dissolve or fall away in social life as it is lived, and how ethical possibility is cultivated within these moments.

MAINTAINING BOUNDARIES

Locksdon, as I have described, was an unpredictable environment with tensions that were peculiar to a secure environment. The uncertainty and volatility of centre life, and the threat emanating from the unknown and possibly dangerous detainees, was 'managed' via classic bureaucratic rational organisation. Locksdon's regime strove towards ideals of impersonality, rationality and formalistic bureaucratic action. Bauman (1993: 18–19) argues that wholly immoral actions can be produced from the bureaucratic fragmentation of tasks wherein individual responsibility becomes linked to a working role rather than a whole person and the overarching authority of 'the system' comes to vouch for all actions. The social life of Locksdon, as I have described it, produced 'the moral' as subordination to the group. This was what made Susan 'dangerous'. The autonomous ethical duty of the individual subject was replaced by a 'heteronomous' ethical duty (see Bauman 1993: 44–5), where individual deviance from accepted moral norms was 'bad'. Conforming with norms of 'fitting in', of displaying loyalty to the group, of placing oneself ahead of the group was how officers could demonstrate 'doing good' (see chapter 3).

Being a 'good officer' was about recognising one's obligations and responsibilities to the group and to one's colleagues, but it was also about being professional towards detainees. The work of an officer at Locksdon involved assuming responsibility for resolving myriad small issues for the detainees, issues that were often of great significance to the men. Work tasks at Locksdon were described as 'like opening a can of worms', as one officer put it. That is, a simple request from a detainee (to retrieve a piece of luggage, to contact a solicitor, to make a phone call) often spiralled into unravelling a series of administrative errors at Locksdon and beyond. Small actions appeared to be favours for the detainees – personal acts of kindness that involved the officers 'going out of their way' – but these 'favours' were construed by officers as central to the ongoing maintenance of the regime, to upholding the 'wiggly lines' (see chapter 3) of the centre.

> Larry is running around for a Jamaican detainee, who wants to send a letter to the Jamaican High Commission in London as soon as possible. The man has recently arrived and has made a name for himself already – he has been mentioned in the Obs book as a possible 'live wire'. Larry, as immigration liaison officer, has decided to give the man an envelope and stamp, despite the fact that these are usually only distributed to detainees once a week. This is an initiative on Larry's part and it could appear that he feels sorry for the man. As he hands over the envelope, he says, 'I've done you a favour now.' The man takes it and nods to Larry, thanking him. I walk with Larry back to the ILO office and he ruminates on his actions:
>
>> You should be interested in what I was doing there. I was clever. That guy fancies himself as a bit of a troublemaker, one of those Jamaicans you get through here that cause trouble. If you do little things for them now and then, then when something kicks off and he starts mouthing off, I'll turn round to him and say, 'Hold on, I was running round for you the other day.' And he'll go, 'Oh yeah.' There'll be some moral obligation there. That's what it's like – you have to make some

> little concessions to them. Have to make then think you're
> doing something for them.

Daily social interaction between officers and detainees tended
to be conducted in a manner that was amiable in appearance, but
which was designed to maintain brittle power relations. Banal acts
of 'personal service' like Larry's 'favour' were used to achieve the
officers' desired ends (a smooth-running regime) and to keep the
initiative. Officers perfected the technique of appearing to treat the
detainees well, while keeping an eye on the 'bigger picture'.

The officers prided themselves on treating 'everyone the same'
and argued that everyone gets 'wound up' at Locksdon. Why not
the detainees? One officer told me how two other officers used to
play jokes on the detainees in reception. These officers told new
detainees that their identity pictures would be used by dentists to
examine their teeth. The detainees opened their mouths wide for
the photo, producing a 'comical' picture that they would have to
carry around with them for the length of their stay at Locksdon.
The practice was discovered by the management and stopped. I
previously outlined the subtleties of language that the officers use
to play to their peers at the expense of the detainees, though the
detainees were also able to engage in jokes about officers in their
own language. I want to emphasise that only some officers engaged
in this kind of 'play', the vast majority viewing it as inappropriate,
unprofessional or boring. The officers who retold these stories to
me half-heartedly insisted that joking with the detainees was a good
way of 'breaking the ice'. Closer to the truth was the way in which
these jokes reproduced unequal power relations in the centre.

> You see, the way I deal with them, I use humour. I have a laugh
> with them. I think it makes things better. If they're coming in and
> surrounded by strange faces, in a strange place, I think having
> a laugh lightens things up. If it happens to be at their expense,
> well, they don't know do they? (Male officer)

Jokes can only 'break ice' if they are mutually understood.
Officers were not keen on the detainees 'becoming too friendly' or
'familiar', assuming an equal social personhood with the officers.
Sharing jokes was seen as ok, in its place, and officers mostly
enjoyed wisecracking detainees with whom they could engage in
banter. However, detainees who become 'too pally' were seen as
inappropriate and insubordinate.

The joke, at Locksdon, was thus a regulatory mechanism. Goffman (1967) has argued that embarrassment is integral to the maintenance of order within social life. Embarrassment is a form of shame emerging from the failure to perform in accordance with norms or expectations, and contradicting our desired impression of self (Billig 2001: 25; Nussbaum 2004: 207). Goffman (1967) argues that witnesses often engage in 'face saving' activities (like humorous joshing) to relieve embarrassment, but Billig (2001: 23–9) argues that this optimistic stance does not address the way that humour can *create* the social reality of embarrassment. People may actively pursue the embarrassment of others. Thus, jokes often express hostility against people, and undermine their dignity and position (Billig 2001: 26, 29, 39). Billig uses Freud's concept of a conflict between the demands of social life and individual desire to argue that social actors are not only motivated to 'fit in', but can desire to seek social disruption. This desire must be curtailed and repressed in most social situations, but people can delight in the disruption of social codes. Thus, embarrassment functions to protect the social order and is also linked to pleasure at social subversion. Making others feel shame or embarrassment is connected to control (Nussbaum 2004: 216). This discussion can go some way to explaining the officers' occasional enjoyment of the embarrassment of the detainees, and their anger at the detainees' own jokes at their expense. In a highly structured environment, there was a strong emphasis on maintaining control of oneself. The pleasure in subverting this structure by 'harmless' jokes was a way of 'keeping the detainees in their place'. Humour was a way of reasserting the officers' control, of retaining the other as other. The detainees' jokes, on the other hand, were subversive 'weapons of the weak' which signalled a disruptive and unruly subject.

Interwoven with these manipulative and humiliating interactions between detainees and officers were more uncalculating and caring encounters.

Just before roll check time in the centre office one wintry day, a detainee stomps into the room. The heating has broken down in his dormitory. The detainee shouts loudly that the conditions are disgusting at Locksdon. What are the officers going to do about it? Stuart, in the detainee's line of fire, is angered: 'Look, we've explained the situation. It's broken. There's nothing I can do right now. I don't carry round a bloody screwdriver.' The man stalks off. Stuart shakes his head. 'What do these bloody people expect?'

he asks. 'They're always whingeing.' An hour later, after lunch, Stuart and I are in the ILO office. There is a knock on the door and the detainee pokes his head round the corner. Workmen are tinkering with the heating along the corridor. The detainee has come to apologise for losing his temper. 'I'm thoroughly ashamed of myself,' he says to Stuart. Stuart is gracious: 'It's forgotten, mate. Everyone gets angry now and then, we all lose our temper, get frustrated. Don't worry about it.' He extends his hand, and they shake on it. Stuart is impressed with the detainee's behaviour, and reflects on the man's case.

> He's usually all right, M. That wasn't like him at all – that was sweet of him wasn't it? He's actually British, you know. He was born in Pakistan, but his parents came over here. He was living in a council flat with his mother, and when she dies, he went to the council, saying he didn't need such a big flat any more, you know, trying to do the right thing, and it all comes out about his immigration papers, he never got registered or something … something's missing and he ends up in here and everything started to go wrong for him. I mean, why keep him here? He had a job, he was getting on all right. He speaks better English than we do. I just don't get the logic of keeping him in here and letting some of those other guys out.

This particular detainee did not 'deserve' to be in Locksdon, whatever his legal status. He was proficient in his performance of 'Britishness'; he spoke English fluently, he had been working and 'fitting in'. He had been quietly conforming to the officers' general expectations about what the ideal 'guest' in Britain should be doing. The fact that these men were detained, while other 'less worthy' detainees were being released, was evidence that the system was untrustworthy. Over my time at Locksdon there was a series of detainees like this man. Their perceived 'deservingness' centred on their behaviour at Locksdon towards the officers, from which the officers generalised about the kinds of lives they would have 'outside in society'. In Nussbaum's (2001) terms, the officers accepted these men into a shared moral community because the officers were able to view them as having similar possibilities and similar values. In Lamont and Aksartova's (2002) terms, and in general, the officers viewed pragmatic activities (such as working hard and leading a quiet, decent life) as meaningful discourses to provide a sense of commonality that was far more important in classifying detainees than legalistic categories of belonging. On one occasion, several officers decried the sudden, last-minute deportation of a detainee who had been at Locksdon for nearly a year. The officers' criticisms centred on the fact that the man had formed relationships with the staff at Locksdon and would have no chance to say goodbye. Several officers took the trouble to wander down to reception to shake the man's hand before he went and wish him luck.

Officers frequently remarked on the impossibility of shirking responsibility when 'confronted with guys everyday'. One of the visiting immigration officers described it thus, 'When you see them here every day, you think, my goodness, can't you [immigration case officer] sort it out? It's more difficult when you can put a name to a face.' The officers frequently begrudged the responsibility that they had to assume in their dealings with detainees. Nevertheless, it was a responsibility that daily confronted them. On one occasion, for example, the ILO officer, Larry, allowed a detainee to make a number of phone calls to his lawyer and family in the ILO office – highly irregular. Larry explained that the man was picked up a few days previously in his minicab. He couldn't prove who he was, so they sent him to Locksdon:

> He's been going on and on since he got here that he's legal, that he's got immigration papers but that he lost them or something. I don't know … There's just something about his story that just rings true to me. Immigration aren't interested. I don't know why, but I trust him. One moment he's in his cab, the next he's in here.

On another occasion, Mandy was in reception chatting to the two reception officers on duty. A new detainee arrived and was halfway through the reception process when the officer asked the required question about self-harm. Mandy cringed and muttered, 'it's such a stupid question to ask.' Suddenly she spotted the detainee was upset. 'Oh dear, he's upset, he's crying.' The two reception officers froze with embarrassment. Mandy immediately took charge. She put her arm around the detainee and said briskly, 'Now then, it's not so bad. There's no reason to cry. It will be ok.' She fetched him a chair as the man sobbed that he was picked up from his home by the police, that he didn't know where he was going, or what was happening to him. His girlfriend was pregnant, he continued, and was due to give birth at any moment. She would be worried about him, what would she think? Mandy took a unilateral decision and allowed the man to use the reception phone to call his girlfriend, against all centre protocols, and called an immigration officer to talk to the man about his case and why he had been picked up. In situations like these, officers and staff at Locksdon found themselves having to cope with 'the effects' of decisions about the detainees taken elsewhere and impinging on the regime. So, while everyday interaction at Locksdon was concerned with maintaining a fragile balance of power and of reinforcing the necessary boundaries that made detention work, and while encounters between officers and detainees (even those that seemed 'kindly' or 'generous') occluded complex manipulative power relations, the officers could not help, despite themselves, assuming responsibility for the care of the detainees, and for their concerns.

ETHICAL ENCOUNTERS

At Locksdon one night in 2003, a man got up from his dormitory bed, walked along the corridor, locked himself in the toilets and strangled himself with his shoelaces. He had been at the centre for some time and had not in any way distinguished himself to officers or staff. Quiet, unassuming, inconspicuous and shortly due to be deported back to his country of origin, his behaviour had not raised any concerns. He was reported missing by his roommate in the middle of the night and was unconscious by the time he was found. When the alarm was raised by a detainee, Tom had been the first officer on the scene. He had sprinted to the toilets and had struggled to open the locked door of the toilet when he realised someone was inside. Tom had clambered over the door and had supported the man while another officer cut the noose. The officers had dragged the man from the cubicle and Tom had attempted to resuscitate him with another officer, keeping up the techniques until the emergency services arrived and the detainee was pronounced dead.

Tom, although later recounting the incident in self-deprecating and darkly comic tones, had found the incident disturbing and it had shaken him: 'It wasn't pleasant. You could basically see he was dead before we'd even started. The resuscitator guard kept slipping. I couldn't be sure. It was exhausting. His eyes were open, staring at me.' The other detainees in the man's dormitory had witnessed the whole incident. Tom told me, 'It was good they saw that – us working hard like that.' As I was talking to Tom, a detainee entered the office and asked about a fax he wanted to send. Tom answered his query and then addressed the man: 'That was a tough business the other night, wasn't it? Bad stuff, a bad evening. How are you feeling?' The detainee, not quite understanding what Tom was saying at first, mumbled something, nodded and left. Tom explained that this man had acted as an interpreter during the incident when the police had questioned witnesses. 'That guy was really good', Tom told me. 'He came up to me afterwards and asked me how I was, whether I was ok. I really appreciated that.'

The aftermath of the suicide saw a series of political struggles at Locksdon. The other detainees used the death of the man as a spur for action to remonstrate against the Home Office and the immigration system. They became angry and restless. Graffiti appeared in the dorms – 'The Home Office killed X' – and there was a spate of suicide threats, self-harm incidents and food refusals. The officers felt a qualitative change in the atmosphere of the establishment: a bubbling of 'trouble' and indiscipline. The fall-out provided openings for other men to stake claims and register protest through their bodies, and officers found themselves responding to increased numbers of food refusals and incidents of indiscipline.

My interest is in the fragile mutual concern between Tom and the detainee in this instance. This encounter, when placed alongside the objectifying, disengaged and antagonistic relationships of the centre, was a qualitatively different kind of engagement. It involved a mutual recognition and care, a spontaneous concern for the other and a dissolving of the boundaries which both officers and detainees saw to permeate life at Locksdon. This encounter was ethical in character, I would argue. Josephides argues that ethical goodness is characterised by 'unmediated recognition and generous action without calculation' (2010: 390). She cites Paul Ricoeur's distinction between ethics and morality, where ethics is the pursuance of ends which are compatible with human flourishing, unconnected to any particular moral code. Acting from a deontological sense of duty within this *telos*, human beings concretise the form of ethical life in moral norms (Josephides 2003a: 63). Ethical aims must legitimate the elevation of the particular moral norm to the universal, while moral norms must legitimate the applicability of the general to the particular. For Ricoeur, the universal in the particular is 'nothing other than the idea of humanity' (in Josephides 2003a: 63). How can this idea of humanity, and its 'unmediated recognition', help us to understand the encounter between Tom and the detainee?

Kant placed 'humanity' centrally in his vision of moral life. More particularly, it is shared human reason, and acting in respect for this shared reason, that is at the heart of acting morally. Ethical action is to act 'in such a way that you always treat humanity, whether in your own person or in the person of another, never simply as a means, but always at the same time as an end' (Kant 1948: 91). In other words, we must ask ourselves in all circumstances whether our actions are 'compatible with the Idea of humanity as an end in itself?' (Kant 1948: 91). With the categorical imperative as a guide, all people, by virtue of their reason alone, are 'well able to distinguish, in all cases that present themselves, what is good or evil, right or wrong ...' (Kant 1948: 69). We are called to obey the moral law and do our duty from a sense of respect for the personhood of others, but also our own personhood. Human goodness comes from struggling to do our duty to others despite the obstacles erected by unruly influences, our desires and our inclinations. This deontological conception of morality, places an emphasis on procedure and duty rather than effects and motives.

Emmanuel Levinas draws a 'radical conclusion' from Kant's solution to the mysteries of the 'moral law inside me', argues Bauman (1993: 49), but only this radicalism may do justice to Kant's conception of morality as a posture guided solely by the concern for the other *for the other's sake*, and the respect for the other as a free subject and the 'end in itself' (1993: 49). Levinas rejects formulaic and deontological concepts of moral life. In contrast to Kant's rational individual, Levinas conjures an uncertain moral subject whose ethical responsibility to others is not a duty, or a matter of following rules, or conforming to norms. Rather, he sees ethics to be a responsibility which constitutes the self. Levinas organises his discussion of ethical life around the approach of the unknown other. As Josephides (2010) summarises, our relation with the other can be defined by difference as foreignness, or else as radical alterity. Otherness as foreignness and difference can, as Kristeva (1982, 1991) argues, be shaped by hatred, fear or unease. This unease emerges from our own unknowable psyche. We are, she argues, 'strangers to ourselves', and in this sense otherness is, in fact, nothing other than an integral facet of sameness and familiarity (Kristeva 1991: 181). As Josephides (2010: 391) argues, 'exteriority and interiority do not define foreignness and ... foreignness is a projection of a part of the self that is feared'.

The approach of the unknown other may prompt fear, hatred and disquiet. The other may prompt me to apply categories and ways of knowing which, in an egocentric way, make the other 'like me' – an extension of my self, or an object to be manipulated for my own ends. Efforts to engage with the other which subsume him or her under categories to make him or her an object in my world is a reductive injustice to his or her uniqueness as a separate entity. Try as I might, however, there is something which always evades capture in the other, and we are drawn towards the other precisely because of the remoteness, unknowability and separation of the other person (Josephides 2010: 393; Wild 1979: 19). This is the other in Levinas' sense – free, separate and unreachable. Living alongside other people in social life might well involve the application of systematic and objectifying ways of knowing and interacting. It might also, however, prompt engagement which respects the absolute difference and unknowability of the other. For Levinas, this is language: true conversation and true engagement comes from 'freely making a choice for generosity and communication, i.e. for the social' (Wild 1979: 15). Reaching toward the other is sociality and it implicates me in an ethical relationship. In responding to the other, Levinas argues, I become responsible and this ethical responsibility constitutes me. That is, I am not a pre-existing social subject who decides to abide by moral codes; I become a subject through my ethical responsibilities to other people, through social life among others. As Keenan summarises:

> I am in the accusative, overtaken and made to answer, because I am exposed to others … from the start, such as it is. Others do not befall me, like a terrible accident that disfigures an integral self. And I do not respond or find myself obligated because some self precedes mine and addresses me, but because I am always already involved and entangled with others, always caught up with answering, from the start: we begin by responding. (1997: 21)

The responsibility that is unleashed by the approach of others is, according to Levinas, a responsibility that only I can bear: '[t]o be a self is to be responsible before having done anything', he argues, and '[t]o be a "self" is always to have one degree of responsibility more' (1996: 94, 91). For those concerned with the 'moral grammar of everyday life' (Critchley 1992: 27), Levinas urges us to think about the pre-eminence of the social relationships between people in everyday contexts. His is a vision of ethical life which appears at odds with Kantian notions of moral duty, and with moral life as a series of norms, merely 'a form of socially sanctioned behaviour' (Parkin 1985: 5). As Bauman argues, the comfort of measuring ourselves by what everyone else is doing and calling it duty will never quiet the conscience, the 'gnawing worm of self-distaste'

(1993: 53). What makes the self moral is not reducible to making 'correct decisions', but is located in the 'unfounded, non-rational, non-calculable urge to stretch towards others' (1993: 247).

Detention centres like Locksdon might appear to be the most inhospitable of places for a consideration of ethical responses. As I have argued, the detention centre is a rationalised, disciplinary institution, in which tasks are broken down and administered upon detainees not as persons but as objects. The ideal detainee is a type of non-presence – a featureless, reduced and abstracted 'body'. Despite their investment in the divisions of the regime, their practised indifference and suspicious stance towards detainees, the Locksdon officers, I argue, could not avoid the approach of the other, in Levinas's terms, and this unleashed a responsibility that was theirs alone. The 'floating responsibility' of the border apparatus system comes to rest with individual officers like Tom, who find themselves in the moment accountable for the life of the other.

Tom and the detainee shared an experience that was disturbing for them both, and which rendered them equally vulnerable in the face of a larger drama. While Tom remained aware of the usefulness of his actions in future dealings with the detainees, he appreciated the fact that the detainee had enquired after his (Tom's) welfare. The detainee had acknowledged the difficulty Tom must have endured in the incident, and had treated him not as an officer and custodian, but as a person. Tom, in turn, felt concern for the detainee. He had seen the detainee acting admirably and generously and had been given cause to reflect on the detainee as a person. Having made this imaginative leap, Tom found it hard not to extend care that was not manipulative or calculating, but which recognised the detainee in his or her singularity. In the act of resuscitating the detainee, the responsibility that Levinas speaks of called to Tom. Tom's presence made him alone answerable in that moment. Within this newly configured space of mutuality, the witness detainee was moved to enquire after Tom's well-being, as an end in himself, a person who may have been shocked, upset and horrified by the death, but who still assumed responsibility and tried his best, despite knowing the man was dead. Tom, in return, reached back to the detainee. I would like to draw out two points from this case.

Bodily vulnerability

I would argue that the detainee's death produced, in Jackson's terms (1998), an intersubjective embodied experience. Tom's efforts to save the man and the detainees' witnessing of the events were an encounter with the extremes of the detention regime, where men every day found (and find) themselves in situations of desperation and complete powerlessness. Unable to legally challenge or refuse his impending deportation to an uncertain and perhaps threatening future, the suicidal detainee took his own life. This act was the logical conclusion of his biopolitical state in detention, and the power that was wielded over him in Agamben's terms (1998) – without the protection of law or sovereign power, yet subject to their full exclusionary power. The staff and detainees who saw the man's death witnessed a single life made completely bare, with no other way to proceed.

I described in chapter 5 the intersubjective experience of violence, and how shared physical struggles and bodily experiences with fellow officers were related to camaraderie, solidarity and loyalty in the moment of being made vulnerable and of suppressing the unruly detainee. In the aftermath of the suicide, I would argue that another kind of intersubjective experience was fostered. The shared witnessing of the man's death produced in detainee and officer alike a disturbed sense of being in the detention centre, one where previous certainties and entrenched judgements about one another fell away. The people gathered to confront a man's death were faced with what Kristeva (1991), after Freud, calls the uncanny – that which has come to light but which should have remained hidden, the unfamiliarity of our mortality revealed to us in the alien and disturbing (see also Kearney 2003). A similar argument is made by Nussbaum (2004) when she claims that feelings of fear towards otherness originate from a dread of mortality, a projection onto others of the fear of our own fleshy vulnerability. In the suicide at Locksdon, the officer and detainee alike came face to face with the uncanny moment of death and also with the biopolitical logic of the detention regime at its limit. This disturbing event shocked those who witnessed it, producing a moment of existential uncertainty and ambiguity.

This ambiguity and rupture from 'the norm' was physically embodied and experienced – by Tom on the cold stone floor, struggling to bear the man's weight, exhausted by the effort of resuscitation, gazing into a dead man's lifeless eyes, and also by the detainees roused from sleep by the alarm bell and gathered helplessly to watch. The embodied and physical sensations of the uncanny moment were important. As Jackson (1998) describes, intersubjectivity involves an unstable interplay between self and other, and is shaped by embodied sensations, dispositions and practices. Viewed as a physical moment of shock and an experience that was intersubjectively shared, the suicide crystallised the relational aspects of self and other in social life. The shared embodied experience of a life at the threshold of death produced a new awareness of the relationship between self and other. No longer divided, or atomised, or kept at a distance, the detainees and officers found themselves located in a space of mutuality and uncertainty. In this sense, the rupture of the death produced, an 'agentive and creative moment' (Grønseth forthcoming) and a sense of estrangement and alienation that disturbed the familiar routines of the centre. As Grønseth argues, entering a zone of 'between' via the physical experience of alienation, pain and suffering (her example is Tamil refugees in Norway) can lead to the creation of 'existential solidarity' that erodes social and cultural divisions between people. Embodied, physical sensations of pain and suffering within and between people, then, can produce shocks or ruptures that force a new sense of relating to the world, a new scopic regime, perhaps, or a new awareness of other people.

At Locksdon, the witnessing of the suicide, and the physical sensations of encountering death forced detainees and officers alike into a new and uncertain moral space. The intersubjective moment shattered the established judgements, assumptions and perspectives that were predominant within social interaction in the centre, and prompted an altered experiential relationship between self and other. That is, shared existential experiences within fraught moments like this produced a heightened awareness of related and shared (bodily) vulnerability and awareness of a mutual capacity for suffering. When Sartre (1975) describes an existential 'human universality of condition', he points to 'the necessities of being in the world, of having to labor and to die there'. 'The human', then, is to be found in our shared embodiment, not in the sense of embodied experience being 'the same', or more fundamental than social and cultural sense-making, but in the 'grounding experiences' of life as it is lived (Josephides 2003b) that we recognise in others (see Honneth 2001; Nussbaum 2001, 2004; Turner 2002: 59). In the uncanny moment of death, and in the unfamiliar and shocking physical experiences forced upon Tom and the detainee, the borders between them dissolved and the unquestioned 'self-evidence' of centre life was thrown into relief and into question. This physical rupture produced a fragile empathetic concern for the other.

Ethics and emotion

The recognition of one's related vulnerability is an important epistemological requirement for empathetic and compassionate responses to the other (Nussbaum 2001). Empathy in Nussbaum's (2004) terms is the imaginative reconstruction of another person's experience. Our empathetic reconstruction of others' experience allows the other to become an object of compassion and concern. Compassion is a belief that the other person's suffering is serious and undeserved, and that the possibilities of the sufferer are in some way similar to ours (Nussbaum 2001: 66, 327, 300–1). That is, compassion is 'eudaimonistic': we understand the experiences of others through what we ourselves have experienced. This is not the same as reductively saying that others' experiences are 'the same as my own', but rather that I understand the world of the other by imaginatively extending outwards from my own social and cultural world.

If compassion and empathy are linked to the acknowledgement of our related and mutual vulnerability, then they are undeniably ethical in character. Deontological conceptions of moral life, with their emphasis on discipline, reason and procedure rather than effects, view emotions as capricious and unruly passions. Kant, for instance, based his moral theory on a criterion from which he believed no rational agent could be excluded: reason (Blum 1980: 15, 34) and saw moral virtue to lie in controlling emotional 'impulses' in order to fulfil one's duty. Yet emotions are far more complex than commonsense characterisations might suggest. Josephides (2003a: 60–1) cites Solomon, who sees emotions not as feelings, but as interpretations and forms of judgement that allow us to constitute the world of our experience. Emotions are functional realms of actions, socially constructed categories, evaluative judgements and ideological discourses reinforcing power relationships (Svašek 2002: 10). They are forms of interpersonal communication, a way of being-in-the-world, of engaging others and constituting selfhood (Parkinson 1995: 4). Nussbaum (2001) sees emotions as intelligent responses and, as such, they are ethical and social/political, related to the questions of what is worth caring about and how people should live: they are appraisals which ascribe importance to things and people outside our control, and thus point to our incompleteness and lack of self-sufficiency.

In the case of the suicide at Locksdon, the physical sensation of estrangement from a normal state of affairs, and a ruptured sense of relating to one another, was productive of, and related to, an empathetic encounter between Tom and the detainee. Having been thrust into an uncanny and disorienting situation, which I have argued was an intersubjectively created and experienced within and between bodies, the extension of empathy to the other was hard to withhold. More than this, having imaginatively reached across the social and political divisions of the detention centre, the extension of empathy became the basis for the commitment to treat the other as an end in moral terms. In the simple, apparently inconsequential, act of enquiring after one another's welfare, the officer and detainee acted, in Josephides' (2010: 390) words, with respect within 'an unmediated and pre-reflective recognition of the other'.

Of course, empathy can be inaccurate or crude and compassion can be inconsistent and exclusionary (Nussbaum 2001: 300–1, 327–8, 336). Compassion towards some people can reinforce boundaries with others and can entrench hierarchies of race, gender and class (Nussbaum 2001: 386–7; see also Ahmed 2004; Berlant 2004). All kinds of social barriers can erode the imaginative link to other people and thus impede compassion (Cohen 2002). Those who wish to foster cruelty remove the conditions for the imagination of similarity. The truth of the accusation that empathy and compassion can be partial and particular responses does not mean that emotions like empathy are not ethical guides. In Locksdon it is clear that emotional states were productive of exclusionary moral discourse and actions in everyday social life (fear exacerbated the craving for control and security, solidarity with colleagues could silence others and make it possible to ignore the moral claims of detainees) but they could also produce inclusive ethical encounters. So, while some emotions involved a strong boundary between self and other, other emotions 'expanded the boundaries of the self' (Nussbaum 2001: 300); empathy and compassion emerging from feelings and experiences of commonality brought about in everyday interaction could lead to the development of a responsible response to the other.

A COSMOPOLITAN MORAL RESPONSE

I argue that a vision of ethics as responsibility for the other, as Levinas describes it, is, in social life, a contradictory and ambivalent phenomenon. The recognition of, and respect for 'humanity' that Levinas and Kant both place at the heart of moral action are grounded within, and emerge from, everyday experiences and embodied dispositions. Despite the techniques and practices enacted at Locksdon to keep the detainees as 'others', some detainees emerged, and were recognised, as *persons* and individuals – like the organiser of the detainee protest described in chapter 5. Although the officers invested in the meaningful barrier between them and the detainees, they could not avoid acknowledging their shared humanity in the fraught daily life of detention. In the case of Tom and the detainee, this acknowledgement took place within an intersubjectively experienced embodied shock of vulnerability, and a fragile emotional extension outwards. The ethical encounter as a recognition and acknowledgement of 'humanity' was thus not an abstract deliberation, nor a reductive move, but one that was grounded in people's experiences of life being led. Without romanticising these occurrences, at Locksdon I would suggest that ethical encounters like these challenged the official politicised moral classifications, and locally produced social and moral boundaries, which saturated centre life and ordered relations between officers and detainees.

These ethical encounters, I argue, were *cosmopolitan* in character, where differences were momentarily overcome, or else folded into a response that had mutuality at its core. Cosmopolitanism is often associated with a kind of 'openness' to cultural difference and orientation to otherness, a dabbling in difference, and expertise in negotiating the unfamiliar or a political engagement beyond local or national frontiers (see Beck 2002; Hannerz 1990). As a moral stance, however, cosmopolitanism can trace its roots back to the Stoics. Refuting the superiority of the *polis*, the Stoics saw the basis of human community to be the shared capacity for reason. Allied to the human capacity for reason is our shared (bodily) vulnerability, our capacity for suffering and our shared fear of death (see Honneth 2001; Nussbaum 2001, 2004; Turner 2002: 59). Given this shared capacity, it makes no sense to differentiate on the grounds of class, locality, nationality or ethnicity, and our moral and political life, they believed, should reflect this. A cosmopolitan moral response, then, is one that, in its experience and enactment, transcends social, cultural and political boundaries and is based instead on what is shared or mutually experienced. Cosmopolitanism, in the case of Tom and the detainee, was an embodied and uncertain reaching towards the other embedded in the existential experience of life (see Josephides and Hall forthcoming). The emergence of mutuality was not self-consciously structured from a respect for diversity and difference, but was based on a mutual acknowledgement and recognition of the other that retained his or her difference.

The emergence of empathy at Locksdon was interesting, not least because it was a more incongruous and unexpected reaction. Empathy and the imagination of similarity were not structured by abstract ideas and ideals about shared humanity or cosmopolitanism, but by everyday moral criteria about good behaviour, a life well led and worthy conduct. The officers 'built bridges' towards those detainees with whom they believed they shared certain moral dispositions and values, or those detainees who had impressed their undeniable personhood upon the officers and who had forced them to acknowledge a shared existence. Locksdon officers used ideas connected to work, personal fortitude and 'deservingness' to build boundaries and differentiate between 'good' people and 'scroungers'. These same ideas became mobilised when seeking to find a common ground and bridge boundaries between themselves and other detainees.

What is the significance of this cosmopolitan moment of recognition between the officer and the detainee? I would like to draw out the way that encounters like the one between Tom and the detainee challenged the politicised and moralised divisions of the securitised immigration system. 'Organisation', as Bauman argues, keeps moral responsibility 'afloat' (1993: 125–6), that is, unattached to a particular person or action. This removal of moral responsibility is achieved by the organisation of distance between action and result. It is also achieved by exempting some 'others' from the class of potential objects of moral responsibility and by 'dissembling' human objects of action into aggregates of specific traits so it becomes hard to recompose the person from the disparate items. Removing the human face from people denies them status as moral subjects and separates moral impulse from social organisation (Bauman 1993: 125–8). In many ways, the entire governmental regime in which 'out-of-place' people find themselves in the UK is organised to preclude the humanity of people like the detainees. The policies of separation and isolation that characterise the reception of people into the UK point to a general ethos of fear, which seeks to maintain the strangers in positions of ambiguity and uncertainty. They are relegated to a 'sphere of irrelevance' and 'emotionally void disattention' (Bauman 1993: 153, 154).

At Locksdon, where the objectification and social isolation of excluded populations found extreme expression, the officers were concerned to maintain the strict boundaries between national and moral insiders and outsiders. However, the officers were placed in close contact with the detainees. This makes the boundary between them even more fraught. Despite the techniques and practices enacted at Locksdon to keep the detainees as 'others', the possibility of an ethical encounter was never wholly effaced. It was the officers in their daily work routines who found themselves burdened with the effects of immigration decisions on men's status, of impending deportation orders and of the anguish of being detained for interminable periods. It was they who had to arrange for a special phone call to a detainee's family member, who had to monitor a depressed man, who had to help a detainee retrieve his lost possessions, or who had to break the news of an impending deportation. The face of the detainees was drawn into focus within the detention regime in fraught moments like the suicide I have described and, once recognised, could not be ignored.

Describing Levinas's account of language, Wild (1979: 15) argues that true speaking 'becomes serious only when we pay attention to the other and take account of him and the strange world he inhabits'. In the choice to respond to the other, I offer something (my view of the world, my assumptions), and in being offered up, these views are exposed to question and 'an escape from egotism becomes possible' (Wild 1979: 14–15). For Levinas, as Josephides (2010) summarises, it is language that allows us to live alongside the other while leaving otherness intact (see Wild 1979: 13). Yet, as Josephides (2010) argues, Levinas's account stops 'at the encounter'. Referring to the interchange that enables us to know and respond to the other in his or her difference, she remains 'unconvinced that a relation of knowing, initiated by exchange, can return to a state of absoluteness for both the knower and the known' (2010: 394). That is, the relationship that is created when I respond to the other transforms us both – the response to the other forces an acknowledgement of my 'arbitrary views and attitudes' (Wild 1979: 15).

Everyday life in detention exposed the arbitrariness of the border that separates 'us' from 'the other', and also exposed the gaps between politics and morality, between the political and social organisation of our relations with others and the existential and ethical experience of life in its complexity. As Kristeva observes, foreigners 'reveal the confrontation between political reason and moral reason' (1991: 96). Certainly life as it was lived in detention threw up situations where officers could not retreat to familiar, comfortable categories and classifications. It was in this way that the ethical response between officer and detainee was a critique in the sense that Foucault describes it – to question that which seems certain, to 'bring into relief the very framework of evaluation' and bringing an 'interrogatory relation to the field of categorization itself' (Butler 2002: 214). The critical potential of ethical encounters like the one experienced by Tom and the detainee lies in the way it throws into question the divisions and differences which are seen to be the self-evident cause of detention and the necessary product of the regime. The possibility of an ethical encounter in the detention centre points to the fragile possibility of transformation and challenge of the biopolitical completeness of the governmental control of risky and out-of-place subjects.

Conclusion

On 8 April 2009, news broke that the UK police and security agencies had foiled a major planned terrorist bomb plot and had arrested twelve men in Manchester under the UK Terrorism Act 2000. The men, all but one of them Pakistani, had been under surveillance since their arrival in Britain on student visas. One of the arrested men was released shortly after, but the remaining eleven men were held for two weeks under the Terrorism Act as the police investigated the plot and the men's alleged terrorist activities. By 22 April, however, Operation Pathway was causing controversy when it emerged that police had failed to find any evidence that could be used to charge the men. One of the suspects, a UK national, was released, but the remaining men were 'transferred into immigration custody' as Lord Carlile (then independent reviewer of the Terrorism Act) put it (2009: 1) – detained pending their deportation in the name of national security.

By early 2010, the men were still in custody, despite not having being charged with any crime. Ten of the men's cases had been before the Special Immigration Appeals Commission (SIAC) but bail had been denied and, by May 2010, these men had left the UK for Pakistan, still protesting their innocence. One of the remaining men, Abid Naseer, was by this time suspected of being an al-Qaida operative. An SIAC hearing concluded that while there was information that strongly suggested Naseer's involvement in terrorist activity (a series of apparently coded emails to a known al-Qaida associate about ingredients for bombs, for instance), he could not be deported to Pakistan because he was likely to be killed or tortured (SIAC 2010). Unable to be prosecuted, or deported, yet still deemed a risk to national security, he remained subject to a control order – a series of restrictions and regulations regarding his movements, communications and associations. By January 2011, when Naseer hit the headlines again, he was to be extradited to the US to stand trial for allegedly planning a series of terrorist bomb attacks.

The Manchester case highlights the difficulties that the police and security agencies encounter in the fight against terrorist threats. 'The authorities', as Lord Carlile summed up, 'had no specific information as to where the suspected terrorist event [in Manchester] was to occur, nor any precise knowledge as to its nature' (2009: 4). More than this, 'none of the arrests were made on a full evidential foundation, as at the time of the arrests no specific offence had been identified'. In the absence of 'an offence' or 'evidence', the authorities instead reported a range of suspicious activities and communications. The Manchester men were arrested, essentially, for 'being terrorists', although 'being a terrorist' cannot constitute the factual basis for any charge without an offence (Carlile 2009: 10). The power of the Home Secretary to detain or deport, in the name of national security, foreign nationals who are suspected of 'being a terrorist', yet against whom no legal evidence can be found, has been roundly criticised by human rights and civil liberties groups (see Justice 2009; Liberty 2010). They condemn, in particular, the used of 'secret material' in such cases – intelligence reports from UK and foreign security agencies, surveillance information such as suspicious emails, travel patterns, information about links to terrorist groups, or known suspects, and associations between people and places. 'Closed information' is regularly heard by the SIAC and frequently forms the basis of judgments about deportation and detention on national security grounds. Crucially, closed and secret material is withheld from the men and their legal advocates. Instead, a 'special advocate' is appointed who argues for the appellant in the closed hearing, but who cannot discuss the information with them. For Liberty (2011: 15) the use of secret material is 'the complete abrogation of the right to fair trial and the presumption of innocence': it places restrictions on liberty based 'on suspicion rather than proof' and renders the subject 'unable to test the case against him'.

The term used in the SIAC judgment to describe what happened to the Manchester suspects – 'released without charge into immigration detention' (SIAC 2010: 1) – captures what is controversial about the contemporary detention and deportation powers wielded in the name of national security. How is it possible for a person be 'released without charge into detention'? What kind of release is this? Inter-disciplinary social and political research has circled this question as an emblem of the politics of the war on terror, asking how the decisions taken about people regarded as 'not being conducive to the public good' are productive of particular exclusionary and exceptional measures. In the case of men like Abid Naseer, the kind of power embodied by the Home Secretary – a power that is shored up by law, and which also seems to 'be in tension' with law (see Carlile 2009) – is sovereign in Agamben's sense. It governs by 'taking outside', yet retaining a hold, by suspending people in a liminal and ambiguous position.

One of the most important elements of the Manchester case, for me, is the way the case revealed a range of authorities – police, security agencies, intelligence authorities, immigration judges – whose 'reasonable suspicion' and 'reasoned decisions' form the frontier of national security. It has always been the case that state policy and state decisions are 'made' at 'street level' by individuals in context (Lipsky 1980; see also Fuglerud 2004; Heyman 1995, 2000; Herzfeld 1992; Shore and Wright 1997). However, the contemporary dispersal and proliferation of 'professionals of unease management' (Bigo 2001, 2002) has made the sovereign security decision more than ever a complex interplay of private and public authorities (Amoore 2008). The self-proclaimed 'capacity to class and prioritize the threats, to determine what exactly constitutes security' (Bigo 2008: 8) is shaping new forms and operations of power and control. The recognition of 'threat' and 'security' – which forms the basis for control orders, deportations and indefinite detentions in the case of the Manchester 'bombers' – is dispersed within a governmental field, but it is also associated with a resurgent and 'resurrected sovereignty' (Butler 2004). As 'the state' appears to dissolve in its unified capacity 'to secure' (the nation, the border, its citizens), so 'petty sovereigns abound' (Butler 2004: 56) in bureaucracies, organisations and administrations.

This book has focused on one particular site of contemporary border politics and national security, and its aim has been to take seriously what people think and believe they are doing in this site. I have examined the micro-political processes of detention from the point of view of staff as one facet of understanding how 'the custody of the immigration and border authorities' operates. People like the officers at Locksdon are not publicly prominent nor do they have the high status associated with traditional bearers of sovereign power and authority. Their role is a difficult one: to create a 'secure but humane' regime for people designated 'illegal', or a security risk, or unidentifiable. Yet I have demonstrated that the power they embody constitutes, in the final instance, the national securitised border. For men like Naseer – 'released into the custody' of the UKBA for indefinite periods – it is people like the Locksdon officers whose judgements, decisions and actions constitute 'security', 'the border', 'exclusion' as it is brought to bear on individual lives. The chapters have collectively argued that a detailed account of how power is used, experienced and resisted in the everyday sites of security (like the detention centre), where security is precariously achieved, might offer a deeper understanding of the production of securitised border controls in the contemporary political terrain.

SECURING THE BORDER

I have shown that the line between security and insecurity in detention is elaborated and produced within fraught social relationships between and among detainees and officers in the everyday routines of centre life. I have argued that actions in the name of security are biopolitical, emerging from, investing and encircling individual bodies, and producing vulnerable and excluded detainee populations. In chapter 2, I described the visual frontiers of security at Locksdon, and how the officers' habits of vigilance produced the detainees as de-individualised and 'object-like' within the regime. At Locksdon, issues of surveillance and invigilation combined in an intimate and concentrated set of bodily practices. Bodywatching, I argued, constituted the difference and distance between the detainees and officers.

On close inspection, the hyper-vigilant gaze of the officers was not a rational application of a disinterested and objective gaze, but a tense, mistrustful and suspicious bodily disposition. As the officers moved around the centre, encountering colleagues and detainees, they experienced feelings and sensations of trepidation, anxiety and unease provoked by the 'unknown' detainee. These feelings and sensations distilled into a precautionary and anticipatory visuality that was indifferent to the detainee as person even as it was highly attentive. The 'politics of fear' and 'neurosis' that are said to shape contemporary political subjectivity in the West (see Isin 2004; Massumi 2005) become intertwined with other kinds of emotions and moods in detention's intimate networks of power. At Locksdon, the officers' desire to keep the initiative and maintain control was infused with apprehension about the unknown capacities of the detainees, but also feelings of anger and frustration. The everyday production of security at Locksdon was as frequently shaped by resentment and irritation as it was by fear and anxiety. As chapter 4 argues, the regularised and predictable detention regime was produced within officers' daily banal struggles to order disobedient bodies, to elicit subservience, to inculcate disciplined movement. These struggles, through which security was precariously achieved, produced humiliation and frustration for detainees, officers and staff alike. The meaning and enactment of security at Locksdon could never be known in advance, but was always emerging from the complex and messy social life of the centre. It was a feeling experienced by individuals in context, and a collective mood that shifted and distilled around individual 'troublemaker' detainees.

I have shown that a consideration of the gender relations of the detention centre illuminated its everyday forms of control. The multiple boundaries at issue in the detention centre (insider/outsider, legal/illegal, secure/insecure) were always gendered and gendering. The officers' sense of maintaining the initiative was frequently a masculine endeavour. This was particularly the case, for instance, in the use of force to uphold the regime – simultaneously the expression of (male) officers' active, forceful and authoritative masculinity and the curtailment and denigration of detainees' capacity to act (see chapter 5). The regime as the set of practices controlling the detainees was shaped by the friendships and relationships between officers, forged within mundane working life and the periodic excitement of crises. As chapter 3 argued, understanding the regime and how it organised boundaries between officers and detainees would be impossible without understanding the (gendered) obligations, solidarities and intimacies that men and women experienced with their colleagues as part of their working life.

My discussion offered a grounded account of how security was produced at Locksdon at a particular time. As a counterbalance to the more abstract accounts of security and the governance of mobility in the contemporary context, it has 'fleshed out' the precise relationship between detainees' mobile bodies (in the sense of being non-national border crossers, but also lively detained subjects) and the concerns of security at Locksdon. It has placed centrally the 'security imagination' of the officers – their active, productive beliefs and thoughts about the detainees and the work they do – and how this security imagination shaped life for everyone in the centre. Paying close attention to the security imagination of the officers within the socio-cultural and micro-political context was important, I argue, because it directed and shaped the enactment of decisions and judgements at the centre.

DECIDING THE BORDER

The officers had a strong sense of their 'Britishness', but seemed uncertain about its meaning, or its future in the contemporary world. More particularly, their sense of 'nationness' was projected outwards from their experiences of solidarity with their colleagues and friends in everyday life. 'Nationness' was understood as an encompassing world order which 'naturally' structured moral, political and social boundaries. The officers' personal experiences of detainees within the border zone of the detention centre contrasted with their feelings of 'home' and 'belonging' to create a sense of threat and encroaching disorder. Their criticisms turned against people in 'the system' and other groups in society ('immigration', the 'do-gooders'), whose actions in relation to border decisions threatened the moral order cherished by the officers. The detainees became tools for thinking about and contesting the kind of social and political world that was being brought into being by the border apparatus of which the officers were a part (see chapter 5).

I showed how issues of solidarity and friendship were strong moral criteria against which people were judged at Locksdon (see chapter 3). I argued that the privileging of 'group' was linked to the strong sense of 'situatedness' that emerged from the officers' life experiences and working relationships. Being moral was a matter of carefully negotiating and privileging webs of relationships in a close-knit milieu. The 'seething' social atmosphere at Locksdon was experienced both negatively and positively; as a form of pressure and conformity, but also as a source of intimacy and attachment. Privileging relevant others had consequences for the detainees, whose outsider status meant they were silenced. The officers emphasised the importance of discipline, self-provision, work and personal responsibility. Against these criteria, the detainees were seen as lacking. The officers had pragmatic ways of thinking about the things that people have in common: work, self-provision, 'fitting in' and 'getting on with it'. These criteria were used to criticise some detainees, while also being used to admit other detainees to the officers' 'imagined moral community'.

The officer's expert eye, then, was constantly working to 'diagnose' what Foucault (2003) calls 'psycho-moral' failings among the detainees. The gaps in knowledge around a man were colonised by officers' expert connoisseurship, masquerading as infallible authority and simple common sense. Bodywatching attentiveness was concerned to locate indiscipline and 'trouble' before its manifestation. It was also concerned to 'double' insubordination to their (the officers') own authority as 'irregularity in relation to certain rules which may be physiological, psychological, or moral' (Foucault 2003: 16). In the detainees' petty misdemeanours, the officers saw moral faults; in the detainees' bodily resistance, the officers found over-emotionality; in the detainees' protests, the officers discovered an inappropriate and wilful subject. Foucault (2003: 18) argues that psychiatric expert opinion transfers the 'point of application of punishment from the offence defined by the law to criminality evaluated from a psycho-moral point of view'. In Locksdon, similarly, the officers doubled the status of being detained under immigration law with a nebulous and imprecise illegality and moral failing. The officer's expert eye could discern the 'truth' about a detainee's character as it revealed itself in everyday activity. More importantly, the officers' expertise was concerned with correcting and punishing infractions against their authority, which in the border zone constituted the line between inside and outside, between national security and threat. As I argued in chapter 5, the officers' discretionary judgements were concerned with upholding the 'wiggly lines' of detention, but they were also concerned with readjusting the detention centre as a punitive probationary zone. Unmoored from legitimate practices of reform associated with the prison, the disciplinary techniques mobilised by Locksdon officers were concerned with producing an ideal type docile detainee *as the officers envisaged him*. The reformatory, penal and rehabilitative ethos of the prison infused the logic of the detention routine – the Seg Unit was as much a punishment for insubordination as a quest for security, a violent encounter was as much a forceful correction of imbalances of power as a protective measure.

The ideal type of detainee (deserving, subservient, compliant) and his antithesis (the wilful, disobedient and undeserving detainee) mobilised a classificatory system that was independent of the official Home Office designations about status and deportations. The sovereign 'drawing of lines' (Edkins and Pin-Fat 2004) between forms of life became, in Locksdon, dispersed into a series of everyday decisions taken by officers – to use force, to isolate from association, to 'ghost out' or 'wrap up'. Quite distinct from the official decision to expel or release – by SIAC, for instance, or at the Immigration and Asylum Tribunal – these banal acts were, nevertheless, sovereign in Agamben's sense. They were productive of a biopolitical body which was 'taken outside' to an ambiguous zone between the *Detention Centre Rules* and the discretionary application of correction and control favoured by the officers. These 'banal sovereignties' created and refreshed the officers' authority anew. Acts to disperse toxic characters, or separate troublemakers, or ghost out detainees was a 'taking of power' that shored up the officers' expertise and power to *decide* against a paradoxical feeling of powerlessness.

The decision, which Agamben, after Schmitt, places centrally within the operation of sovereign power, becomes in the detention centre a fraught notion. William Connolly, in his call for a more nuanced view of sovereign power and 'the exception', argues that '[s]overeign is that which decides an exception exists and how to decide it', but 'the that' is 'composed of a plurality of forces circulating through and under the positional sovereignty of the official arbitrating body' (2005: 145). Doty (2007) similarly questions the coherence of 'the decision'. She uses the example of border vigilantes in the US–Mexican desert to describe how citizens take the law into their own hands and invoke a different distinction between friend and enemy than that made by 'the sovereign'. 'The decision' might reinforce or change the law rather than suspend it and, she asks, 'can we ever ultimately pinpoint "the decision" or is it more accurately a conglomeration of dispersed decisions whose significance often goes unrecognized?' (Doty 2007: 116). In the case of Locksdon, the multiple decisions taken and judgements made by officers, and the forms of political subjectivity they produce, are 'more littered, layered and complex than Agamben allows' (Connolly 2005: 137). A focus on the social world of the detention centre places 'the exception' in a socio-cultural context, and reveals the way that decisions slip and slide between contested notions of friend, enemy, emergency, security. The officers, as state agents invested in the sovereign power to unleash violence, do not simply police the lines that have already been drawn between lives, but draw new ones in the biopolitical border zone of detention.

ENCOUNTERS AND ETHICS

The detention centre routine, as I have described it, was objectifying and unable to recognise men in their particularity, in the sense of acknowledging their individual experiences, traumas and suffering. The abstraction and division that is produced in the 'organisation' and 'administration' of out-of-place lives keeps moral responsibility detached from individuals and actions (Bauman 1993: 125). This detachment of moral responsibility is achieved by the organisation of distance between action and result. It is also achieved by 'disassembling' human objects of action into aggregates of traits so it becomes hard to recompose the person from the disparate items, and so tasks set for action on each item can be exempt from moral evaluation. Removing the human face from people denies them status as moral subjects and separates human moral impulse from social organisation (Bauman 1993: 125–8). At Locksdon, the disassembly of the detainee into a series of biological processes and social requirements (food, association, exercise) enabled the 'humane regime' to be achieved while still ignoring the detainee as a person.

For the officers, however, the practicalities of everyday life, and occasional experiences of mutuality with the detainees, led them to bridge political and moral boundaries, despite their continued investment in these boundaries that separated the detainees, placing them on the moral and political 'outside'. The extending of moral concern between officer and detainee contextually challenged the politicised distinctions made by the border regime. I have argued that this moral stance was cosmopolitan in character, in that it reflected in ethical action what is shared across political, social and cultural boundaries – an embodied exposure, a shared vulnerability, a mutual experience of the world. As a remedy against the indeterminacy and 'imaginary utopianism' of many studies of cosmopolitanism, Skrbis et al. (2004: 120–1) argue for empirical studies of mundane *existing* cosmopolitanisms to reveal the pragmatic nature of cosmopolitanism as a moral stance in mundane life. Recent studies have shown cosmopolitanism to be pragmatic schema required by (and resulting from) ordinary people's encounters with 'difference' as they make their way in the world, as well as an aesthetic framing of individual experience in shifting social contexts (see, for instance, Lamont 2000; Lamont and Aksartova 2002; Wardle 2000). 'The cosmopolitan' can also be found in shared capacities of mind and body and their associated existential predicaments (Wardle 2010: 384; see also Josephides and Hall, forthcoming). My discussion of Locksdon has demonstrated that empathy and the imagination of shared worlds are not structured by abstract ideas and ideals about 'universal humanity', but by everyday moral criteria about good behaviour, a life well led and worthy conduct, and also by emotions and the experience of life being led. The officers 'built bridges' towards those detainees with whom they believed they shared certain moral dispositions and values, or those detainees who impressed their undeniable presence as persons upon the officers. The production of 'cosmopolitan' dispositions among people (in this case, officers and detainees) was developed using personal experience and concerns, and mutuality at everyday levels. It also arose, as described in chapter 6, from a shared experience of shock or vulnerability, from physical sensations, and from an empathetic extending outwards towards the other.

In a discussion about the completeness and the impossibility of resistance that is often suggested by readings of Agamben, Jenny Edkins argues that Agamben himself suggests a way out of the political impasse conjured by his vision of sovereign power. Bare life, Agamben argues, can become a 'form-of-life' – a being 'which is only its own bare existence' and which 'being its own form remains inseparable from it' and 'over which power no longer seems to have any hold' (1998: 188). It is the very lack of identity that constitutes a 'threat the State cannot come to terms with' (Agamben 1993: 85). As Edkins and Pin-Fat suggest, the grammar of sovereign power is not effectively contested by counter-identity claims, for such actions merely fight over 'where the lines are drawn' (2004: 13). Instead, they argue, it is by neither refusing nor accepting the biopolitical distinctions that sovereign power seeks to draw that its logic may be interrupted. Bare life, then, has the potential to become 'explicitly and immediately political' (Agamben 1998: 153) – as Edkins has it, bare life is the constitutive outside of sovereignty which may also form 'the element that threatens its disruption from within' (2007: 86).

In the case of the suicide I described in chapter 6, banned, bare life offered a 'disruption from within'. The witnessing of a man's death, I argued, precipitated an ethical moment between detainee and officer that challenged the 'grammar of sovereign power' as it was lived in the detention centre. This was a hopeful, incongruous and unexpected reaction, and one that points to the complexity of ethical responsibility and recognition within social life. Presented as a counterbalance to the distressing and difficult work of the centre, and the desperation caused by detention, ethical encounters like these represented a critique and challenge to the logic of detention. This book has paid attention to the lived experience of detention, and it has shown that bare life – as a lived socio-political reality and as an embodied fleshy vulnerability – can potentially become the grounds for a fragile ethical recognition and acknowledgement that troubles the certainties of political exclusion and differentiation upon which the politics of contemporary mobility and security frequently rests. The social, cultural and political conditions in which ethical recognition and concern are produced in everyday life demand as much attention as the troubling proliferation of detention techniques described in this book.

Notes

1 INTRODUCTION: GOING INSIDE

1. All names are pseudonyms.
2. The experiences of asylum seekers and refugees in Britain and beyond have been the subject of a growing body of social science and policy literature (see, for example, Amnesty International 2005; Farah 2003; Knudsen 1995; Malkki 1995a, 1995b; Matlou 1999; McSpadden 1999).
3. As the London Detainee Support Group (2009: 10, 2010) has demonstrated, those who have been convicted of crimes in the UK (often in direct consequence of being rendered destitute by a rejected claim for asylum) have increasingly found themselves facing indefinite detention, with the Home Office operating a tacit presumption of detention for those who are subject to a deportation order following criminal conviction. The increase in the number of foreign-national ex-prisoners in immigration removal centres constitutes a marked development from the situation in 2002.
4. Despite ongoing efforts to harmonise member states' security and immigration initiatives (the Schengen Information System II, Frontex, the Common European Asylum System), there remains a reluctance to relinquish full and ultimate control over immigration, border and asylum policy to the EU (see Guild 2006; Guild and Bigo 2005; Guild et al. 2008). Detention practices are variable. Despite the existence of common standards of treatment pertaining to the reception and detention of people claiming asylum and the detention of migrants who do not have legal status, member states have variable procedures for administering asylum seekers, refugees and illegal immigrants, with distinct detention regimes. Migreurop's 2010 map of European detention facilities shows a 'chicken pox' of long- and short-term detention, reception and holding facilities for asylum seekers and illegal migrants spreading across EU member states, into EU-candidate countries and spilling over into North Africa, Russia and the Canary Islands in extra-territorial holding facilities (Conflitti Globali 2007). The Reception Conditions Directive 2003/9/CE, 2003 and Council Directive 2005/85/C, 2005 outline a legal framework for reception of asylum seekers and minimum standards for granting and withdrawing refugee status. Standards of care for the detention of migrants and asylum seekers are governed by the International Covenant on Civil and Political Rights (which protects people from arbitrary detention), as well as the European Convention on Human Rights, which does not prohibit the detention of these categories of person, but stipulates that it must be in accordance with law and a fair process. In essence, the administrative detention of asylum seekers in the West is highly controversial because it appears to be a 'penalty' and punishment of those who are asylum seekers under the terms of the 1951 United Nations Geneva Convention Relating to the Status of Refugees, on which international refugee protection standards are based.

5. Britain is known to have the largest immigration detention estate in Europe, but it is not alone in bolstering its detention capacity in recent years. In the US, for example, the civil detention of non-citizens has steadily increased since the 1996 Illegal Immigration Reform and Immigrants Responsibility Act and legislative shifts in the war on terror, notably the US Patriot Act and the Real ID Act (see Welch 2003; Welch and Schuster 2005a, 2005b; Zolberg 2006). Immigration and Customs Enforcement (ICE), the investigative branch of the Department of Homeland Security, detains over 230,000 non-citizens each year. Most detainees have no criminal history or terrorist connections, but are held under civil immigration law in Service Processing Centres, Contract Detention facilities and Intergovernmental Service Agreement facilities (mostly county jails and local prisons). The American Civil Liberties Union (ACLU 2008: 69) has previously labelled the conditions for immigration detainees 'punitive and unconstitutional'. Canada also has gradually solidified the legal basis for detention: the 2002 Immigration and Refugee Protection Act and the 2001 Anti-Terrorist Act have expanded immigration officers' powers to detain various categories of people, part of its tough new stance towards illegal immigration, organised crime and terrorists (see Pratt 2001, 2005). Australia has perhaps the most infamous record of 'mandatory detention' for those subject to immigration law. Anyone arriving without a visa, or passport, or necessary documentation is liable to be detained, including asylum seekers who make onshore applications. Australia's sustained policy of 'off-shoring' border controls and 'excising' sovereign territory from national law to prevent asylum seekers reaching national territory has attracted vehement international criticism (Hyndman and Mountz 2008) and in 2003, the United Nations High Commission for Refugees accused Australia of jeopardising 'the proper functioning of the international [refugee] protection regime' by its policies.

6. The UK Detention Estate includes designated IRCs like Locksdon, but also short-term holding facilities at ports of entry. People detained under the 1971 Immigration Act may also be held in police custody, or in prisons.

7. These members of staff are not prison officers, but wear uniform and perform security tasks and administrative duties in the establishment.

8. The detainees can take English courses leading to Pitman's qualifications, classes in business skills, numeracy skills, 'Training for Work' modules in health and safety, food hygiene and gardening, as well as computer courses, and art and music lessons.

9. Contemporary UK detention resonates with historical efforts to rationalise the border regime over the twentieth century by consolidating powers of confinement, detention and internment, which persistently invoked the 'threat' posed by the alien non-national and the need to secure the homeland, through emergency powers if necessary. The control of immigrants has frequently been bound up with concerns about protecting the limits of national welfare (Cohen 2002). The bases of British border controls, and the power to intern and deport non-nationals, were originally laid down amid anxious anti-alienism directed towards Russian and Jewish refugees leading up to the First World War (Burleston 1992; Pirouet 2001: 14; Stevens 1998: 10–16). These powers have been successively strengthened ever since, with emergency measures deemed necessary during wartime (such as internment during the Second World War) frequently being extended into peacetime (see Cesarini 1992). Contemporary detention, like wartime internment, confronts the ambiguous risk posed by

mobile or anomalous populations with forcible confinement and isolation (Bashford and Strange 2002). For a history of early British immigration and detention controls, see Cesarini 1992; Dummett and Nicol 1990; Holmes 1991; Panayi 1992, 1994; Schuster and Solomos 1999.

10. See HM Inspectorate of Prisons' immigration removal centre inspections: http://www.justice.gov.uk/publications/inspectorate-reports/hmi-prisons/immigration-removal-centres.

11. After the formal designation of Locksdon as an immigration removal centre in 2002, the governor of Locksdon was officially re-titled 'manager'. However, none of the officers at Locksdon used this term.

2   VISUAL PRACTICE AND THE SECURE REGIME

1. A new detainee could have arrived from a prison having completed a sentence for a criminal conviction, or from a police holding cell or another IRC. A range of documentation should have ideally accompanied the man, and could include: a movement notice from the detainee escorting and population management unit (DEPMU); files from a prison establishment; a detainee transferable document (DTD) from another removal centre. These files would contain information about a man's risk with regard to violence and self-harm. He would also be accompanied by an IS91 form, the authority to detain form from the immigration authorities, with details of a man's passage through the immigration estate and escort agencies.

2. Paragraph 7 of the *Detention Centre Rules* (2001) outlines the statutory instruments for searching detainees. Searching is '[f]or reasons of security and safety' and should be undertaken, 'in as seemly a manner as is consistent with discovering anything concealed'. Strip searching should never be 'in the sight of another detained person, or in the sight or presence of an officer or other person not of the same sex'. At the time of my fieldwork (2002–3), this strip search took place for all new detainees, and was performed behind a curtain. It involved the officer asking the detainee to pull down his trousers and pants, and take off his shirt and socks (not at the same time) to locate concealed weapons and note any distinguishing tattoos or scars, which were called out to the other officers for documentation. When I was at reception, officers would ask me to go into a side office for the process to make sure the detainees' privacy was protected. Towards the end of my time at Locksdon, the practice of strip searching all detainees at reception was abandoned. It belonged to the Prison Service set of rules and was not performed in other IRCs. See Crawley (2004) for a description of the strip search in prisons.

3. A copy of the photograph was passed to the establishment's police liaison officer for checks with criminal databases, another copy was sent to the immigration authorities, one was kept in a man's 'stat card' and one was attached to his summary sheet. Another photo was sent to health care.

4. A frequent cause of irritation for Locksdon staff at the time of my fieldwork was when escort contractor vans arrived too late to admit new detainees to Locksdon. If men arrived after 16.15, they were not accepted because the nursing staff were off duty. Detainees who had spent the best part of a day travelling in the back of an escort van could thus find themselves simply being returned to their original location.

5. Biometric identification systems aim precisely to lock down identity to the materiality of the body, but were not in widespread use in 2002.

6. The number of detainees was noted in a ledger in the centre office and movements in and out of the establishment were recorded as the day proceeded. Detainee numbers were also noted on a white board in the centre office for general reference. This number was checked with the gate area through the day, to ensure numbers of men going in and out were constantly tracked.

7. The lunchtime roll check was altered in spring 2003. Detainees were not locked in their dormitories at lunch. This brought Locksdon in line with other IRCs.

8. I take the notion of 'transposability' from Feldman (1991).

9. It was absolutely second nature for officers never to be alone with detainees, in case of accusations of abuse or because of the potential for violence or attack. This was not a verbalised or conscious organisation of bodies, but became an unspoken choreography through which officers were accompanied by colleagues in certain peripheral zones of the establishment (notably reception) that were hard to reach.

10. At the time, this was a self-harm document that was 'opened' on detainees who were known to be possible self-harm or suicide risk cases.

3   BEING THERE: SOCIAL LIFE IN THE CENTRE

1. During my fieldwork, Locksdon had one governor (male), one deputy governor (female), three POs (two males, one female), four SOs (male), approximately thirty-three normal grade officers (including five women).

2. Prison work also enables entrepreneurial 'fiddle jobs'. The shift system at Locksdon allowed some officers (usually men) to engage in secondary jobs usually based on skilled manual trades such as plumbing, carpentry, decorating or taxi-driving. There was a pleasure and pride in 'fiddling' in this way – a way of 'getting one over' on the system by supplementing prison wages.

3. A form of punishment in the navy, where a person must take the worst guard watch in the middle of the night.

4. For more on the distinction between friendship and 'mates' see Pahl (2000), Allan (1996), Carrier (1999).

5. See Rapport (2009) for a discussion of similar processes.

6. This role covered responsibilities relating to 'Race Relations', 'Equal Opportunities' and GAYLIPS (Gay and Lesbian in the Prison Service). Susan organised training and awareness sessions, implemented race and discrimination complaints procedures and dealt with individual detainees (or staff) who had experienced discrimination of any kind.

4   COMPLIANCE AND DEFIANCE: CONTESTING THE REGIME

1. An App is an application – a small sheet of paper which a detainee fills out when requesting something: for example, he wants a fax sent, an appointment with the governor to complain about some aspect of Locksdon's regime, or to ask for special permission to retrieve something from his stored luggage.

2. There has been increased concern about the number of cases of self-harm and suicide in the British immigration detention estate, reflecting the larger number of people held in detention facilities. In 2004, the Joint Committee on

Human Rights noted that there were five deaths in UK immigration detention centres between 1989 and mid-2003, four of which were self-inflicted. In 2004 alone, three apparently self-inflicted deaths were recorded, with evidence of numerous incidents of self-harm (2004: para. 82). More recently, the Home Office (2010) released statistics which reported that in December 2010, 128 detainees were considered on formal self-harm at-risk, with 10 people requiring medical attention for self-harm incidents. See, for example, reports by Medical Justice (Burnett et al. 2010), Liberty (2010) and Lorek et al. (2009)

3. De Genova (2002: 45) argues that state law *creates* illegality as a juridical relationship to the state. Immigration laws are instruments of discipline and coercion. The deployment of these laws as tactics of control aims to make a disciplined and manageable object out of an 'unruly' social group, immigrants, although the realisation of this aim is never complete. Illegality is a shifting category with a specific history. Heyman and Smart (1999) also argue that states and illegal practices are counterparts. There is indeterminacy, ambiguity and duplicity in the state creation and control of illegality.

4. Since my fieldwork, detainees are allowed to engage in work in IRCs and are paid a small amount in return for that work.

5. Recent thought has also increasingly decoupled citizenship as a status from acts of citizenship which constitute political subjects (Isin and Nielsen 2008; Squire 2009).

5   DRAWING THE LINE: DISCRETION AND POWER

1. The death of a deportee being forcibly restrained during removal by private security contractors at Heathrow airport in October 2010 shone a spotlight on the dangers of the use of C&R techniques during deportation, and the apparent lack of training and management of private guards. Detention custody officers employed in IRC or as escorts are trained by control and restraint instructors accredited by the National Offenders Management Service (NOMS). Prison officers regularly undergo C&R refresher courses and may take advanced C&R courses. However, a 2008 independent report (Birnberg Peirce & Partners et al., 2008) *Outsourcing Abuse* and an HM Inspectorate of Prisons report (2009) both highlighted serious concerns about the use of force in escorted removals by security contractors. Indeed, a Ministry of Justice manual (2010) on physical control in care stated that 'it has been known for those in custody to die as a result of physical restraint if the correct procedures are not followed or if a previously undetected health condition is worsened by the restraint'. One of the risks of C&R is the restrained person being unable to breathe (see Guardian 2010).

2. Similarly, Prison Service Order (PSO) 1600, makes clear that, '[a]ll reasonable efforts must be made to manage violent, refractory or disturbed behaviour by persuasion or other means which do not entail the use of force' and '[t]he use of C&R techniques must be regarded as a matter of last resort' (paras 1.1.3 and 2.2.3).

3. See: http://pso.hmprisonservice.gov.uk/pso1600/default.htm.

4. 'Nonce' is a prison term for a sex offender, someone who is not safe in the main part of a prison because other prisoners pose a threat to him or her. Generally, the term signifies morally repugnant 'deviant' tendencies that cannot be countenanced by the dominant group.

6   ETHICS AND ENCOUNTERS

1. Only two detainees entered the essay competition, though there were plenty of entries in the art competition. One detainee wrote about Nigerian wedding ceremonies. The other, the Algerian student, with whom I had been sitting at the start and who went on to win the competition, wrote about being an asylum seeker and missing life back home, ignoring Susan's initial instructions.
2. It was not clear whether this was due to lack of willing participants, apathy or lack of information. Detainees at Locksdon woke daily with the hope of getting out. Men arrived and departed all the time. Perhaps only longer-term residents were motivated to participate.

References

Abrams, P. (1988) 'Notes on the difficulty of studying the state', *Journal of Historical Sociology* 1: 58–89.

Abu-Lughod, L. (1990) 'The romance of resistance: tracing transformations of power through Bedouin women', *American Ethnologist* 17(1): 41–55.

Agamben, G. (1993) *The Coming Community*, trans. M. Hardt. Minneapolis: University of Minnesota Press.

Agamben, G. (1998) *Homo Sacer: Sovereign Power and Bare Life*. Stanford, CA: Stanford University Press.

Agamben, G. (2002) 'Security and terror', *Theory and Event* 5(4).

Agamben, G. (2005) *State of Exception*. Chicago, IL: University of Chicago Press.

Agamben, G. (2006) 'We refugees', available at: http://roundtable.kein.org/node/399 (accessed 15 December 2011).

Agar, M. (1980) *The Professional Stranger: An Informal Introduction to Anthropology*. London: Academic Press.

Ahmed, S. (2004) *The Cultural Politics of Emotion*. London: Routledge.

Ahmed, S. (2011) 'Willful parts: problem characters or the problem of character', *New Literary History* 42: 231–53.

Allan, G. (1996) *Kinship and Friendship in Modern Britain*, 2nd edn. Oxford: Oxford University Press.

American Civil Liberties Union (2008) *Detention and Deportation in the Age of ICE*. ACLU of Massachusetts, available at: http://www.aclum.org/sites/all/files/education/aclu_ice_detention_report.pdf (accessed 15 March 2008).

Amnesty International (2005) 'Seeking asylum is not a crime: detention of people who have sought asylum', available at: http://www.amnesty.org.uk (accessed 15 June 2011).

Amnesty International (2011) 'United Kingdom: the Terrorism Prevention and Investigation Measures Bill 2011: Control Orders Redux', available at: http://www.amnesty.org.uk (accessed 15 September 2011).

Amoore, L. (2007a) 'Vigilant visualities: the watchful politics of the war on terror', *Security Dialogue* 38(2): 139–56.

Amoore, L. (2007b) 'There is no Great Refusal: the ambivalent politics of dissent', in M. de Goede (ed.) *International Political Economy and Poststructural Politics*. Basingstoke: Macmillan, pp. 255–75.

Amoore, L. (2008) 'Consulting, culture, the camp: on the economies of the exception', in L. Amoore and M. de Goede (eds) *Risk and the War on Terror*. London: Routledge, pp. 112–31.

Amoore, L. and M. de Goede (2005) 'Governance, risk and dataveillance in the war on terror', *Crime, Law and Social Change* 43: 149–73.

Amoore, L. and M. de Goede, M. (2008a) 'Transactions after 9/11: the banal face of the preemptive strike', *Transactions of the Institute of British Geographers* 33(2): 173–85.

Amoore, L. and de Goede, M. (2008b) 'Introduction: governing by risk in the war on terror', in L. Amoore and M. de Goede (eds) *Risk and the War on Terror*. London: Routledge, pp. 5–21.

Amoore, L. and A. Hall (2010) 'Border theatre: on the arts of security and resistance', *Cultural Geographies* 17(3): 299–319.

Anderson, B. (1983) *Imagined Communities*. London: Verso.

Anderson, B. (2007) 'Hope for nanotechnology: anticipatory knowledge and governance of affect', *Area* 19: 156–65.

Anderson, B. (2010) 'Preemption, precaution, preparedness: anticipatory action and future geographies', *Progress in Human Geography* 34: 777–98.

Andreas, P. and T. Biersteker (2003) *The Re-Bordering of North America: Integration and Exclusion in a New Security Context*. London: Routledge.

Andreas, P. and T. Snyder (eds) (2000) *The Wall around the West: State Borders and Immigration Controls in North America and Europe*. New York: Rowman and Littlefield.

Appiah, K. (1994) 'Identity, authenticity, survival: multicultural societies and social reproduction', in C. Taylor, *Multiculturalism and the Politics of Recognition*, edited and introduced by A. Gutmann. Princeton, NJ: Princeton University Press, pp. 149–63.

Aradau, C. and R. van Munster (2007) 'Governing terrorism through risk: taking precautions (un)knowing the future', *European Journal of International Relations* 13(1): 89–115.

Arendt, H. (2004 [1951]) *The Origins of Totalitarianism*. New York: Schocken Books.

Aretxaga, B. (1997) *Shattering Silence: Women, Nationalism and Political Subjectivity in Northern Ireland*. Princeton, NJ: Princeton University Press.

Bacon, C. (2005) 'The evolution of immigration detention in the UK: the involvement of private prison companies', Refugee Studies Centre Working Paper no. 27, available at: http://www.rsc.ox.ac.uk/PDFs/RSCworkingpaper27.pdf (accessed 3 June 2010).

Baigent, D. (2001) *One More Last Working-Class Hero: A Cultural Audit of the UK Fire Service*. Published by fitting-in ltd, http://www.fitting-in.com.

Bal, M. (2003) 'Visual essentialism and the object of visual culture', *Journal of Visual Culture* 2: 5–32.

Balibar, E. (2002) *Politics and the Other Scene*. London: Verso.

Bashford, A. and C. Hooker (2001) 'Introduction: contagion, modernity and postmodernity', in A. Bashford and C. Hooker (eds) *Contagion: Historical and Cultural Studies*. London: Routledge, pp. 1–15.

Bashford, A. and C. Strange (2002) 'Asylum seekers and national histories of detention', *Australian Journal of Politics and History* 48(4): 509–27.

Bashford, A. and C. Strange (2003) 'Isolation and exclusion in the modern world: an introductory essay', in A. Bashford and C. Strange (eds) *Isolation: Places and Practices of Exclusion*. London: Routledge, pp. 1–19.

Bauman, Z. (1993) *Postmodern Ethics*. Oxford: Blackwell.

Bauman, Z. (2000) *Liquid Modernity*. Cambridge: Polity.

Bauman, Z. (2001) *The Individualised Society*. Cambridge: Polity Press.

Beck, U. (2002) 'The cosmopolitan society and its enemies', *Theory, Culture & Society* 19(1–2): 17–44.

Bennett, J., B. Crewe and A. Wahidin (eds) (2008) *Understanding Prison Staff*. Cullompton, Devon: Willan Publishing.

Berlant, L. (1998) 'Intimacy: a special issue', *Critical Inquiry* 24(2): 281–8.

Berlant, L. (2004) 'Compassion (and withholding)', in L. Berlant (ed.) *Compassion: The Culture and Politics of an Emotion*. London: Routledge, pp. 1–15.

Bigo, D. (2001) 'The Möbius ribbon of internal and external security(ies)', in M. Albert, D. Jacobson and Y. Lapid (eds) *Identities, Borders, Orders*. Minneapolis: University of Minnesota Press, pp. 91–117.

Bigo, D. (2002) 'Security and immigration: toward a critique of the governmentality of unease', *Alternatives* 27(1): 63–92.

Bigo, D. (2008) 'Globalised (in)security: the field and the ban-opticon', in D. Bigo and A. Tsoukala (eds) *Terror, Insecurity and Liberty: Illiberal Practices of Liberal Regimes after 9/11*. London: Routledge, pp. 10–49.

Billig, M. (1995) *Banal Nationalism*. London: Sage.

Billig, M. (2001) 'Humour and embarrassment: limits of "nice-guy" theories of social life', *Theory, Culture & Society* 18(5): 23–43.

Birnberg Peirce and Partners, Medical Justice and the National Coalition of Anti-Deportation Campaigns (2008) 'Outsourcing abuse: the use and misuse of state-sanctioned force during the detention and removal of asylum seekers', available at: http://www.libertysecurity.org/IMG/pdf_outsourcing_abuse.pdf (accessed 15 June 2010).

Bleiker, R. (2000) *Popular Dissent, Human Agency and Global Politics*. Cambridge: Cambridge University Press.

Bloch, M. (2003) 'Authority', in J. Kreinath, J. Snoek and M. Stausberg (eds) *Theorizing Rituals*, vol. 1: *Issues, Topics, Approaches, Concepts*. Leiden: Brill.

Bloch, A. and L. Schuster (2005) 'At the extremes of exclusion: deportation, detention and dispersal', *Ethnic and Racial Studies* 28(3): 491–512.

Blum, L. (1980) *Friendship, Altruism and Morality*. London: Routledge and Kegan Paul.

Bordo, S. (1999) *Unbearable Weight: Feminism, Western Culture and the Body*. Berkeley: University of California Press.

Bourdieu, P. (1977) *The Logic of Practice*. Cambridge: Polity Press.

Brouwer, E., P. Catz and E. Guild (2003) *Immigration, Asylum and Terrorism*. Nijmegen: Instituut VoorRechtssociologie.

Burleston, L. (1992) 'The state, internment and public criticism in the Second World War', in D. Cesarini and T. Kushner (eds) *Alien Internment in Britain during the Twentieth Century*, Special Issue of *Immigrants and Minorities* 11(3): 102–25.

Burnett, J., J. Carter, J. Evershed, M. Kohli, C. Powell and G. de Wilde (2010) *State Sponsored Cruelty: Children in Immigration Detention*. London: Medical Justice, available at: http://www.medicaljustice.org.uk/images/stories/reports/sscfullreport. pdf (accessed 15 December 2010).

Butler, J. (1988) 'Performative acts and gender constitution: an essay in phenomenology and feminist theory', *Theatre Journal* 40(4): 519–31.

Butler, J. (1990) *Gender Trouble: Feminism and the Subversion of Identity*. London: Routledge.

Butler, J. (1993) *Bodies that Matter: On the Discursive Limits of 'Sex'*. London: Routledge.

Butler, J. (2002) 'What is critique? An essay on Foucault's virtue', in D. Ingram (ed.) *The Political: Readings in Continental Philosophy*. London: Basil Blackwell, pp. 212–26.

Butler, J. (2004) *Precarious Life: The Powers of Mourning and Violence*. London: Verso.

Buzan, B. and O. Wæver (1997) 'Slippery? Contradictory? Sociologically untenable? The Copenhagen School replies', *Review of International Studies* 23: 241–50.

Campbell, D. (1998) *Writing Security: United States Foreign Policy and the Politics of Identity*. Minneapolis: University of Minnesota Press.

Caplan, P. (2003) 'Introduction: anthropologists and ethics', in P. Caplan (ed.) *The Ethics of Anthropology*. London: Routledge, pp. 1–25.

Carlile, Lord of Berriew (2009) *Operation Pathway: Report Following Review*, available at: http://www.irr.org.uk/pdf2/Carliles_report_Pathway.pdf (accessed 12 September 2011).

Carrier, J. (1999) 'People who can be friends: selves and social relationships', in S. Bell and S. Coleman (eds) *The Anthropology of Friendship*. Oxford: Berg.

Carrithers, M. (1992) *Why Humans Have Cultures*. Oxford: Oxford University Press.

Cesarini, D. (1992) 'An alien concept? The continuity of anti-alienism in British society before 1940', in D. Cesarini and T. Kushner (eds) *Alien Internment in Britain during the Twentieth Century*, Special Issue, *Immigrants and Minorities* 11(3): 25–53.

Certeau, M. de (1984) *The Practice of Everyday Life*, trans. S. Rendell. Berkeley: University of California Press.

Cockburn, C. (1983) *Brothers: Male Dominance and Technological Change*. London: Pluto Press.

Cohen, A.P. (1985) *The Symbolic Construction of Community*. Chichester: Harwood.

Cohen, A.P. (1996) 'Personal nationalism: a Scottish view of some rites, rights, and wrongs', *American Ethnologist* 23(4): 802–15.

Cohen, A.P. (2000) 'Discriminating relations: identity, boundary and authenticity', in A.P. Cohen (ed.) *Signifying Identities: Anthropological Perspectives on Boundaries and Contested Values*. London: Routledge.

Cohen, S. (2002) 'The local state of immigration controls', *Critical Social Policy* 22(3): 518–43.

Conflitti Globali (2007) 'Foreword. Internments: CPT and other camps', available at: http://www.libertysecurity.org/article1356.html (accessed 3 May 2008).

Connell, R. (1987) *Gender and Power: Society, the Person and Sexual Politics*. Cambridge: Polity.

Connell, R. (1995) *Masculinities*. London: Allen and Unwin.

Connell, R. (2005) *Masculinities*. Cambridge: Polity Press.

Connolly, W. (2005) *Pluralism*. London: Duke University Press.

Cooley, H. (2004) 'It's all about the fit: the hand, the mobile screenic device and tactile vision', *Journal of Visual Culture* 3: 133–55.

Cooper, R. (1995) 'The fireman: immaculate manhood', *Journal of Popular Culture* 28(4): 139–70.

Cornwall, A. and N. Lindisfarne (1994) 'Dislocating masculinity: gender, power and anthropology', in A. Cornwall and N. Lindisfarne (eds) *Dislocating Masculinity: Comparative Ethnographies*. London: Routledge, pp. 11–48.

Coutin, S.B. (2007) *Nation of Emigrants: Shifting Boundaries of Citizenship in the United States and El Salvador*. Ithaca, NY: Cornell University Press.

Coutin, S.B. (2010) 'Confined within: national territories as zones of confinement', *Political Geography* 29(4): 200–8.

Coutin, S.B. (2011) 'Legal exclusion and dislocated subjectivities: the deportation of Salvadoran youth from the United States', in V. Squire (ed.) *The Contested Politics of Mobility: Borderzones and Irregularity*. London: Routledge, pp. 169–48.

Cowan, J. (1992) *Dance and the Body Politic*. Princeton, NJ: Princeton University Press.

Crary, J. (1992) *Techniques of the Observer: On Vision and Modernity in the 19th Century*. Cambridge, MA: MIT Press.

Crary, J. (1994) 'Unbinding vision', *October* Spring: 21–44.

Crary, J. (2001) *Suspensions of Perception: Attention, Spectacle and Modern Culture*. Cambridge, MA: MIT Press.

Crawley, E. (2004) *Doing Prison Work: The Public and Private Lives of Prison Officers*. Cullompton, Devon: Willan Publishing.

Crawley, H. (1999) *Breaking Down the Barriers: A Report on the Conduct of Asylum Interviews at Ports*. London: Immigration Law Practitioners' Association.

Crick, M. (1992) 'Ali and me: an essay in street corner anthropology', in J. Okely and H. Callaway (eds) *Anthropology and Autobiography*. London: Routledge, pp. 175–93.

Critchley, S. (1992) *The Ethics of Deconstruction: Derrida and Levinas*. Oxford: Blackwell.

Csordas, T. (1994) *Embodiment and Experience: The Existential Ground of Culture and Self*. Cambridge: Cambridge University Press.

Dasgupta, P. (1988) 'Trust as a commodity', in D. Gambetta (ed.) *Trust: Making and Breaking Cooperative Relations*. Oxford: Basil Blackwell, pp. 49–72.

Daston, L. and P. Galison (1992) 'The image of objectivity', *Representations* 40: 81–128.

Daston, L. and P. Galison, P. (2007) *Objectivity*. Cambridge, MA: Zone Books.

De Genova, N. (2002) 'Migrant "illegality" and deportability in everyday life', *Annual Review of Anthropology* 31: 419–47.

De Genova, N. (2004) 'The legal production of Mexican/migrant illegality', *Latino Studies* 2: 160–85.

De Genova, N. (2007) 'The production of culprits: from deportability to detainability in the aftermath of "homeland security"', *Citizenship Studies* 11(5): 421–88.

De Genova, N. and N. Peutz (eds) (2010) *The Deportation Regime: Sovereignty, Space and the Freedom of Movement*. Durham, NC: Duke University Press.

de Goede, M. (2008) 'The politics of preemption and the War on Terror in Europe', *European Journal of International Relations* 14(1): 161–85.

de Goede, M. and S. Randalls (2009) 'Preemption, precaution: arts and technologies of the actionable future', *Environment and Planning D: Society and Space* 27(5): 859–78.

Dean, M. (1999) *Governmentality: Power and Rule in Modern Society*. London: Sage.

Derrida, J. (2001) *On Cosmopolitanism and Forgiveness*. London: Routledge.

Detention Centre Rules (2001) Statutory Instruments No. 238, available at: www.legislation.hmso.gov.uk (accessed 15 December 2010).

Dikeç, M. (2002) 'Pera pera poros: longing for spaces of hospitality', *Theory, Culture & Society* 19(1–2): 227–47.

Diken, B. (2004) 'From refugee camps to gated communities – biopolitics and the end of the city', *Citizenship Studies* 8(1): 83–106.

Diken, B. and B.C. Laustsen (2006) *The Culture of the Exception: Sociology Facing the Camp*. London: Routledge.

Donnan, H. and T. Wilson (1998) 'Nation, state and identity at international borders', in H. Donnan and T. Wilson (eds) *Border Identities: Nation and State at International Frontiers*. Cambridge: Cambridge University Press.

Donnan, H. and T. Wilson (1999) *Borders: Frontiers of Identity, Nation and State.* Oxford: Berg.

Doty, R. (2007) 'States of exception on the Mexico–U.S. Border: "decisions" and civilian border patrols', *International Political Sociology* 1(2): 113–37.

Douglas, M. (1966) *Purity and Danger: an Analysis of Concepts of Pollution and Taboo.* London: Routledge.

Douzinas, C. (2002) 'Identity, recognition, rights, or what Hegel can teach us about human rights', *Journal of Law and Society* 29: 379–405.

Douzinas, C. (2007) *Human Rights and Empire: The Political Philosophy of Cosmopolitanism.* London: Routledge Cavendish.

Dowler, L. (2001) 'Till death do us part: masculinity, friendship and nationalism in Belfast, Northern Ireland', *Environment and Planning D: Society and Space* 19: 53–71.

Dummett, A. and A. Nicol (1990) *Subjects, Citizens, Aliens and Others.* London: Weidenfeld.

Edensor, T. (2002) *National Identity, Popular Culture and Everyday Life.* Oxford: Berg.

Edkins, J. (2007) 'Whatever politics', in M. Calaraco and S. Decaroli (eds) *Giorgio Agamben: Sovereignty and Life.* Stanford, CA: Stanford University Press, pp. 70–92.

Edkins, J. (2011) *Missing: Persons and Politics.* Ithaca, NY: Cornell University Press.

Edkins, J. and V. Pin-Fat (2004) 'Introduction: life, power, resistance', in J. Edkins, V. Pin-Fat and M.J. Shapiro (eds) *Sovereign Lives.* London: Routledge, pp. 1–23.

Fabian, J. (1983) *Time and the Other.* New York: Colombia University Press.

Farah, R. (2003) 'Reinscribing exile: a case study of al-Baq'a refugee camp', in A. Bashford and C. Strange (eds) *Isolation: Places and Practices of Exclusion.* London: Routledge, pp. 181–97.

Farnworth, L. (1992) 'Women doing a man's job: female prison officers working in a male prison', *Australian and New Zealand Journal of Criminology* 25: 278–95.

Feldman, A. (1991) *Formations of Violence: The Narrative of the Body and Political Terror in Northern Ireland.* Chicago, IL: University of Chicago Press.

Feldman, A. (2005) 'The actuarial gaze: from 9/11 to Abu Ghraib', *Cultural Studies* 19(2): 201–26.

Flynn, D. (2005) 'New borders, new management: the dilemmas of modern immigration policies', *Ethnic and Racial Studies* 28(3): 463–90.

Foucault, M. (1977) *Discipline and Punish: The Birth of the Prison.* London: Penguin.

Foucault, M. (1982) 'The subject and power', in H. Dreyfus and P. Rabinow (eds) *Michel Foucault: Beyond Structuralism and Hermeneutics.* New York: Harvester Wheatsheaf.

Foucault, M. (2000) *Essential Works of Foucault 1954–1984*, vol. 3: *Power*, edited by J. Faubian, trans. R. Hurley and others. London: Penguin Books.

Foucault, M. (2003) *Abnormal.* New York: Picador.

Foucault, M. (2007) *Security, Territory, Population.* Houndmills: Palgrave Macmillan.

Fuglerud, O. (2004) 'Constructing exclusion: the micro-sociology of an immigration department', *Social Anthropology* 12(1): 25–41.

Gambetta, D. (1988) 'Can we trust trust?', in D. Gambetta (ed.) *Trust: Making and Breaking Cooperative Relations.* Oxford: Basil Blackwell, pp. 213–27.

Garland, D. (1990) *Punishment and Modern Society.* Oxford: Clarendon.

Garland, D. (2001) *The Culture of Control.* Oxford: Oxford University Press.

Geertz, C. (1973) *The Interpretation of Cultures: Selected Essays*. New York: Basic Books.

Gibney, M. (2001) *The State of Asylum: Democratisation, Judicialisation and the Evolution of Refugee Policy in Europe*. Oxford: Refugee Studies Centre, Queen Elizabeth House, University of Oxford, available at: www.rsc.ox.ac.uk (accessed 13 September 2003).

Gibney, M. (2004) *The Ethics and Politics of Asylum: Liberal Democracy and the Response to Refugees*. Cambridge: Cambridge University Press.

Gill, N. (2009) 'Governmental mobility: the power effects of the movement of detained asylum seekers around Britain's detention estate', *Political Geography* 28: 186–96.

Goffman, E. (1961) *Asylums: Essays on the Social Situation of Mental Patients and Other Inmates*. New York: Doubleday.

Goffman, E. (1967) *Interaction Ritual*. New York: Pantheon.

Goffman, E. (1969) *The Presentation of Self in Everyday Life*. London: Penguin.

Good, A. (2004a) '"Undoubtedly an expert"? Country experts in the UK asylum courts', *Journal of the Royal Anthropological Institute* 10: 113–33.

Good, A. (2004b) 'Expert evidence in asylum and human rights appeals: an expert's view', *International Journal of Refugee Law* 16: 358–80.

Good, A. (2007) *Anthropology and Expertise in the Asylum Courts*. London: Routledge-Cavendish.

Good, A. (2008) 'Cultural evidence in courts of law', *Journal of the Royal Anthropological Institute* 14: S47–S60.

Gregory, D. (2006) 'The black flag: Guantánamo Bay and the space of exception', *Geografiska Annaler B* 88(4): 405–27.

Gregory, D. and A. Pred (2007) 'Introduction', in D. Gregory and A. Pred (eds) *Violent Geographies, Fear, Terror, and Political Violence*. London: Routledge.

Grønseth S. (forthcoming) 'Experiences of pain: a gateway to cosmopolitan subjectivity?', in L. Josephides and A. Hall (eds) *Cosmopolitanism, Existentialism and Morality: Anthropological Perspectives*. London: Berghahn.

Grosz, E. (1994) *Volatile Bodies: Toward a Corporeal Feminism*. Bloomington: Indiana University Press.

The Guardian (2010) 'Deportation death raises questions over "proportionate force"', 14 October.

Guild, E. (2003) 'Exceptionalism and transnationalism: UK judicial control of the detention of foreign "international terrorists"', *Alternatives/Special English Language Issue of Cultures and Conflits* 28(4): 491–515.

Guild, E. (2006) 'The Europeanisation of Europe's asylum policy', *International Journal of Refugee Law* 18(3–4): 630–51.

Guild, E. (2009) *Security and Migration in the 21st Century*. Cambridge: Polity Press.

Guild, E. and D. Bigo (eds) (2005) *Controlling Frontiers: Free Movement into and within Europe*. Aldershot: Ashgate.

Guild, E., S. Carrera and T. Balzacq (2008) 'The changing dynamics of security in an enlarged European Union', Research Paper No.12. Brussels: CEPS, available at: http://www.ceps.eu/index3.php (accessed).

Gupta, A. (1995) 'Blurred boundaries: the discourse of corruption, the culture of politics, and the imagined state', *American Ethnologist* 22(2): 375–492.

Hall, A., J. Hockey and V. Robinson (2007) 'Occupational cultures and the embodiment of masculinity', *Gender, Work and Organisation* 14(6): 534–51.

Hannerz, U. (1990) 'Cosmopolitans and locals in world culture', *Theory, Culture & Society* 7: 237–51.

Harrison, P. (2000) 'Making sense: embodiment and the sensibilities of the everyday', *Environment and Planning D: Society and Space*, 18: 497–517.

Harvey, C. (2000a) *Seeking Asylum in the UK: Problems and Prospects*. London: Butterworths.

Hay, W. and R. Sparks (1991) 'What is a prison officer?', *Prison Service Journal* summer.

Hearn, J. (1993) 'Emotive subjects: organizational men, organizational masculinities and the (de) construction of "emotions"', in S. Fineman (ed.) *Emotion in Organizations*. London: Sage, pp. 142–66.

Herzfeld, M. (1985) *The Poetics of Manhood: Contest and Identity in a Cretan Mountain Village*. Princeton, NJ: Princeton University Press.

Herzfeld, M. (1992) *The Social Production of Indifference*. New York: Berg.

Heyman, J.McC. (1995) 'Putting power in the anthropology of bureaucracy', *Current Anthropology* 36(2): 261–87.

Heyman, J.McC. (2000) 'Respect for outsiders? Respect for the law? The moral evaluation of high-scale issues by U.S. immigration officers', *Journal of the Royal Anthropological Institute* 6: 635–52.

Heyman, J.McC. (2004) 'Ports of entry as nodes in the world system', *Identities: Global Studies in Culture and Power* 11(3): 303–27.

Heyman, J.McC. (2009) 'Trust, privilege, and discretion in the governance of the US borderlands with Mexico', *Canadian Journal of Law and Society* 24(3): 367–90.

Heyman, J.McC. and A. Smart (1999) 'States and illegal practices: an overview', in J.McC. Heyman and A. Smart (eds) *States and Illegal Practices*. Oxford: Berg.

HM Inspectorate of Prisons (2009) *Detainee Escorts and Removals: A Thematic Review*, available at: http://www.justice.gov.uk/inspectorates/hmi-prisons/docs/Detainee_escorts_and_removals_2009_rps.pdf (accessed).

Hochschild, A.R. (1983) *The Managed Heart: Commercialization of Human Feeling*. Berkeley: University of California Press.

Holmes, C. (1991) *A Tolerant Country? Immigrants, Refugees and Minorities in Britain*. London: Faber.

Home Office (2002a) *Safe Haven, Secure Borders: Integration with Diversity in Modern Britain*, available at www.official-documents.co.uk (accessed 15 September 2003).

Home Office (2002b) 'Immigration and asylum statistics 2002', available at: http://rds.homeoffice.gov.uk/rds/immigration-asylum-publications.html (accessed 15 September 2003).

Home Office (2010) 'Self-harm in immigration detention', available at: http://www.homeoffice.gov.uk/about-us/freedom-of-information/released-information1/foi-archive-immigration/13738-selfharm-immig-deten/ (accessed 15 December 2011).

Honig, B. (2001) *Democracy and the Foreigner*. Princeton, NJ: Princeton University Press.

Honneth, A. (2001) 'Recognition or redistribution? Changing perspectives on the moral order of society', *Theory, Culture & Society* 18(2–3): 43–55.

Howe, L. (1990) *Being Unemployed in Northern Ireland*. Cambridge: Cambridge University Press.

Howe, L. (1998) 'Scrounger, worker, beggarman, cheat: the dynamics of unemployment and the politic of resistance in Belfast', *Journal of the Royal Anthropological Institute* 4(3): 531–50.

Howell, S. (1997) 'Introduction', in S. Howell (ed.) *The Ethnography of Moralities*. London: Routledge, pp. 1–25.

Humphrey, C. (1997) 'Exemplars and rules: aspects of the discourse of moralities in Mongolia', in S. Howell (ed.) *The Ethnography of Moralities*. London: Routledge, pp. 25–47.

Humphrey, C. (2004) 'Sovereignty and ways of life: the *marshrut* system in the city of Ulan-Ude, Russia', in D. Nugent and J. Vincent (eds) *A Companion to the Anthropology of Politics*. New York: Blackwell, pp. 418–36.

Huysmans, J. (2006) *The Politics of Insecurity*. London: Routledge.

Hyndman, J. and A. Mountz (2008) 'Another brick in the wall? Neo-refoulement and the externalisation of asylum in Australia and Europe', *Government and Opposition* 43(2): 249–69.

Inda, J. (2005) 'Analytics of the modern: an introduction', in J. Inda (ed.) *Anthropologies of Modernity: Foucault, Governmentality, and Life Politics*. Malden, MA: Blackwell, pp. 1–23.

Inda, J. (2006) *Targeting Immigrants: Government, Technology, and Ethics*. Oxford: Blackwell.

Indra, D. (1999) 'Not a "room of one's own"', in D. Indra (ed.) *Engendering Forced Migration*. London: Berg, pp. 1–23.

Isin, E. (2004) 'The neurotic citizen', *Citizenship Studies* 8(3): 217–35.

Isin, E. and G. Nielsen (eds) (2008) *Acts of Citizenship*. London: Zed Books.

Isin, E. and K. Rygiel (2007) 'Abject spaces: frontiers, zones, camps', in E. Dauphinee and C. Masters (eds) *Logics of Biopower and the War on Terror*. New York: Palgrave Macmillan, pp. 181–203.

Itzin, C. (ed.) (1992) *Pornography: Women, Violence and Civil Liberties*. Oxford: Oxford University Press.

Jackson, M. (1989) *Paths toward a Clearing: Radical Empiricism and Ethnographic Enquiry*. Bloomington, IN: Indiana University Press.

Jackson, M. (1998) *Minima Ethnographica: Intersubjectivity and the Anthropological Project*. Chicago: University of Chicago Press.

Jackson, M. (2005) *Existential Anthropology: Events, Exigencies and Effects*. Oxford: Berghahn Books.

Jay, M. (1993) *Downcast Eyes: the Denigration of Vision in Twentieth Century French Thought*. Berkeley: California University Press.

Jay, M. (2002) 'Cultural relativism and the visual turn', *Journal of Visual Culture* 1(3): 267–78.

Jean-Klein, I. (2001) 'Nationalism and resistance: the two faces of everyday activism in Palestine during the Intifada', *Cultural Anthropology* 16(1): 83–126.

Johns, F. (2005) 'Guantánamo Bay and the annihilation of the exception', *European Journal of International Law* 16(4): 613–35.

Joint Committee on Human Rights (2004) 'Deaths in custody', available at: http://www.publications.parliament.uk/pa/jt/jtrights.htm (accessed 13 September 2010).

Josephides, J. (2003a) '"Being there": the magic of presence or the metaphysics of morality?', in P. Caplan (ed.) *The Ethics of Anthropology*. London: Routledge, pp. 55–77.

Josephides, J. (2003b) 'The rights of being human', in R. Wilson and J. Mitchell (eds) *Human Rights in Global Perspective: Anthropological Studies of Rights, Claims and Entitlements*. London: Routledge, pp. 229–50.

Josephides, L. (2008) *Melanesian Odysseys: Negotiating the Self, Narrative, and Modernity*. London: Berghahn.

Josephides, J. (2010) 'Cosmopolitanism as the existential condition of humanity', *Social Anthropology* 18(4): 389–95.

Josephides, L. and A. Hall (eds) (forthcoming) *Cosmopolitanism, Existentialism and Morality: Anthropological Perspectives*. London: Berghahn.

Justice (2009) *Secret Evidence*. Available at: http://www.justice.org.uk/data/files/resources/33/Secret-Evidence-10-June-2009.pdf (accessed March 2012).

Kant, I. (1948) *The Moral Law: Groundwork of the Metaphysic of Morals*, trans. and analysed by H.J. Paton. London: Routledge.

Karp, I. (1991) 'Culture and representation', in I. Karp and S. Lavine (eds) *The Poetics and Politics of Museum Display*. London: Smithsonian Institution Press, pp. 120–25.

Kauffman, K. (1988) *Prison Officers and their World*. Cambridge, MA: Harvard University Press.

Kearney, R. (2003) *Strangers, Gods and Monsters: Interpreting Otherness*. London: Routledge.

Keenan, T. (1997) *Fables of Responsibility: Aberrations and Predicaments in Ethics and Politics*. Stanford, CA: Stanford University Press.

Kelly. T. (2009) 'The UN Committee against Torture: human rights monitoring and the legal recognition of torture', *Human Rights Quarterly* 31(3): 777–800.

Kimmel, M. (2001) 'Masculinity as homophobia: fear, shame and silence in the construction of gender identity', in S. Whitehead and F. Barrett (eds) *The Masculinities Reader*. Cambridge: Polity, pp. 266–88.

Kirshenblatt-Gimblett, B. (1991) 'Objects of ethnography', in I. Karp and S. Lavine (eds) *The Poetics and Politics of Museum Display*. London: Smithsonian Institution Press, pp. 80–112.

Knudsen, J. (1995) 'When trust is on trial: negotiating refugee narratives', in E. Valentine and J. Knudsen (eds) *Mistrusting Refugees*. Berkeley: University of California Press, pp. 13–36.

Kristeva, J. (1982) *Powers of Horror: An Essay on Abjection*, trans L.S. Roudiez. New York: Columbia University Press.

Kristeva, J. (1991) *Strangers to Ourselves*. London: Harvester Wheatsheaf.

Lamont, M. (2000) *The Dignity of Working Men: Morality and the Boundaries of Race, Class and Immigration*. New York and Cambridge, MA: Russell Sage Foundation and Harvard University Press.

Lamont, M. and S. Aksartova (2002) 'Ordinary cosmopolitanism: strategies for bridging racial boundaries among working-class men', *Theory, Culture & Society* 19: 1–25.

Lavine, S. and I. Karp (1991) 'Introduction: museums and multiculturalism', in I. Karp and S. Lavine (eds) *The Poetics and Politics of Museum Display*. London: Smithsonian Institution Press, pp. 1–15.

Levinas, E. (1996) *Basic Philosophical Writings*, edited by A. Peperzak, S. Critchley and R. Bernasconi. Indianapolis: Indiana University Press.

Liberty (2010) *Submission to the Review into Ending the Detention of Children for Immigration Purposes*, available at: http://www.liberty-human-rights.org.uk (accessed 15 December 2011).

Liberty (2011) *Second Reading Briefing on the Terrorism Prevention and Investigation Measures Bill*. Available at: http://www.liberty-human-rights.org.uk/pdfs/policy11/liberty-s-second-reading-briefing-on-the-terrorism-prevention-and-investigat.pdf (accessed March 2012).

Liebling, A. (2000) 'Prison officers, policing, and the use of discretion', *Theoretical Criminology* 3(2): 173–87.

Liebling, A. and D. Price (2001) *The Prison Officer*. HMP Leyhill: The Prison Service Journal.

Lipsky, M. (1980) *Street Level Bureaucracy: Dilemmas of the Individual in Public Services*. New York: Russell Sage Foundation.

London Detainee Support Group (2009) *Detained Lives: The Real Cost of Indefinite Immigration Detention*, available at: www.detainedlives.org (accessed 15 September 2010).

London Detainee Support Group (2010) *No Return, No Release, No Reason: Challenging Indefinite Detention*, available at: www.detainedlives.org (accessed 15 December 2010).

Lorek, A., K. Ehntholdt, A. Nesbitt, E. Wey, C. Gitinj, E. Rossor et al. (2009) 'The mental and physical health difficulties of children held within a British immigration detention center: a pilot study', *Child Abuse and Neglect* 33(9): 573–85.

Lui, R. (2004) 'The international government of refugees', in W. Larner and W. Walters (eds) *Global Governmentality: Governing International Spaces*. London: Routledge, pp. 116–35.

Lutz, C. (1998) *Unnatural Emotions*. Chicago: University of Chicago Press.

MacCormack, C. and M. Strathern (1980) *Nature, Culture and Gender*. Cambridge: Cambridge University Press.

McDowell, L. (2001) 'Men, management and multiple masculinities in organisations', *Geoforum* 32(2): 181–98.

McSpadden, L. (1999) 'Negotiating masculinity in the reconstruction of place', in D. Indra (ed.) *Engendering Forced Migration*. London: Berg.

Makaremi, C. (2008) 'Border detention in Europe: violence and the law', paper presented at the annual meeting of the ISA's 49th Annual Convention, 'Bridging Multiple Divides', San Francisco, March.

Makaremi, C. (2009) 'On technologies of control of foreigners', Centre for European Policy Studies CHALLENGE Programme. Available at: http://www.libertysecurity. org/article2464.html (accessed March 2012).

Malkki, L. (1995a) 'Refugees and exile: from "refugee studies" to the national order of things', *Annual Review of Anthropology* 24: 495–523.

Malkki, L. (1995b) *Purity and Exile*. Chicago: University of Chicago Press.

Malkki, L. (1997) 'Speechless emissaries: refugees, humanitarianism, and dehistoricisation', in K. Hastrup and K. Fog Olwig (eds) *Siting Culture: The Shifting Anthropological Object*. London: Routledge.

Malloch, M. and E. Stanley (2005) 'The detention of asylum seekers in the UK: representing risk, managing the dangerous', *Punishment and Society* 7(1): 53–71.

Massumi, B. (2005) 'The future birth of the affective act'. Conference proceedings 'Genealogies of Biopolitics', available at: http://browse.reticular.info/text/ collected/massumi.pdf (accessed 15 September 2010).

Massumi, B. (2007) 'Potential politics and the primacy of preemption', *Theory and Event* 10(2).

Matlou, P. (1999) 'Upsetting the cart: forced migration and gender issues, the African experience', in D. Indra (ed.) *Engendering Forced Migration*. London: Berg, pp. 128–46.

Merleau-Ponty, M. (2004) *The World of Perception*, trans. O. Davies. London: Routledge.

Messner. M. (1992) *Power at Play: Sports and the Problems of Masculinity*. Boston, MA: Beacon Press.

Migreurope (2010) '"The encampment" in Europe and around the Mediterranean Sea', available at http://www.migreurop.org/ (accessed 15 September 2010).

Miller, P. and N. Rose (2008) *Governing the Present: Administering Economic, Social and Personal Life*. Oxford: Polity Press.

Minca, C. (2005) 'The return of the camp', *Progress in Human Geography* 29: 405–12.

Ministry of Justice (2010) *Physical Control in Care Training Manual*, available at: http://www.justice.gov.uk/physical-control-in-care-training-manual-2010.pdf (accessed 15 September 2010).

Misztal, B. (1996) *Trust in Modern Societies: In Search for the Bases of Social Order*. Cambridge: Polity Press.

Mitchell W.J.T. (2002) 'Showing seeing: a critique of visual culture', *Journal of Visual Culture* 1: 165–81.

Mitchell W.J.T. (2005) 'There are no visual media', *Journal of Visual Culture* 4(2): 257–66.

Modood, T. and P. Werbner (eds) (1997) *The Politics of Multiculturalism in the New Europe*. London: Zed Books.

Moore, H. (1994) *A Passion for Difference: Essays in Anthropology and Gender*. Cambridge: Polity Press.

Morgan, D. (1994) 'Theater of war: combat, the military, and masculinities', in H. Brod and M. Kaufman (eds) *Theorizing Masculinities*. Thousand Oaks, CA: Sage, pp. 165–80.

Mountz, A. (2010) *Seeking Asylum: Human Smuggling and Bureaucracy at the Border*. Minneapolis: University of Minnesota Press.

Mountz, A. and J. Hyndman (2008) 'Another brick in the wall? Neo-refoulement and the externalisation of asylum in Australia and Europe', *Government and Opposition* 43(2): 249–69.

Newman, D. (2001) 'Boundaries, borders and barriers: changing geographic perspectives on territorial lines', in M. Albert, D. Jacobson and Y. Lapid (eds) *Identities, Borders, Orders: Rethinking International Relations Theory*. Minneapolis: University of Minnesota Press, pp. 137–53.

Nield, S. (2006) 'On the border as theatrical space: appearance, dis-location and the production of the refugee', in J. Kelleher and N. Ridout (eds) *Contemporary Theatres in Europe*. London: Routledge, pp. 61–73.

Nussbaum, M. (2001) *Upheavals of Thought: The Intelligence of Emotions*. Cambridge: Cambridge University Press.

Nussbaum, M. (2004) *Hiding from Humanity: Disgust, Shame, and the Law*. Princeton, NJ: Princeton University Press.

Nyers, P. (2003) 'Abject cosmopolitanism: the politics of protection in the anti-deportation movement', *Third World Quarterly* 24(6): 1069–93.

Nyers, P. (2006) 'The accidental citizen: acts of sovereignty and (un)making citizenship', *Economy and Society* 35(1): 22–41.

Ortner, S. (1996) *Making Gender: The Politics and Erotics of Culture*. Boston, MA: Beacon Press.

Ortner, S. (2006) *Anthropology and Social Theory: Culture, Power and the Acting Subject*. London: Duke University Press.

Pahl, R. (2000) *On Friendship*. Cambridge: Polity Press.

Paine, R. (1967) 'What is gossip about? An alternative hypothesis', *Man* 2(2): 272–85.

Paine, R. (1999) 'Friendship: the hazards of an ideal relationship', in S. Bell and S. Coleman (eds) *The Anthropology of Friendship*. Oxford: Berg.

Panayi, P. (1992) 'An intolerant act by an intolerant society', in D. Cesarini and T. Kushner (eds) *Alien Internment in Britain during the Twentieth Century*, Special Issue, *Immigrants and Minorities* 11(3): 53–75.

Panayi, P. (1994) *Immigration, Ethnicity and Racism in Britain: 1815–1945*. Manchester: Manchester University Press.

Parkin, D. (1985) *The Anthropology of Evil*. Oxford: Basil Blackwell.

Parkinson, B. (1995) *Ideas and Realities of Emotion*. London: Routledge.

Pirouet, M. (2001) *Whatever Happened to Asylum in Britain? A Tale of Two Walls*. Oxford: Berghahn.

Powdermaker, H. (1966) *Stranger and Friend: The Way of an Anthropologist*. New York: W.W. Norton.

Pratt, A. (1999) 'Dunking the doughnut: discretionary power, law and the administration of the Canadian Immigration Act', *Social and Legal Studies* 8(2): 199–226.

Pratt, A. (2001) 'Sovereign power, carceral conditions and penal practices: detention and deportation in Canada', *Studies in Law, Politics and Society* 23: 45–78.

Pratt, A. (2005) *Securing Borders: Detention and Deportation in Canada*. Vancouver and Toronto: UBC Press.

Pratt, A. (2010) 'Between a hunch and a hard place: making suspicion reasonable at the Canadian Border', *Social and Legal Studies* 19(4): 461–80.

Pratt, A. and L. Sossin (2009) 'A brief introduction to the puzzle of discretion', *Canadian Journal of Law and Society* 24(3): 301–12.

Rancière, J. (1999) *Dis-agreement: Politics and Philosophy*. Minneapolis: University of Minnesota Press.

Rancière, J. (2004) 'Who is the Subject of the Rights of Man?', *South Atlantic Quarterly* 103(2–3): 297–310.

Rapport, N. (2002) 'The body of the village community: between Reverend Parkington in Wanet and Mr Beebe in "A Room with a View"', in N. Rapport (ed.) *British Subjects: An Anthropology of Britain*. London: Routledge.

Rapport, N. (2003) *'I am Dynamite': An Alternative Anthropology of Power*. London: Routledge.

Rapport, N. (2009) *Of Orderlies and Men: Hospital Porters Achieving Wellness at Work*. Durham, NC: Carolina Academic.

Rapport (forthcoming) 'The capacities of anyone: accommodating the universal subject as value and in space', in L. Josephides and A. Hall (eds) *Cosmopolitanism, Existentialism and Morality: Anthropological Perspectives*. London: Berghahn.

Rapport, R. and J. Overing (2000) *Social and Cultural Anthropology: The Key Concepts*. London: Routledge.

Rose, N. (1996) 'The death of the social? Refiguring the territory of government', *Economy and Society* 25(3): 327–56.

Rose, N. (1999) *Powers of Freedom: Reframing Political Thought*. Cambridge: Cambridge University Press.

Rose, N. and P. Miller (1992) 'Political power beyond the state: problematics of government', *British Journal of Sociology* 43(2): 173–205.

Sabo, D., T. Kupers and W. London (eds) (2001) *Prison Masculinities*. Philadelphia, PA: Temple University Press.

Said, E. (1978) *Orientalism*. New York: Pantheon.

Sales, R. (2002) 'The deserving and the undeserving? Refugees, asylum seekers and welfare in Britain', *Critical Social Policy* 22(3): 456–78.

Sales, R. (2005) 'Secure borders, safe haven: a contradiction in terms', *Ethnic and Racial Studies* 28(3): 445–62.

Salter, M. (2008) 'When the exception becomes the rule: borders, sovereignty, citizenship', *Citizenship Studies* 12(4): 365–80.

Sartre, J.-P. (1975) 'Existentialism is a humanism', in W. Kaufman (ed.) *Existentialism from Dostoevsky to Sartre*. New York: Plume, pp. 345–69.

Schuster, L. (2003a) 'Asylum seekers: Sangatte and the Tunnel', *Parliamentary Affairs* 56: 506–22.

Schuster, L. (2003b) *The Use and Abuse of Political Asylum in Britain and Germany*. London: Frank Cass.

Schuster, L. and J. Solomos (1999) 'The politics of refugee and asylum policies in Britain', in A. Bloch and C. Levy (eds) *Refugees, Citizenship and Social Policy in Europe*. London: Macmillan.

Scott, J. (1985) *Weapons of the Weak: Everyday Forms of Peasant Resistance*. London: Yale University Press.

Scott, J. (1990) *Domination and the Arts of Resistance: Hidden Transcripts*. New Haven, CT: Yale University Press.

Sekula, A. (1986) 'The body and the archive', *October* 39: 3–64.

Shapiro, M. (1999) 'The ethics of encounter: unreading, unmapping the imperium', in D. Campbell and M. Shapiro (eds) *Moral Spaces: Rethinking Ethics and World Politics*. Minneapolis: University of Minnesota Press.

SIAC (Special Immigration Appeals Commission) (2010) *Open Judgement, Abid Naseer, Ahmad Faraz Khan, Shoaib Khan, Abdul Wahab Khan and Tariq Ur Rehman versus Secretary of State for the Home Department*. Available at: http://www.siac.tribunals.gov.uk/Documents/outcomes/1_OpenJudgment.pdf (accessed March 2012).

Sibley, D. (1995) *Geographies of Exclusion*. London: Routledge.

Skrbis, Z., G. Kendall and I. Woodward (2004) 'Locating cosmopolitanism: between humanist ideal and grounded social category', *Theory, Culture & Society* 21(6): 115–36.

Spijkerboer, T. (2000) *Gender and Refugee Status*. Aldershot: Ashgate.

Squire, V. (2009) *The Exclusionary Politics of Asylum*. London: Palgrave Macmillan.

Squire, V. (ed.) (2011) *The Contested Politics of Mobility: Borderzones and Irregularity*. London: Routledge.

Stafford, B. (1993) *Body Criticism: Imaging the Unseen in Enlightenment Art and Medicine*. Cambridge, MA: MIT Press.

Stanley, N. (1998) *Being Ourselves for You: The Global Display of Cultures*. Middlesex: Middlesex University Press.

Stolcke, V. (1995) 'Talking culture: new boundaries, new rhetorics of exclusion in Europe', *Current Anthropology* 36(1): 1–21.

Stoler, A. (1991) 'Carnal knowledge and imperial power: gender, race and morality in colonial Asia', in M. di Leonardo (ed.) *Gender at the Crossroads of Knowledge: Feminist Anthropology in the Postmodern Era*. Berkeley: University of California Press, pp. 51–102.

Stoler, A. (1996) *Race and the Education of Desire: Foucault's History of Sexuality and the Colonial Order of Things*. Durham, NC: Duke University Press.

Strathern, M. (1987) 'The limits of auto-anthropology', in A. Jackson (ed.) *Anthropology at Home*. London: Tavistock, pp. 16–38.

Thomas, R. (2006) 'Assessing the credibility of asylum claims: EU and UK approaches examined', *European Journal of Migration and Law* 8: 79–96.

Thomas, R. (2008) 'Consistency in asylum adjudication: country guidance and the asylum process in the United Kingdom', *International Journal of Refugee Law* 20: 489–532.

Turner, B.S. (2002) 'Cosmopolitan virtue, globalisation and patriotism', *Theory, Culture & Society* 19(1–2): 45–63.

Turner, S. (1995) 'Torture, refuge, and trust', in E. Valentine and J. Knudsen (eds) *Mistrusting Refugees*. London: University of California Press, pp. 56–73.

Turner, V. (1969) *The Ritual Process: Structure and Anti-Structure*. London: Routledge and Kegan Paul.

Tyler, I. (2006) '"Welcome to Britain": the cultural politics of asylum', *European Journal of Cultural Studies* 9: 185–202.

UKBA (2008) Enforcement and Instructions Guidance 55.1.2, 9, available at http://www.ukba.homeoffice.gov.uk/policyandlaw/guidance/enforcement/ (accessed 13 March 2010).

UKBA (2009) Enforcement Instructions and Guidance para. 55.4, available at: http://www.ukba.homeoffice.gov.uk/policyandlaw/guidance/asylumprocess/ (accessed 13 March 2010).

UKBA (2012) 'Enforcement instructions and guidance – detention and removals', chs 46–51. Available at: http://www.ukba.homeoffice.gov.uk/sitecontent/documents/policyandlaw/enforcement/detentionandremovals/ (accessed 15 September 2010).

Valverde, M. and M. Mopas (2004) 'Insecurity and the dream of targeted governance', in W. Larner and W. Walters (eds) *Global Governmentality: Governing International Spaces*. London: Routledge.

Van Gennep, A. (1960) *The Rites of Passage*. Chicago: University of Chicago Press.

Walby, S. (1988) *Patriarchy at Work*. Oxford: Polity Press.

Waldram, J. (1998) 'Anthropology in prison: negotiating consent and accountability with a "captured" population', *Human Organisation* 57(2): 238–44.

Walters, W. (2002) 'Deportation, expulsion, and the international police of aliens', *Citizenship Studies* 6(3): 265–92.

Walters, W. (2004) 'Secure borders, safe haven, domopolitics', *Citizenship Studies* 8(3): 237–60.

Walzer, M. (1994) *Thick and Thin: Moral Argument at Home and Abroad*. Indiana: Notre Dame Press.

Wardle, H. (2000) *An Ethnography of Cosmopolitanism in Kingston, Jamaica*. Lewiston: Edwin Mellen Press.

Wardle, H. (2010) 'Introduction. A cosmopolitan anthropology', *Social Anthropology* 18(4): 381–88.

Weber, L. and L. Gelsthorpe (2000) *Deciding to Detain: How Discretion to Detain Asylum Seekers is Exercised at Ports of Entry*. Cambridge: Institute of Criminology.

Welch, M. (2003) *Detained: Immigration Laws and the Expanding I.N.S. Jail Complex*. Philadelphia, PA: Temple University Press.

Welch, M. and L. Schuster (2005a) 'Detention of asylum seekers in the UK and USA: deciphering noisy and quiet constructions', *Punishment and Society* 7(4): 397–417.

Welch, M. and L. Schuster (2005b) 'Detention of asylum seekers in the US, UK, France, Germany, and Italy: a critical view of the globalizing culture of control', *Criminal Justice* 5(4): 331–55.

Werbner, P. (2005) 'Islamophobia: incitement to religious hatred – legislating for a new fear', *Anthropology Today* 21(1): 5–9.

Whitehead, S.M. (2002) *Men and Masculinities*. Cambridge: Polity.

Wikan, U. (1999) 'Culture: a new concept of race?', *Social Anthropology* 7(1): 57.

Wikan, U. (2002) *Generous Betrayal: Politics of culture in the New Europe*. Chicago: University of Chicago Press.

Wild, J. (1979) 'Introduction', in E. Levinas, *Totality and Infinity*. Pittsburgh, PA: Duquesne University Press, pp. 11–21.

Williams, B. (1989) 'A class act: anthropology and the race to nation across ethnic terrain', *Annual Review of Anthropology* 18: 401–44.

Williams, S. (2001) *Emotion and Social Theory*. London: Sage.

Woodward R. (1998) '"It's a man's life!": soldiers, masculinity and the countryside', *Gender, Place and Culture* 5(3): 277–300.

Wright, S. (1994) '"Culture" in anthropology and organisational studies', in S. Wright (ed.) *Anthropology of Organisations*. London: Routledge.

Young, M. (1991) *An Inside Job: Policing and Police Culture in Britain*. Oxford: Clarendon Press.

Žižek, S. (2008) *Violence: Six Sideways Reflections*. London: Profile Books.

Zolberg, A. (2006) *A Nation by Design: Immigration Policy in the Fashioning of America*. Cambridge, MA: Harvard University Press and New York: Russell Sage Foundation.

Zureik, E. and M. Salter (eds) (2005) *Global Surveillance and Policing: Borders, Security, Identity*. Cullompton: Willan Publishing.

Index